I Do,
Now What?

I Do, Now What?

Secrets,
Stories,
and Advice

from a
Madly-in-Love
Couple

Giuliana and Bill Rancic

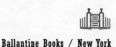

Ballantine Books / New York

This is a recollection about a certain time in our lives. The names of some characters have been changed, and some are composites of various people, experiences, and conversations we've had with them. If you think that's wrong or unfair, you may change your mind after reading what we have to say. We wrote this book to reveal what makes our great marriage work— not to make people from our past cringe. This is an ode to love, after all.

Published in the United States by Ballantine Books, an imprint of The Random House Publishing Group, a division of Random House, Inc., New York.

BALLANTINE and colophon are registered trademarks of Random House, Inc.

The "Style" logo is a registered trademark of E! Entertainment Television, Inc.

All interior photos were taken by Kusha Alagband Photography (www.kushaphotography.com) and are from the author's collection

Library of Congress Cataloging-in-Publication Data

Rancic, Giuliana.
    I do, now what? : secrets, stories, and advice from a madly-in-love couple / Giuliana and Bill Rancic
        p. cm.
    ISBN 978-0-345-52499-7 (hbk. : alk. paper)—
ISBN 978-0-345-52515-4 (electronic)
    1. Marriage.   2. Married people—Psychology.
3. Couples—Psychology.   4. Man-woman relationships.
5. Rancic, Giuliana   6. Rancic, Bill.   I. Rancic, Bill.   II. Title.
    HQ734.R176 2010
646.7'8—dc22
                        2010031012

Printed in the United States of America on acid-free paper

www.ballantinebooks.com

9876543

Book design by Susan Turner

*To our wonderful parents, Gail and Edward,
Anna and Eduardo, whose marriages inspired us to search
for the love of our lives and never settle for less*

If the grass looks greener on the other side,
it's because they take care of it.

—CECIL SELIG

Contents

Why a Couple Like Us Wrote a Book Like This

If you're anything like we are, your heart gets warm and fuzzy when you meet a married couple who's madly in love. What's more endearing than watching a husband subtly reach for his wife's hand as she tells a story, or a wife smile at her husband as they share an inside joke? Their energy is palpable to those around them. And as outsiders, we don't exactly know what makes these great marriages work, but we do imagine they're hoarding all the good secrets to themselves.

Well, somehow we've managed to convince a lot of people that we're one of these lucky couples. Maybe it's the way we gush about each other's accomplishments at dinner with peers and loved ones, or banter like best friends with benefits on our reality show *Giuliana & Bill*. Having good chemistry probably doesn't hurt, either. But all that said, we're here to tell you that our marriage isn't the result of discovering the truth behind a mystery we can't wait to share with the world. No, it's much simpler than that. Our marital success stems from small but significant efforts we've made to improve our relationship, starting as far back as our first date. The result is a bond built on a foundation of shared values that allow our marriage to thrive.

Call us old-fashioned, but we've learned that tried-and-true basics, similar to what our grandparents looked to for guidance, are what work in today's world, too. For instance, we're kind to each other, have fun, and laugh a lot. We've learned how to diffuse tension before fights become explosive, and we lean on friends, family, and God for support when we need to call in backup. We also know how to forgive and forget. We do our best to trust each other, try not to tell white lies, and deal with money and housework issues in a way that feels fair. We have delicious sex as often as we can. We try new and different things to keep our relationship fresh, and we honor our commitment every single day. We talk (but not too much) about what matters in between, and we've come to discover that marriage isn't about "work" as the saying goes, but "effort." As a result our marriage is healthier today than when we first said, "I do."

When we first met, we had no idea we were in for such a whirlwind romance. As would soon become a running theme in our relationship, this initial encounter was full of ridiculousness.

Giuliana: I first fell hard for Bill when he won *The Apprentice,* though we didn't officially meet until two years later when I'd overheard in the *E! News* newsroom that we were shooting an interview with him. He was doing charity work in Santa Monica for the Boys and Girls Club, which offers positive programs and services to underprivileged kids, and we wanted to cover the details to support the cause. My assignment manager, Maureen, was about to give the story away to a junior reporter, but I immediately elbowed my way to the front of the line. I knew from watching Bill on TV that he was a catch, and I wanted a shot at this hottie with a body.

"Whoa, whoa, whoa, whoa, whoa," I said to Maureen. "What's this about a shoot with Bill Rancic?" Maureen gave me all the details, and said that she didn't ask me to cover the event because I was busy anchoring at the time, and the interview was an afterhours gig forty minutes from the studio. "Well, I *do* want to get involved in more charity work," I told her. She threw me a knowing smirk (I later found out that she also had a crush on Bill) and then gave me the assignment. I ran to the bathroom to touch up my makeup.

Just before leaving for the interview, I did some quick investigative research on Bill by Googling three words: "Bill Rancic girlfriend." You better believe I did, but not only for the reason you think. Sure, I wanted to know if Bill was available for my own single girl purposes, but if you've ever seen my interviews, I love to get personal with my subjects . . . and the more intimate the questions, the more memorable the Q&A.

As I clicked the "Search" button, I secretly hoped that nothing would pop up about Bill's love life, but something did. A few gossip blogs reported that he'd been dating a producer in New York City for the past few months. This seriously bummed me out, since my motivation for doing the interview wasn't entirely professional. But with an hour before the shoot, it was too late to squirm out of the assignment, so when I finally sat down with Bill, I remember copping an attitude with my tone and body language. My arms were crossed, and my voice sounded indifferent, even though all I could think was, "Damn, this guy is gorgeous!" After a series of questions about boys, girls, and clubs, I prepared to dash the hopes of single women like me. Donald Trump had just had a son and seemed very settled and content with his beautiful wife Melania, so it seemed like the perfect segue to get my viewers the scoop on Bill and that chick in NYC.

"So, are you going to settle down soon with your *girlfriend*?" I asked him, while simultaneously planning how to act shocked when he told me about the producer. Instead, Bill surprised me. "My girlfriend?" he asked. "We broke up." My heart skipped a beat, and my cheeks got rosy. I was excited. *"Really?"* I asked, as I unfolded my arms and leaned-in closer to Bill. "Do you plan to settle down, eventually?" Bill turned on the charm. "I'm holding out," he said. And when I asked him what for, he said, "I'm holding out for you."

I nearly swallowed my Trident. We both laughed nervously since we weren't sure what would come next. I couldn't tell whether Bill wanted to woo our TV audience or me, but it really didn't matter. We ended up hanging out for an hour once the cameras were off, and we just couldn't stop talking. We covered everything that mattered—our families, our hometowns, our exercise habits, you name it. And at the end of the conversation, I thought, *OK, that was fun. But I guess this isn't going anywhere, since he's not asking me out.* I told Bill I needed to leave, but as I walked to my car, I heard him call my name. "Giuliana?" he yelled, and I thought, *Ah-ha! Here it comes. He's going to ask me to grab a beer.* But when I turned around, he hit me with an unusual request. "Want to go for a run sometime?"

Now, I don't know how they do it in the Midwest, but when the women of Los Angeles go out with a handsome stranger for the first time, we prefer dim lighting, alcohol, high heels, and plenty of makeup. Why would I ever want to meet Bill at ten a.m. wearing unflattering spandex, a clean face, and my hair in a ponytail?

"Or . . . we could grab drinks or dinner?" I suggested. "That would be great, too," Bill said. So we exchanged numbers, went out the next week, and by the third date we began planning our future together. "So what are you doing in two months?" we'd ask each other during marathon phone calls late at night. "I have a trip to New Zealand," Bill would say. "Maybe if we're still together, you'll come." And then I'd say,

"OK. Well, I have a premiere in New York in three months, so maybe if we're still together, you'll come with me to that?"

For me, it was love at first interview—though I can say for a fact that I fell for Bill while watching him every week on *The Apprentice*. Bill never tuned-in to *E! News* because he doesn't care who Gerard Butler is banging from week to week, but I liked having the advantage. I was already impressed with Bill's character from the way he won Trump's competition with utmost class. Actually, a lot of what I needed to know about my future husband I learned from watching *The Apprentice*. For instance, Bill didn't backstab, and he was intelligent, funny, and business-savvy on that show. He also looked hot in a two-piece suit. Bill's too sensible to say that he fell in love with *me* at first sight, but he'll be the first to admit that what turned his head was that I made him laugh and seemed very authentic, like him. Those were important qualities to Bill.

From that point on, our long-distance relationship managed to move at breakneck speed—everywhere, we should say, but in the bedroom. Since we lived in two different cities (Bill in Chicago and Giuliana in L.A.), we were careful to build intimacy and anticipation slowly, since establishing a relationship based on shared values was our biggest priority, even back then. We didn't even kiss until our third date, and we didn't take things further, if you know what we mean, until several months later. We were intent on pacing our relationship and were respectful of each other's timelines and hesitations. We only took steps forward when it felt right, and maybe a little serendipitous, including the first time we said, "I love you."

Bill: Three months after we met, I flew to New York City to escort Giuliana to the Gracie Awards, which recognizes successful women in the media, where she was a presenter. We walked the red carpet together for the first time, and had a blast schmoozing the night away. We met Giuliana's sister Monica and her husband B.Z. for dinner after, and I was impressed with how warm and comfortable they were with me and how much fun they had with Giuliana. Monica is Giuliana's best friend, which was endearingly obvious, as Monica told me hilarious stories about how frugal Giuliana was as a kid and how close they are as a family—both of which were music to my ears. Lying in bed with Giuliana that night, I was so excited about our relationship that I wanted to tell her how much she meant to me. I told her I loved her for the first time and she said she loved me, too.

Eight months after we met, I repeated those same three words to her when I asked her to marry me while flying over Chicago in a private helicopter, and then nine months later when we were joined as husband and wife in Capri. Long-distance dating and marriage have certainly had its challenges, but I wouldn't trade the course of our relationship for the world.

Cut to today, and we feel more deeply in love than when we first met, mostly because our passion is joined by a sense a security and calm that reminds us that "home" is where we are. A big part of our dynamic, too, is our shared desire to lead a "normal" life, even if our long-distance and public relationship seems unconventional. When you live among crazy entertainment types the way we do, we count our blessings every day that we found each other. It's rare to meet, and then marry, someone who shares our traditional values and down-to-earth priorities in Hollywood. Bad plane food and expensive phone bills are the price we're happy to pay to have each other.

As Bill likes to say, "Marriage is the one choice that will impact every decision you'll make for the rest of your life." And so far, he's been right: each day reminds us that we made the right choice, because knowing each other makes us better people. Giuliana's brought a sense of ease and humor to our lives, with a free-spirited, live-for-today attitude; and Bill enforces empathy, boundaries, and pragmatism every moment he gets. We listen, laugh, and learn from each other's quirks, always focusing on our partnership. Is this a radical approach to marriage? Not really. But when our priorities are put into action, day after day, the result changes our lives.

What does all this mean to you? In the following pages, you'll read about the experiences we've had, and the lessons we've learned, that influence and make up the amazing marriage we have today. We've broken this book down by some of the bigger themes that have always run throughout our relationship— such as money, honesty, commitment, communication, and so on—so you can zero-in on the topics you're most interested in. We even talk about food and gift-giving here, since they play a fun role in creating memories but can also cause couples stress. And just so we don't sound like we're talking entirely out our tush, we've grounded some of our thoughts in research about happy unions. We hope the end result paints a clear, amusing, and helpful picture of what our loving marriage looks like.

So pour yourself a glass of wine, cuddle-up next to your honey, and promise that if you have a laugh at our expense, you'll try to learn something, too. We hope this book urges you to highlight and share the better parts with friends, and even read a few sections aloud to your spouse. We think everyone's marriage has the potential to be the type that others notice and admire. All you may need is a gentle nudge, from a couple that's truly, madly, and hilariously in love.

I Do,
Now What?

1 Baby, You're So Money

Without a doubt, money conversations are one of the shakiest topics that come up in any marriage (again and again). We love shiny new things as much as the next couple, but problems creep up when we don't see eye-to-eye on our spending habits. In fact, the most common reasons we argue over money are less about the actual cash, and more about what the green stuff means. What a change from when we were single and only accountable to ourselves. . . .

We can totally relate when we hear that research out of the University of Virginia finds that money evokes feelings of freedom, control, trust, security, and self-worth—and that these things can really impact how we think and feel about ourselves and our spouses. Money issues can cause us to question how compatible we feel with our partners, make us judge the way he/she handles money, and make us look for someone to blame when our bank account's low or we've missed a cable bill payment. Though newer studies find that money is no longer the top reason for divorce, it still causes blow-outs and squabbles

over incompatible spending
habits, materialism, and
consumer debt. When ei-
ther one of us bitches about
finances, just talking about
the subject raises the stress
level in our home. And the

> *"The best money advice I
> ever got was from my dad.
> He said, 'It's not what you
> earn, it's what you save.' I live
> by those words."* —**Bill**

more time we spend arguing, the less time we spend together.
On the flip side, when we have a solid and open understanding
of the role money plays in our relationship, our financial confidence trickles into other areas of our life in a positive way. Suddenly, our sex life is better and our jobs feel more manageable!
Which would you prefer to experience?

Now, by no means do we think money buys happiness,
because we've met our share of miserable rich folks; and if
anything, they remind us that it's important to be grateful
for your spouse and the life we share, even if there's room for
improvement. But we do suggest that the next time you
sneak away to Barneys or Best Buy for a shopping spree, consider how your spending will affect your partner, plus the
consequences it might have on the short- and long-term
health of your marriage. Even before we said "I do," both of
us had money matters on the mind—though we had very different opinions on this touchy topic. Here's how we found
our way.

Bill: My friends and family all agree: money changes everything. And in most marriages, the subject of money can be the
cause of some ugly conversations. It doesn't matter if you're
liquid, live on credit, or thrive somewhere in between: When
you decide to join your life and wallet with another person's,
there's always the question of what's fiscally mine, yours, and
ours—and a lot of it's based on what you earned before meeting each other and the assets acquired during and after. Nobody likes to talk about money, even if you're rich, because in

the big picture, it affects trust levels, not to mention how safe or free we feel in our relationship. So to me, it was really important to map out my money situation with Giuliana before we walked down the aisle together. It felt like a really wise and husbandy thing to do.

When couples get married in their early twenties, both the husband and wife are usually broke, so it doesn't matter where they are financially. You grow together, and build your nest egg from the ground up. But when I married Giuliana, I was thirty-six and Giuliana was thirty-one, so our situation was a little different. I'd spent eight years slaving away, eighteen hours a day, building my company before I even knew Giuliana's name. I had heard that one of the top things couples argue about is money, specifically debt, and it's stressful on marriages. I wanted to make sure we had as little stress as possible in ours.

I spent three years working for Donald Trump after I won season one of *The Apprentice*. All day, and all night, our conversations were about how to protect and make money.

> "The worst cash advice I ever got came from my brother Pasquale (who owns a red Ferrari and drives it wearing a red Ferrari tracksuit, Ferrari baseball cap, and red shoes): 'Spend your money like it's your last day on Earth.' I love my bro, but Bill's taught me it's better to die with cash in the bank than live without a dime. PS: I don't take Pasquale's fashion advice, either." —Giuliana

So when Trump heard I was engaged, I shouldn't have been too surprised when he called to offer his advice. The golden words? "Make sure you get a pre-nup." Donald's always been a good friend and mentor to me, so I was open to hearing him out.

Giuliana: Gee, lucky us . . .

Bill: I'd already thought about a pre-nup, and I even made jokes about it to Giuliana before we got engaged. "Hey, when we get married, we've got to sign a pre-nup—it's part of the program," I'd half-tease her. I thought it was a good idea to just keep things as clean, documented, and clearly defined as possible, and it helped to hear a happily married multibillionaire second that. When I spoke to Giuliana the night after I talked to Donald, I told her, "Trump says we should get a pre-nup"—and she said fine. Fine! So I researched a bunch of good lawyers and had an agreement drawn up by one of the best: a really good, trustworthy guy named David. The document basically stated that what I owned prior to September 1, 2007—the date we got married—was mine and what Giuliana owned prior to September 1, 2007 was hers. Everything from September 1 on would be part of the marriage and ours to share. It was pretty basic.

Giuliana: Wait, the pre-nup said all of that? I have to confess: I never read it. I gave it to, um, "my lawyer" to review. And by lawyer, I mean my older brother Pasquale, who sells plane parts to the military by day and is a classically trained opera singer by night. He's always had strong opinions about my relationships, which is a nice way of saying he's hated all my past boyfriends and threatened their lives if they ever hurt me, until Bill came along.

Bill: This is when I learned about the Neapolitan way. Especially in business, many Italians like to put things off as if they don't exist, until they're ready to deal with them on their watch. For five months, I asked Giuliana for feedback on the latest draft of the pre-nup, and for five months, she fed me excuses: *My lawyer is out of town. I had to work the red carpet at the Oscars. . . .*

Giuliana: When I mentioned the pre-nup to Pasquale, he was disgusted. The word *pre-nup* isn't even in my family's vocabulary: he never signed one, my sister never signed one, and my parents certainly didn't sign one. To me, marriage is about becoming one—money, feelings, families. What's mine is yours, what's yours is mine. My brother feels the same way. So he was blunt about the document: "If Bill really loves you, he wouldn't ask you to sign this. I didn't ask *my* wife to sign a pre-nup. . . ."

Bill: Because he didn't have anything when he got married at twenty-four!

Giuliana: Well, that's true—he didn't have much when he married my sister-in-law Nikki. But he sure had an opinion on the topic. "Italian men don't give their women pre-nups, and Italian women sure as hell don't sign them," he said. "Tell your American husband to shove that pre-nup up his ass." And that was basically the advice from my lawyer-slash-consigliere. I don't think Bill asked his friends and family what they thought about asking me to sign that pre-nup, but maybe he should have.

Bill: My friends assumed I'd have one, but I don't think my mom would have cared either way.

There's Nothing Funny About Money

Giuliana: I have to admit that when Bill first brought up the idea of a pre-nup, I thought he might be joking around. I even joked that I'd sign the pre-nup if he put a fidelity clause in there about how much I'd get if he cheated, and a weight clause about how much he'd pay me if he put on fifty pounds of man boobs and a beer gut. Because we laughed about it so much, I guess part of me thought it would go away. It made me too upset to think that Bill would attach a dollar-and-cents value to our marriage. So we danced around the topic for a long time, or at least I did.

Bill: I wish Giuliana had been honest with me about how unhappy the papers made her before I dropped five grand on them in legal fees—I felt like a schmuck, and I lost money. And I didn't think she was kidding about the fidelity clause, because it cost me another $1,200 to add it in!

Giuliana: Look, I'm not this Beverly Hills chick who spends her afternoons on Rodeo Drive. I work really hard, and I don't spend money I don't have . . . at least, I haven't since my twenties. When a woman looks like a financial assassin who is gonna rob you blind, then a man should absolutely consider a pre-nup, but that was never me. If God forbid we broke up tomorrow, and Bill were to remarry some hoochie, I would definitely tell him to get a pre-nup because most women can't be trusted with a fat wallet. But I knew I'd never screw him, and I knew he would never screw me. I just had that feeling, and it was enough for me. I didn't need it on paper. I knew I could be trusted.

Bill: Let me tell you something: I've known Giuliana for four years, and if things broke badly in this relationship, she'd go for my throat. She would try to take me for every red cent I have and make sure I ended up homeless.

Giuliana: If Bill cheated on me or did something really awful like leave me for another woman, I would one hundred percent ruin his life and take him for all he's worth, but this isn't news to anyone who knows me. I'm a crazy Italian chick, so if my man wrongs me, I will absolutely take him to the cleaners and destroy him. That may sound harsh, but it's better than what I would really want to do to Bill, which is chop his balls off and feed them to the lions at the zoo. (Actually, I'd never do that. I'd get thrown in jail and where would that leave me, except with a kick-ass *True Hollywood Story?*) Bottom line, I knew Bill was a good person because I dated a lot of dogs before him. I had faith in him and in us. He can't fault me for that.

Bill: Aww, that's sweet, honey. I think.

Giuliana: What really put the period on this issue for me is when I bumped into the world-famous financial guru Suze Orman at the Gracie Awards, in New York City. Suze was so sweet, even when she practically cornered me in the elevator. "I hear you're getting married!" she said, and then: "You're signing a pre-nup, right?" I told her about how Bill really wanted one and how I was hesitant to sign it. She started shaking her head furiously. "No, no, no. I'm talking about *you* giving *him* a pre-nup. What if you land *The Today Show,* or just start making more money? Your fame could explode! How will you protect yourself?" Bill had Trump on his team; Suze Orman was on mine: Team Blue vs. Team Pink. This was starting to feel like an episode of *Celebrity Apprentice.*

That night, I couldn't sleep because, despite the well-intentioned advice that Suze gave me, the pre-nup still didn't feel right to me for two big reasons. For one, I worried about how Bill's mine-versus-yours point of view would play out in other financial aspects of our marriage. If we were going to divvy up what we had before we got hitched, how would we want to structure our money as husband and wife? I'm not a fan of having separate accounts—you pay for the kids' tuition, I'll cover family vacations. Does that ever work? I also didn't want our marriage to get off to such a litigious, unromantic start. We may have been engaged, but we still didn't know each other well enough at that point to be painfully honest about such explosive topics like how much we were or weren't worth *and how that might impact our hypothetical divorce*!

In the end, I decided not to sign the papers, but I didn't tell Bill right away. I continued to feel really awkward about the pre-nup topic and dodged it whenever I could. It was clear Bill felt weird badgering me about it, though he really wanted an answer. Looking back, I should have been more honest with him, but we don't really talk about money in my family, so why would I start with Bill? To me, money is a by-product of working hard. It's what you use to pay bills, fund dreams, and help out the people you care for. I didn't see the point of hashing all this out with Bill, and I was a little afraid that if we did, we'd second guess whether we were really meant to be together if this was a big issue for him and not for me. I also wasn't comfortable planning how our marriage would end before it began. The whole topic freaked me out.

Bill: So she waited until a week before our wedding to tell me she wouldn't sign. At that point, it probably wouldn't have even been valid because a lawyer could say she signed it under duress!

Giuliana: Hmmm, I never thought about that. When Bill called me for a final answer, I was just off a shoot and really stressed out. I didn't tell him how sad it made me to think about life without him, that I found his need for financial structure to be totally unromantic, and that I was sorry for avoiding a topic that was really important to him.

Bill: No, she definitely didn't say any of that. She just said, "Italians don't sign pre-nups."

Giuliana: Yeah, that was it.

Bill: It wasn't quite the response I had hoped for, but I was relieved to finally get any response from Giuliana, and while I didn't entirely buy her Italian excuse, I realized it was the closest thing I'd get to a straight answer from her. I didn't want to be right or wrong, I just wanted us to be happy. It felt too frustrating to not connect the way we usually do, and I just wanted it to be over. You make sacrifices in marriage, and while this was something that I thought would be wise, it made Giuliana upset, so maybe it wasn't the best idea after all. You don't need a PhD in psychology to know that feeling this awkward before a wedding is no way to kick off a life together.

The pre-nup made me feel protected in case something went wrong, financially or otherwise. I never *expected* something to happen, but how could I know? Giuliana is a Hollywood girl, and everyone knows most Hollywood marriages don't last. If I lost DePandi, plus all the money I'd worked for my whole life, it would have been too overwhelming for me. I'd be left with nothing, so I don't think I acted so strange. I think every guy with a dime to his name has wondered whether a woman wants to be with him for his ability to buy her nice things or for the person he really is. Marriages can get messy when things go wrong, and I really believe you can eliminate a lot of future issues when you address problems before they happen. That was my goal with the pre-nup: to put a plan in place so I didn't have to worry about how things might spiral out of control if Giuliana ran off with a scuba diving teacher. Or George Clooney.

Giuliana: I don't scuba dive, since the ocean scares me. Seeing fish that close up is creepy, but Clooney, well, that's another story.

I knew my love for Bill was deep and true. Come to think of it, I should have asked Bill to sign an *emotional* pre-nup. At their core, our concerns are mostly emotional, anyway. The

Most expensive item in Giuliana's closet: *"Louis Vuitton suitcase ($3,000) for regular four-hour flights to Chicago."* **Least:** *"Flats ($7) that roll up and fit in my purse. I hate running errands in heels after work."*

stuff we really needed to feel good about before pledging our lives to each other were about trust, respect, and promising that neither of us will walk out when things get tough. If I could have an emotional pre-nup drafted, I'd also put something in about making an effort to do something nice for your spouse every day and having realistic expectations of what your partner can deliver—mostly for Rancic, not me. Bill surprises me with flowers and fills up my car with gas all the time. I love him so much for that; he's really giving about the amount of energy he puts into our marriage. But I'm not nearly as generous that way, and it's a flaw that I'm trying to fix. For instance, he thinks I'm a TV host during the day and a masseuse at night—and I repeatedly prove him wrong. He wants full-body massages almost every evening, but I give him certificates to a spa instead. I hate giving massages more than anything in this world. I have dainty hands, and they get very tired after two minutes.

The Deal with Our Dinero

Giuliana: We talked about money so much before we were married that afterward, I think we were both a little afraid to approach the topic—so at first nothing changed, at all, about how we handled our individual funds. I had my bank account, Bill had his bank account, and we both seemed fine with doing our own thing; and it's certainly not like *me* to say,

"Sweetie, let's go talk to a money manager!" I am a full-on paesano, an off-the-boat Italian who'd stash her cash under her mattress if Bill would let me. I have no idea what's in my bank account from one day to the next, and people think I'm crazy for not balancing my checkbook. I think that made Bill a little nuts, too—he probably kept better mental tabs on my bank account than I did.

When I first met Bill, with all his talk about planning and finances, I just kept thinking: *What if we die tomorrow, and we've spent all this time saving our money and not enjoying it to the fullest?* But I was so focused on how *I* don't want to live my life that I never stopped to think about how *Bill* didn't want to live his life. His fears are just as legit as mine. I can't blame him for thinking I was some flaky chick who'd spend all his money, because my money track record practically screamed, well, "flaky chick."

Bill: Don't even get me started. There was so much drama over Giuliana's taxes.

Giuliana: I used to think taxes were unfair, but Bill talked some sense into me. I remember when I told him that I wanted to write off dresses and shoes that I'd bought for interviews, and he was like, "You can't write off Nordstrom. It's a red flag." I secretly doubted him. "I'll go to court and prove it with receipts and copies of my interviews wearing those outfits."

Bill: I can see it now: "Your honor, do you watch *E! News*? These are the Gucci shoes I wore when I interviewed Angelina Jolie."

Giuliana: Very funny . . . and they were Dior. Anyway, when Bill explained how horrible (and expensive) it is to get audited, I backed down.

Bill: She had this whole imaginary defense about how she'd go to court, bring her lawyer, and try to defend why she tried to write off M.A.C lipstick and skinny jeans from the mall. She swore she'd win. Giuliana had no idea how much money it would cost her to go to court and sue the government—the government?! In life, you pay taxes. It sucks. End of story.

Giuliana: See how he looks out for our family?

Bill: Part of being a family is realizing a long-term plan for our lives, and money is an element of that equation. I didn't want either of us to ever have a reason to criticize the other person for spending too much or putting our family's finances at risk. I also wanted to stop thinking about the pre-nup situation and start talking about how we can be pro-active about our monetary goals. So after a year of doing our own thing, we decided we should meet with a financial adviser to learn how to set financial goals for now and for retirement—plus establish smart spending habits while we still have jobs that earn us some play money. My parents were schoolteachers, so they had pension plans. Giuliana's dad is seventy-two, and he still works. We don't have a pension and basically work for ourselves, so we had to figure this stuff out. Money represents security, trust, and devotion to me, but it can also be the source of fear or conflict if it's not handled appropriately. It's important to have a financial road map that helps us act more responsibly with our spending. If we want to live our life with certain privileges, we need to figure out the best way to do it. A new financial plan would act as a nice little reminder, too, that we're working toward a common goal. I now think twice before picking up the check with ten guys at dinner, and Giuliana might do the same the next time she thinks about buying $1,200 Balchiogo boots.

Giuliana: He means Balenciaga boots.

> **Most expensive item in Bill's office:** *"Apple laptop ($1,500)"* **Least:** *"Photo taken minutes after we got engaged. We have cheesy grins on our faces, and I'm so happy that we could capture how elated we felt in that exact moment. Giuliana had it framed and inscribed with the date."*

Bill: Sorry . . . Balenciaga. I must have missed the brand. All I saw were dollar signs on that credit card statement.

Giuliana: What made *me* want to go to the finance guy was that combining our money made us feel like a family. Bill and I still have our separate business accounts, which makes tax time less complicated, but we now have a joint account that we use for travel, play, or even dinner money. It also tells me Bill's in it for the long haul.

Bill: I think a big reason why it took me awhile to come around to the idea of sharing our funds—from both before and after our marriage—is that I never thought I'd get married. So I didn't want to start off on Day One by saying "Here's the checkbook, honey!" That would require too much of me, too soon—I'd be giving over myself, plus the money I worked so hard to make on my own, all at once. But I love the idea of building a family, and a family fund, with Giuliana. It just took me a minute to realize and accept how much I needed her in my life, because I never expected that I'd feel this way about anyone.

Giuliana: We are totally open about all of our money and spending habits now. I can't believe that in wanting to avoid an argument with Bill over the pre-nup, I could have caused some big-time problems with financial trust issues. Problems don't go away if you don't talk about them! I know the more experience we have with learning to handle the new and strange things about each other, the better we'll get at it—financially

and otherwise. We learn from each other's pet peeves and become better because of it.

We don't keep tabs on each other's spending now, or keep
money secrets from each other. There's no reason for it, with
our financial plan. Having shared financial goals also moti-
vates us to work harder, land more gigs, and make more
money for our future family. We know what we have to make
every year to get to that goal, and the end is financial freedom,
which equals spending time together and enjoying retirement—
hopefully in a villa in Tuscany.

Bill: Financial confidence will also allow us to be the parents
we want to be, and that's very important to each of us. Personally, I want to have the monetary freedom to not miss out
on coaching the football team and soccer teams because I have
a bunch of meetings somewhere, and Giuliana wants to be
able to take time off to be a PTA mom in six-inch heels. Sometimes we have minor regrets about waiting so long to get married at our age, but I'll tell you this much: it did afford us the
luxury of becoming financially equipped parents someday. I
only hope it makes up for the fact that we'll also be the oldest,
and slowest, parents on the playground.

Giuliana: Speak for yourself, Rancic. I can run in heels like no
other; it's amazeballs! That said, it is really nice knowing that
Bill has our best future interests at heart—and I like to think
it's my job to keep us in the present. Bill may be teaching me
how to save money, but I like to think I'm teaching *him* how to
enjoy his cash in the moment a little more. He works so hard
that he forgets to reward himself with a vacation or the more
expensive iPod once in a while. That said, we don't need a private plane or to eat out every night at the best restaurant in
town. I always assure Bill: if life ever rained on our financial
parade, I'd be happy in a cozy one bedroom apartment for the
rest of our lives. As long as we're together, we're fine.

TIPS FOR TWO: Talking About Your Finances

• Learn your spouse's financial hot buttons—spending habits, saving and planning philosophies, financial history, and earning potential. Use these details to inform your talks about money.

• To reach financial goals, consider the impact of credit card debt, a savings account, mutual funds, separate spending accounts, or a joint household account. Talk to an objective pro for help!

• Create a financial plan for your marriage. Where do you see yourself in five, ten, fifteen years? How can you afford to get there?

• Choose a relaxing, distraction-free time and place to review your finances at least once a month. We like to review our statements together online; knowing that the other person will see everything we've bought in the past month keeps us on point.

• It may take time to develop the communication skills necessary for your partner to really hear you on money issues. If you're met with silent treatments or arguments, don't give up.

• Don't be afraid to take a break in the middle of a tense money conversation; they can get exhausting. Just be sure you pick up where you left off when you're ready to tackle the issue again.

2 Tell Me No Lies

A wise stylist once told Giuliana that the only secrets you should keep in your marriage are beauty secrets (details about getting Botox around the eyes or having your lips pumped with Juvéderm are better left unsaid). And though nobody likes to hear it, psychologists insist that telling small fibs, concealing information, and even editing the details of a story to spare your partner's feelings all count as big fat lies. Even dancing around the truth to avoid confronting an ugly situation qualifies as dishonesty. After all, betrayals come in all shapes and sizes, but their end result is the same: they chip away at trust and intimacy, and can cause damage to a marriage.

We had a rough time with secrets when we first met. As far as Giuliana knew, white lies were harmless if intentions were pure and nobody seemed to get hurt. Bill, however, was a hard ass when it came to telling lies, no matter what their size, and drew a more severe line between truth and dishonesty, right and wrong. The juxtaposition of these values was jarring for us, since slight indiscretions rubbed us in different ways. We eventually had to learn how to rely on direct communication to quiet our anxieties and suspicions. Does the occasional exaggeration or fib still manage to slip through the cracks? Sure. But does Bill always have a logical plan that helps us get back on track with the truth? He sure does, and we're always appreciative of it.

We do our best to be open and honest in our marriage now, because it scares us to think about being with a spouse who doesn't have your back. But as you'll soon learn, it took us awhile to get to this place. Read on for one of our favorite stories about secrets, truth, and consequences.

Giuliana: It was our second date when Bill casually asked me how old I was. We were at dinner, and I was caught by surprise—mostly because people in Hollywood do their best to avoid this topic. But Bill is from Chicago, so he didn't think like my L.A. friends or the age-obsessed guys I'd dated. On my third glass of cabernet, I told him I was twenty-nine—even though I was really thirty-one at the time. Two years. Big deal, right? The fib seemed harmless enough, since entertainment people always shave a few years off their age. And when I asked Bill's age in return, he told me he was thirty-five. It never dawned on me to doubt Bill, because I was just making conversation. I didn't really care one way or the other.

We had a really good time on our date, so we planned our next rendezvous before we left the restaurant, and when I got home, I did what any girl-in-lust does after a fabulous night out with a mystery man: I Googled him. Bill had told me all about his life at dinner, and I hung on every word. But I also figured that he must have been exaggerating a little because he seemed too perfect to be true. My suspicions were wrong. Online, Bill's profile matched up to his talking points at dinner. I read about how he studied criminal justice in college, how his favorite musical group was indeed the Dave Matthews Band,

and how he grew up a middle-class kid from the 'burbs who was lousy in school and used his street smarts to start a successful company at the age of twenty-three, which he later sold for a lot of money.

Best and worst of all, I noticed time and time again that he copped to his real age: thirty-five.

Something inside made my stomach flip-flop. *Please God,* I thought. *Don't let him Google me.* For a second, I wondered if it was too late to tweak my Wikipedia page. But I figured it was a bad idea to type while tipsy, went to bed, and forgot the whole fib even happened.

Bill: We'd started dating in April, and Giuliana's birthday was four months later, on August 17, so after she mentioned she was twenty-nine, I got excited that her thirtieth was just around the corner. I'd had an incredible party for my Big 3–0 and wanted to make sure, if we were still together in a few months, that Giuliana would also have a party she'd never forget. In late July, with no mention of any plans, I began to think it was so sad that nobody was planning something for this nice girl's thirtieth birthday. Not her sister Monica, not her mom . . . nobody. I thought, *I'll put something together for her—a big surprise. She'll be psyched.* So I called Monica, I called her good friends Pam and Colet, and it was the weirdest thing—none of them called me back. I tried a few times, and after days of radio silence, I decided that maybe they were just horrible people. It was so strange to me that nobody seemed to care about Giuliana enough to help me celebrate her big day.

Giuliana: Bill left a few messages for my family and friends rambling on about my upcoming thirtieth birthday. When they called me to ask me what the hell was going on, they were pissed at me because they obviously knew I wasn't headed for a milestone year. In fact, Monica called one day and before she

even said hello, she dead-
panned into the phone:
"I just heard from Bill.
How old did you tell him
you are?" I was silent,
confused. "Bill's been calling everyone," she ex-
plained. "He wants a list
of friends and family to
invite to your thirtieth
birthday party. Giuliana,
you turned thirty two

> ### To Tell You the Truth . . .
>
> • We think honest people have less reason to feel insecure and uncertain.
> • We hope that trying to be honest in our marriage will set a good example for our children.

years ago." I didn't know what to process first: that Bill already cared enough to throw me a party, or that he might
freak out if he learned my real age and that I'd lied to him
about it. I froze and ignored my phone as it rang off the hook
from friends and family. It was enough to give me a nervous
breakdown. (I didn't know it at the time, but Bill loves planning surprises for people. He's very thoughtful that way—
birthdays, getaways, excursions.)

"Don't call him back," I finally told Monica. "I'll tell him,
I'll tell him"—but she wouldn't let it go. "Giuliana, this isn't
just about you. He's going to think we're all assholes," she
said, and it was true. I'd begun to suspect that he thought my
friends were a bunch of selfish losers. We'd be eating Thai
food, and Bill would casually slip in, "So, how close are you to
Pam? What about your sister?" and I'd act oblivious to his in-
sinuations: "Close, you know." And he'd just say, "*Really*?
Huh."

Bill: It was the weirdest thing ever. I was so confused; I didn't
know what to think. I was blowing up these peoples' phones.
The few times I'd met Giuliana's friends and family, they
seemed like fun and caring people—or at least polite enough
to return a phone call. Finally I called Monica, and left her a

serious message. My voice meant business: "Monica, please call me. Giuliana's birthday is two weeks away, and I've booked a venue. The money's down, we're ready to go. We just need to send out Evites . . ."

Giuliana: My sister called me immediately. "You have *got* to call him," she said, in her bossy big sister voice. "We can't even go to dinner with you at this point because we're too embarrassed to see Bill. We're dodging him like a stray bullet." Meanwhile, I could hear her husband Bryan, who we also call B.Z., in the background: "Tell her Bill's calling me, too, and I'm sick of throwing him to my voice mail!" My little white lie had snowballed out of control.

Bill: So here's what I did to put this issue to bed. I insisted we go to dinner with Monica and B.Z. at this sushi restaurant called Katsuya—their baked crab rolls are off the charts. If I couldn't get them on the phone, I figured I'd get some information from them over crispy rice tuna. All night, I gave Monica the stink eye because I couldn't say anything about the party in front of Giuliana, so I just kept staring at her, hoping she could read my mind. *Is this party on, or what?* It was so uncomfortable, and I was confused at how Monica could act so pleasant during dinner after having ignored my urgent calls about her own sister for two weeks. What kind of family was this?

After I stared her down for an hour straight, Monica turned to Giuliana and said, "You'd better tell him now, Giuliana. You have to tell him now." *Oh, hell,* I thought. *What's going on? Is she pregnant? Married? Does she have an STD?* My heart fell to my stomach. I had no idea what bomb was about to drop, but it didn't look good.

Giuliana: At this point, it was, like, ten days before my birthday.

Bill: The clock was ticking. And again, I was losing more money!

Giuliana: So my sister said, "Tell him!" And I just couldn't do it. I stared at her, pissed yet petrified, like a deer in headlights until B.Z. says, "Tell him, Giuliana. *He deserves to know.*" Bill looked so frightened, more panicked than I've ever seen him. "What's going on?" he asked, with big eyes and nervous laughter. So I said: "You're going to die, Bill. This is *so* funny! Are you ready?" I took a deep breath and a gulp of my sake. "Remember how I told you I was twenty-nine?" I started. "Well, I'm actually thirty-one, so I'm not having a thirtieth birthday! It's my thirty-second! *How funny is that?*"

Bill: You could hear a chopstick drop at our table. It wasn't funny at all.

When Little Lies Lead to Big Problems

Giuliana: When I originally lied about my age, I didn't think it was a big deal. I really didn't. *This is only our second date,* I thought. *It's not like he'll be my husband some day.* I figured Bill could be gone next week, and if we were ever in a situation where he could learn my real age—like from a passport or my driver's license—I figured I'd come up with some way to conceal it. I actually have a way of holding my passport and license so you can't see my age—I just put my finger over the birth date. I've always had lots of clever ways of never letting people know how old I am.

Bill: And when we went to Mexico together, just before Giuliana's birthday, she did hold her passport that way! She told me I couldn't see it because she hated her picture.

Giuliana: I did! See, I told you I was slick. Bill loves to keep things organized because he doesn't have the patience to watch me dig through my giant handbag in the security line, so when he offered to hold my passport, I refused: "I'd rather not. My photo's hideous. The lighting was terrible, and I was experimenting with bangs that month. I can't bear to show it to you."

Bill: Anyway, when I learned the truth about Giuliana's age at dinner, it rubbed me the wrong way. In fact, it was a big turning point for me in our relationship. I thought, *If this girl is lying about such a little thing, what huge* crap *is she lying about?* That night, when we were back at her apartment after dinner, I told her straight-out: "Lying doesn't work with me. I don't care what it's about. No more secrets. They may work for you in Hollywood, but I'm not from Hollywood. I'm from the Midwest, and here's how we do it: we say what we mean, and we don't make other people look foolish. Get with the program, or we're cutting this thing off." I was really pissed.

Giuliana: The thing is, I truly didn't have any kind of malicious intent—at all. I just wanted this guy I was dating to think I was younger than I was. That's it. I wasn't trying to trick him into anything or act like a sneaky chick. It wasn't as if I told him I had a job that I didn't or hid some kind of terminal illness. It was amazing to me that Bill could make such a big deal out of what I thought was a little itty-bitty lie, and immediately saw me as a girl he couldn't trust—a crazy compulsive liar. (I never used to tell anyone my real age, not even my hair and makeup girls at work, and I tell those ladies *everything*.) "But you could tell me your real age," Bill said, though I didn't buy it at the time. When I first met him, he was just some guy, and if we broke up, I didn't want him rolling around town saying I was thirty-one. Like he would do that, but that's how I think, you just never know. I also loved having a two before my age, when I went on a first date. I wasn't ready to dive into thirty-something territory just yet.

It took me a while to come around to Bill's point of view, and my stubbornness started to cause problems. I tried lots of different tactics to endear myself to him and get him to soften up, like folding his socks the way he likes them, winking at him in public, and making my cutest kissy faces at him—but none of my old tricks worked. Bill still held me at a distance, it felt terrible to be so disconnected. What I thought was a harmless white lie fed newer spats that always managed to link back to our unresolved issue. I remember sitting down with Bill to discuss a completely unrelated problem we'd had about where to go on vacation, and Bill somehow found a way to loop it back to the age thing. I told him to lighten up. "Don't you see?" he said. "This isn't just about a number. It's about you feeling the need to be dishonest with me for such a long period of time. It really makes me wonder what else you're lying about!"

Bill: Man, that lie left a bad taste in my mouth. Whether she meant to or not, keeping a secret—whether that means withholding information, downplaying the truth, or outright lying—is deceptive and sneaky. It wasn't a trait I'd expect from Giuliana, because she always says what's on her mind and had been really honest about more personal issues like childhood fears she still carried with her and insecurities about her body when she wasn't feeling sexy. So I felt the need to reinforce my expectations as often as I could. If we were going to move forward with our relationship, I wanted to let her know what I expected from a partner and that honesty wasn't something I took lightly. Without trust, you have nothing. That's paramount to me.

Giuliana: He saw the white lie as a real character flaw.

Bill: And I wanted to make sure I wasn't being duped. I was just waiting for more secrets to tumble out, and that's a bad feeling to have.

Giuliana: The funny thing is, there really isn't much else that I kept secret. He'll admit it.

Bill: No, but that's why I said, "This is it. This is your opportunity to tell me anything else that you need to get out right now."

You *Can* Handle the Truth

Bill: When Giuliana and I were first dating, I disclosed a lot of personal things those first few months, including the pain and heartache of losing my father when I was twenty-nine years old. We had to open up—we were long distance, so I didn't want us to waste each other's time. We knew we had a lot of chemistry right out of the gate, and neither of us had ever experienced that in other relationships.

Giuliana: Even if I thought Bill overreacted at first, I later realized that melodramatic or not, keeping a secret from Bill was something that really bothers him—no matter how innocent my intentions may be at the time. I may have learned a lesson about Bill's intolerance for secrets before I signed our marriage license, but there isn't a day that I don't think about this hot button and how it affects him and our relationship now, and even my relationships with other people. Bill and I only dated for eight months before we got engaged—it was a whirlwind romance. So testing our limits and setting some early boundaries was important.

Bill: You really set the ground rules for the rest of your life that first year of marriage. For me, I felt it was important to establish boundaries even earlier than that—when we were in the first year of *dating,* especially with subjects that I felt strongly about. Will there be minor changes as you grow together? Of course, but it takes effort and you have to be consistent. I have a lot of friends who let their wives turn them into prisoners of war, and they're like that forever because they never established what they expected from their relationship and each other. That's not for me. I've seen guys make the wrong turn, and just think, "Ah, maybe next year I'll tell her how that makes me feel," and they live in a constant state of torment and confusion.

Giuliana: When it comes to secrets, especially, I've learned that there's no room for misinterpretation. I like to say that we Mapquested our marriage early on—and now we get to where we need to go faster and more efficiently because we've shared and verbalized what's important to us. Without a road map, there is constant confusion. Had Bill not made such a big deal out of the age issue, I probably would have thought it was OK to tell more fibs in our marriage about things that didn't matter to me, even if they secretly mattered to him. It's those little details that tell you where you stand with each other.

Bill: Marriage is the great partnership, but secrets can chip away at that bond. I think couples keep secrets because they hope they'll go away, or that they'll make memories that supersede them, or because they're ashamed of their past and just want a new beginning, but lying doesn't work, because any "fresh start" will have been built on a shaky foundation. And if there's anything I've learned in my real estate career, buildings built on shaky foundations have major issues later on. Your problems are going to find you.

Giuliana: I've read a few times that instead of keeping a secret, you should figure out why you're afraid of telling the truth and then address *that* issue. Experts say that it will make the actual secret become less important. I love that advice!

The good thing about confessing the truth, too, is that after I told Bill my real age, I felt so much closer to him—and I think he felt the same way. It added a layer of intimacy to our relationship, maybe since realizing someone else knew me so well made me feel like it was safe to show my vulnerable side. And it's nice knowing he really does know me better and more intimately than anyone else in my life. Even better, Bill never used my lie against me. He never made me feel ashamed for keeping something inside, though he did make me face and explain it. He still teases me about the age stuff now, but never in a way that makes me feel bad.

You know what else? Beyond feeling closer, I found it really liberating to be so honest with him. Every time I hand Bill my passport now, I'm always really proud of it. I'll say with a big old smile: "Want my passport? Want my license?"—like, *Look how honest I'm being!* You feel such relief when you disclose a secret; and you don't live in fear, and

---

Secret-Keeping Celebs, and the Lessons They've Taught Us

Tiger Woods and Elin Nordegren: Hoochies can't keep a secret for long.

Kobe Bryant and Vanessa Laine: Touch another woman and it will cost you a big, fat diamond.

Brad Pitt and Jennifer Aniston: "Honey, I swear I'm not falling for my co-star. And yes, of course I think she's ugly." Trust has its limits.

Jesse James and Sandra Bullock: See Tiger and Elin.

you don't have anxiety nightmares. Who wants to look over their shoulder all the time? That's just crazy. A relationship based on fear is going to seep into every aspect of your life—at work, with your in-laws . . . and you're just going to become a paranoid and unfulfilled person. You really need to be one hundred percent square at home, in order for the rest of your life to work. That's what I think anyway.

Technological secrets are something else we're against: Bill's free to look at any of my emails, and we read each other's texts if we're bored. I have never been like that with any guy, and frankly, I never thought I could be that open with anyone. I used to guard emails with my life, as did a lot of the guys I dated, and you know what? We were all up to no good. Giving your spouse carte blanche to fumble through your personal info eliminates the need to snoop, and in our minds, snooping is the sleuthy stepsister to secrets—try saying that five times fast!

Bill: Saying "I do" affects everything—your friendships, work, family life, money . . .

Giuliana: . . . where you live, what you eat for dinner . . .

Bill: . . . kids, how many you have . . . the simplest things.

Is There Such a Thing as Oversharing?

Bill: No matter how many talks you have, there's always going to be some information you didn't know about that pops up. We're constantly learning that about each other, like it or not.

Giuliana: Like the time we took a walk in New York City, and Bill said, "I used to live in that building around the time that I won *The Apprentice.*" He lived at 100 Central Park South. So I said, "Wow, that's a nice place. Did you used to take walks with a lot of girls at night like this?" He never gave me a straight answer.

Bill: It was a weird time in my life. I was a young entrepreneur from Chicago, and the next thing you know I'm on the cover of *People* and *US Weekly* every week. It was weird. Everything was so new, so I was very cautious and I didn't know who to trust. I wasn't rolling girls back to my room, but I'm not saying I didn't meet *some* women while I lived in New York, because of course I did.

Giuliana: But my question about the ladies made me realize that for all Bill and I talk about not having secrets, there are things about his past that I don't know . . . and don't really need to know. I don't want to ask for too many details, because I think we're all entitled to a certain degree of privacy and independence after we're married (and he doesn't know details about certain guys I've been with). But if there's something fishy in your personal history that you suspect could impact your marriage, address it ASAP. Otherwise, I say skip it. Some things are better left unsaid.

Bill: I completely disagree, because what you may feel you don't need to disclose, the other person may feel that you should. I think: better safe than sorry, lay it out.

Giuliana: Oh yeah? Then by those standards, I should insist you tell me what went on at 100 Central Park South, but I won't. I think that if you have a love child, have been in jail, or at some point declared bankruptcy—big stuff that affects your marriage—then you need to tell your partner about it. Otherwise, I think things like your previous sex life on the eighth floor of that building should remain private.

Bill: I lived on the tenth floor. But listen, if you're going to spend the rest of your life with someone, make sure there are no surprises. Cover your ass, is what I'm saying. Marriage is about building a foundation. You can build a high-rise on it, but make sure you have a solid bedrock foundation, not swamplands.

Giuliana: Back to my point: I've never asked Bill what his "number" is, and I don't need to know. His sexual past means nothing to me. He could have slept with one girl or one thousand girls before me. I seriously don't care. Bill's a good-looking guy, he was having fun, he was making money—and I would do the same thing in his situation.

Bill: Wait a minute. I'd want to know if Giuliana were some call girl out on the streets, banging ten guys a night. I wouldn't want her to keep that to herself to "protect me."

Giuliana: Well, yeah, if that was my job, and if I were some sort of a call girl . . .

Bill: No, I don't mean literally. I mean, if I walk down the street and hear some guy say "I used to bang your wife," I'd want to know that. I'd want to know if she slept with the NY Giants!

Giuliana: But you can find that out on the Internet . . .

Bill: I'd like to find it out from her. See, there she goes assuming—it's the Neapolitan way.

Giuliana: The key is to know your spouse. If you think he'll care, tell him what you suspect he'll want to know.

Bill: OK, but if you think there's even the *slightest* possibility that your spouse may think something's not kosher, lay it out before you get married or early in the marriage. You don't want it to come out two years later when you have a kid, and you drop the bomb that you used to be a slut. If you start peeling off the layers of the onion several years into the marriage, it's like, *Crap, I've been bamboozled.*

Giuliana: Like poor Sandra Bullock and Elin Nordegren.

Bill: Exactly. They got screwed and ended up with lemons. If I'm not buying the perfect car, I'd want to know about the kinks and dents beforehand. Then I'd be OK with them.

Giuliana: Bill always says that you have to pick your spouse wisely and really know what you're getting yourself into— and that includes knowing if there are any skeletons in the closet. If, in the end, you feel you've made the right decision, then you've got to really work on the choices you make together from that point on, to make sure you're both happy.

TIPS FOR TWO: Keys to an Open Relationship
(No, Not That Kind)

• The size of a secret or fib is rarely proportionate to its consequences. Secrets, white lies, editing, and withholding info are all forms of dishonesty and betrayal that can really harm a relationship.

• To build trust and intimacy, you need to be truthful with your spouse. Early in your relationship, share incidents from your past and present that you suspect your partner will want to know about.

• If something makes you feel guilty, this may be a sign that you should share it with your spouse.

• Say what you mean, mean what you say—and don't ever cause your spouse to feel duped.

• Create a roadmap for your life together and establish rules that establish honest expectations.

• Good intentions mean a lot, but they shouldn't blind you from seeing your spouse's point of view.

3 **Love in the Time of Clorox**

et's face it: nobody likes folding her husband's socks or pulling his wife's hair out of the shower drain. We commit to household duties because they keep our lives in working order and provide us with good collateral for barters (for example, "You do my laundry, I do you"). But chores can also be the fodder for fights and grievances, since they can make couples feel overwhelmed, underappreciated, and even inadequate if they're not very good at the task. Add to this two people who've spent their whole lives doing housework their way or no way, and it's suddenly not so hard to think of at least one other place to store the broom other than the hall closet.

Neatness was a sore subject for us during our first two years of marriage. Bill carefully guarded his type A precision, and Giuliana defended her disorganization with real vehemence. We also found ourselves belittling the way one of us left empty glasses on the coffee table and the other loaded the dishwasher so often that it felt like a wicked competition to

call the other person out. A few years into sharing household duties, we still aren't in full agreement about who's responsible for doing what and how, but we've managed to work out enough kinks to keep the peace. We basically make sure our homes are orderly enough for us to cohabitate without losing our keys, cell phones, and minds. We also do the best we can by leaning on each other's strengths—and on our occasional housekeeper Ana Georgina. She can fold a hospital corner better than anyone we know.

When it comes to housework, everyone wants to feel they got a fair deal at the end of the day. Whether that equality means taking turns with trash duty or volunteering for chores you don't loathe, there's a good chance your spouse will interpret your efforts as selfless. Unlike our generation's parents and grandparents, who felt pressure to keep a perfect house for show, we're working hard to make our home warm and comfortable for each other. For now, that's more than enough. Here's a major turning point in Giuliana's battle against her piggish ways:

Giuliana: My sister Monica is five years older than me, and when we were growing up, she was an insane neat freak. Come to think of it, she's still the most regimented person I know—besides Bill, of course. And as her annoying little sister, all I wanted to do was go shopping in her perfectly kept closet. Monica had flawless taste as a kid, and she owned the most grown-up stuff at age sixteen: tweedy Ralph Lauren blazers, pastel Izod polos, big leather belts. She was such a young sophisticate. No wonder she grew up to have a big job for Versace.

When I was in the seventh grade, my classes began an hour later than my sister's did in high school, and I was let out an hour earlier. So when Monica left the house every day, I'd sneak into her room, open the lock on her closet (yes, she kept it locked, and yes, I found the key), and pick something special to borrow. I wouldn't wear the least bit of perfume or even deodorant, because I didn't want Monica to smell any trace of me on her clothes. Then I'd confidently walk though my day in her capri jeans and oversized blazers, and when school was done, I'd sneak back to her room and return everything to her wardrobe. The minute I'd hear the doorknob turn after school, I'd think: *She's home. I hope she doesn't realize I stormed her closet.* But then I'd hear Monica yell: "Mamaaaaaaa!"

Monica's cry was always my cue to brace myself, as my sister rushed down the hall. My heart would practically beat out of my chest. *It* can't *be the clothes,* I'd think. *How could she know?* Then she'd burst into my room and always begin her tirade the same way: "You BITCH!"

Bill: I love Monica.

Giuliana: So a couple of years ago over dinner at Mr. Chow in Beverly Hills, Monica and I were telling this story to Bill—and she spilled her trick for busting me for the first time ever. Apparently, Monica channeled James Bond and booby-trapped her closet so she could catch me in the act of stealing her stuff. She had strategically placed items and even laid small pieces of string under her closet door so that I'd accidentally move them when I opened it—and she'd have the evidence to prove it. To this day, Monica still keeps her Valentino and Chanel pieces immaculately hung in her wardrobe, just like when we were kids. But now, as an adult, I'd never think to borrow from her closet for an event or opening without asking her first. Her traps would be much more sophisticated now—my psycho sister lives close to a Home Depot.

If a Phone Gets Misplaced, and Nobody Hears It Ring, Did You Lose It?

Giuliana: Since Monica's confession, I can't stop myself from wondering whether her Mean Girl reprimands and harsh actions left a mark on my young and impressionable tween psyche. When she called me names and yelled at me about poaching her outfits, I'd always spit back: "You value clothes too much! You're materialistic! Who cares, it's just stuff?"— and apparently it stuck with me, because that's how I felt about my things when I first moved in with Bill. Sometimes I even caught myself saying some variation of these very words to him—minus the bitchy-little-sister tone.

When Bill and I were first married, his apartment was suddenly mine, and mine was suddenly his. So during those first few months together, I acted like my normal self in both places. I left cashmere sweaters all over our home, expensive bags in the middle of the bathroom floor—to me they were all just material objects, and none of it really mattered. When I'd visit Chicago after an exhausting four-hour flight, I liked knowing that I could just drop my stuff wherever I wanted to. If Bill grimaced, I'd whine, "But I feel free this way, honey— like a bird. I am free like a bird." I thought I could do what I wanted, so I told him I didn't want to be as regimented as him (hello, Monica flashbacks). "Regimented?" Bill would ask. "Since when is hanging something up so regimented?" I knew my laissez-faire habits could make our place messy, but I wasn't *dirty* about it. Everything's clean, just . . . misplaced. I didn't understand why it was a big deal.

Bill: Giuliana's sister and I are birds of a feather. She knows things last longer when you take care of them. Growing up, my dad always said you have to make things last. I really believe that.

Giuliana: Bill is such a neat freak, and it used to really annoy me. He's like the captain of the neat police. It's hard enough to live with someone new, never mind someone with new priorities about how you should coexist from here to eternity. At first it was hard for me to feel comfortable in Bill's immaculate Chicago space—and it was difficult to pretend I was OK with him encroaching on my relaxed L.A. pad. Our awkwardness manifested in small spats about who had the healthiest views on how to live well. I'd admonish Bill about how he was too disciplined about being neat and insist that what he saw as my messiness was really the result of living a superior, carefree life—a positive thing! I told him my habits had nothing to do with being raised in a barn, or willing to live in one now.

But Bill called me out, time and time again. In so many words, he said my lax attitude toward cleanliness was nothing more than willful ignorance, since no matter what he, Oprah, or science said about the mental and physical benefits of de-cluttering, I insisted on adding more stress and aggravation to my "carefree" life by refusing to change my ways and get myself organized. Bill made some good points; I could never find things when I looked for them.

Bill: Her phone, her house keys . . .

Giuliana: . . . important papers, my favorite leggings, even my *wedding band*, which I can't find to save my life (and makes Bill sick with disappointment each time I mention it). Everything was lost in mounds of crap I'd accumulated that managed to make me crazy several times a day.

Until one morning, I was headed to work at six a.m. because I had a really early meeting about yet another celeb who'd checked into rehab, and I realized that I didn't have my cell phone on me. So I tried to think where I'd last left it. On my dresser? In my purse? Nope and nope—that would have made too much sense. I couldn't go to work without my cell, so for twenty frantic minutes I searched high and low for it—and finally enlisted Bill's help. We looked under mattresses, on closet shelves, even in the refrigerator (I did leave it there once, while making a protein shake)—and it was nowhere to be found. By now, of course, I'd missed my meeting and begun to really freak out. I cursed my demanding job, messy apartment, and hectic life. I almost turned on Bill for just being there, but I held my tongue. This was everyone else's fault but mine!

After the longest thirty minutes of my adult life, I finally found my freaking cell in the pocket of my bathrobe, which was hanging over my desk chair, covered by two blouses and a pair of jeans that I'd tried on that morning for the meeting I never attended. I must have woken up, washed my face, checked my messages, and then shoved my phone in my bathrobe pocket while getting ready. My carelessness nearly caused me a psychotic break.

When I found my phone, I was embarrassed that I'd made such a scene in front of Bill. I expected a lecture from him, but he wasn't as smug about the situation as he could have been. "If you were just neater, you could be happier and saner," he said. "Please consider decluttering."

Since then, I've tried to keep track of my life a bit more—keep my keys on the table near the front door, hang my clothes up when I'm not wearing them. It's easy for me to see the value in this when I watch how effortless little things are for Bill. He always knows where his phone, keys, and wallet are when he wants them because he has a place for each. Life seems so perfect and manageable in Bill's tidy world. It just took a minute for me to decide I wanted to live there.

Cluttered Home, Cluttered Mind

Bill: If you have clutter in your real life, your tangible life, then it really adds to the emotional clutter in your mind. A neat woman is a sane woman. Who wouldn't want that in a wife?

Giuliana: From hearing Bill talk, you'd think the way to a man's heart is through his vacuum. But it's not the actual lack of sweeping or mopping that upsets Bill; it's not like he gets off seeing me with a duster in my hand. I think he gets upset about the reasons I don't clean (he doesn't like lazy people) and he hates the result of not keeping a tidy house (we become disorganized). And if Bill feels like he's doing all the housework on his own, he becomes resentful real fast.

He's a super neat person, but there are two things he won't do . . .

Bill: Make a bed.

Giuliana: And pick up towels.

Bill: You know why? I travel so much, I'm used to hotel living.

Giuliana: Well, the last time I checked there wasn't a maid wheeling a little cart around our homes. The bed and towel stuff annoys the crap out of me, even though everything else Bill does is really neat. So in the morning, I'll sometimes make the bed with him in it just to be annoying. Or I'll wait until he walks by to start making the bed just to show him how, once again, I'm the one fluffing the pillows. I will huff and puff, pull and tuck, and then throw in a little "Oh hey, how's it going? Everything good?" to make a scene. I'd rather teach by example than criticize.

Bill: Don't let her fool you. Giuliana is a borderline candidate for that show *Hoarders*. I open up drawers and stuff will just fall out everywhere.

Giuliana: It's called being a woman.

Bill: It's called being a slob—there's stuff she'll never ever use. Like a Walkman from 1982. And an old laptop computer from ten years ago that she won't throw away.

> **Giuliana's worst bathroom offense:** *"She leaves her underwear on the doorknob."* **Bill's grossest blunder:** *"Little dribbles of urine on the floor, next to the toilet. How hard is it to aim for the giant hole in front of him, and if he misses it, grab some toilet paper and wipe it up?!"*

Giuliana: Well, I don't know what to do with a laptop computer.

Bill: Throw it away.

Giuliana: I don't want to just throw away a laptop in any old garbage can. I have files and pictures on there . . .

Bill: Then give it to charity, or destroy it. I don't know what to tell you.

Giuliana: I was going to maybe send it to Haiti or something.

Bill: I can't live that way. It drives me crazy. Until the cell phone incident, she used to overlook the fact that I lived in the house, too. I had to live with, and among, Giuliana's mess.

Giuliana: Bill just had a hard time accepting that he didn't live in a model home. I'll never forget the first time I saw Bill's house—it freaked me out. The place looked like a decorator had just staged it for an open house, and since Bill worked in real estate, he saw this as an acceptable way to show off his single living style. I'd never spend money on a decorator. I'd think I could do it myself and then never get around to buying the tables, artwork, or sofas. But Bill had his little dining room table set with two salad plates on top of two main entrée plates, with napkins on top of those—all on beautiful place mats! What thirty-five-year-old bachelor owns a beautiful set of place mats? Meanwhile, I didn't even have matching silverware or plates or even glasses at the time. When we met, my dishes were from CVS pharmacy.

> ### Fates (Mildly) Worse Than Housework
>
> • Standing in the security line at LAX airport
> • Getting caught in a Chicago windstorm
> • Babysitting other people's two-year-olds

Bill: I didn't want to move the place settings, because I might not know how to reset the table if someone came over for dinner. Cut me some slack?

Home Is Where Our Housekeeper Is

Bill: Giuliana has tried to be neater since the phone incident, but outside the home, she's still a mess, especially with her car. Growing up, I didn't have the best car, but it was a clean car. I'd wax it every week, and treat it with respect because I had to work for it; I had to earn it. But Giuliana's car? I have a nickname for it: the dirty diaper. There's stuff everywhere. Once a month, I have it cleaned for her, and I'm embarrassed when I take it to the lube center—it's vile inside. There are random papers stuck to empty food containers, used tissues, gum wrappers, hair elastics with little hairs still caught in them—disgusting. And her gas tank? No matter what day of the week it is, it's always bone-dry empty. She must put two dollars of gas at a time into that tank, because after she uses my car, the gas light is always on. So I shouldn't have been too surprised when Giuliana called the other day to tell me she was driving to the studio and became nervous that she was going to run out of gas in the rain. She took that chance during a rare thunderstorm in rush-hour traffic on the Los Angeles freeway!? Woah, I don't like living that way. I like knowing that I'll make it to work without having to call AAA or hitchhike with a stranger.

Giuliana: I totally agree. AAA takes forever to come. They're so annoying.

Bill: I like a full gas tank and a clean house. Is that too much to ask? My dad always said, "It doesn't matter what you have, but what you have, take good care of it." It really stuck with me.

Giuliana: With Bill, I think neatness is a control thing, too. I suspect he likes when everything is in its place, because he feels in control of it, of himself. That's how my sister Monica is, too. I don't need to feel in control as much as they do, so I'm kind of flightier. I try hard to avoid arguments about housework or my car with Bill—or at least learn from them. I really believe that in a marriage, one person's deficiencies can be another's strengths.

Bill: How is being messy a strength?

Giuliana: Bill has clearly never made love on a giant pile of fresh laundry. If he knew what this was like, he'd change his tune.

Listen, for me, our biggest housework-related problems aren't about whether the floor's swept or the laundry's folded. I've established that I'm doing my best with keeping our homes in order, regardless of whether Bill agrees. Housework conjures issues for me about fairness, respect, and an appreciation for how much effort the other person puts into what keeps a home running smoothly. Gratitude is also a big deal for me. When I load the dishwasher or empty the bathroom trash can, I want Bill to notice. When I make the bed in the morning, I'd like him to say

> "I like a clean car that shines like a Rolex, an organized closet that resembles a men's clothing store, and a garage that looks like the showroom of a dealership. Yes, I'm that husband." —**Bill**

"You make a nice bed, honey." I don't make a *bad* bed; I arrange all the throw pillows in a decorative fashion, I make it pretty. I feel like without the bed made, the whole room looks messy. But I'd like Bill to acknowledge what I've done, even if he doesn't care about beds.

Equality is another big theme with housework. Bill likes to grocery shop because he has favorite cereals and peanut butters, so I'll unpack the bags. When Bill cooks, I clean up after us; it's a nice way to share responsibilities. If I don't chip in somehow, Bill feels like he's hired help. I think that's the case for most chores: housework doesn't have to be divided equally in terms of numbered tasks. But you need to feel as if everyone's doing their fair share to contribute.

Bill: What's fair to one couple, though, isn't always fair to another—so there isn't one system that always works. You want to know that you can count on your spouse, and it's important that we both feel that. I have friends whose wives do all the housework to keep things in order, but this can breed resentment, and the annoying thing is, most guys know this and just watch it happen because their wives won't let them re-jigger the system or the men don't know how to offer their help without getting in the way. Here's what I say: Establish priority cleaning duties, split up chores depending on which you can tolerate, ask for help, or hire someone to clean up every few weeks. Just get the housework done in a way that makes everyone feel at peace. If both a husband and wife feel they're working toward a shared goal—in this case, a clean house—and the tasks are split up fairly, their housework won't seem like such a chore, because they won't be in it alone.

You know what I really appreciate? If I'm folding the laundry, and Giuliana starts to help without me having to ask her for it, or when she offers to run to Whole Foods for me when I'm in the middle of cooking dinner, because I've forgot-ten an ingredient. That stuff never goes unnoticed.

Giuliana: I think you have to know when to intuitively offer your help and when to let go of doing things your way so stuff gets done. Bill used to do both our laun-dry until he put my lights and darks into the same washer, which resulted in a load of light blue T-shirts that used to be white. I told Bill I thought he'd made a really sweet effort, but we resolved to do our own laun-dry from then on. Some-times I'll do his clothes, but

> *"The worst casualty of my clutter is my wedding band. I can't find it to save my life. I was convinced it was in a pocket or handbag stashed somewhere in my messy closet, but after searching for months, I've given up. I'm so sad and disappointed in myself for losing it, but the worst part was telling Bill that it was gone because I'm such a disorganized ditz. He's still disappointed, and it kills me."*
> —Giuliana

I never let him do mine, so I do the laundry much more than he does.

Bill: Uh, we have someone who does our laundry most of the time.

Giuliana: OK. Well, I do it when our housekeeper Ana Georgina isn't available. I don't book her as much as Bill would like to. At some point, I'd like to help him with the laundry situation, the way he helped me find my keys. It was actually Monica who told me that if I want Bill to help around the house, I'd have to let him do chores his way, even if they're not perfect.

For me and Bill it's not about saying "Do it my way" or "I'll let you be messy"; it's more like: "Here are the benefits of trying it another way. Let me help you get there." And you know what? We always do. Freud said women marry their fathers, but when it comes to keeping a clean house, I think I married my sister.

TIPS FOR TWO: How to Lighten the Load

- Do your best to get organized. A clutter-free home leads to a clutter-free mind.
- Determine a fair way to split chores so neither person feels they're doing more than the other.
- Consider divvying up tasks based on your strengths and/or preferences.
- Tell your spouse how grateful you are after noticing a job well done.
- Don't be afraid to ask for help, and if you delegate, accept how your spouse does his duty.
- Offering to help, especially when you haven't been asked, never goes unnoticed.

4 Radio Ca-Ca

Forget what you've learned from years of watching cheesy romantic comedies and reading trashy novels: we're here to tell you that as a happily married couple, we require more than love to thrive. We've learned how to commit to our love, every day, with gestures that demonstrate our loyalty. While this may sound claustrophobic to couples still dating, our guess is that married duos find it refreshing. According to a University of Virginia study, when husbands and wives recognize and talk about their shared, long-term commitment, they feel more emotionally invested in each other and their life together. In fact, women, specifically, feel happier with the amount of affection and understanding they get from their husbands when there's a sense of mutual dependability.

We realize that a number of factors influence commitment, but one of the big ones for us is that we've pledged to do whatever it takes to make our spouse feel special—now and forever. We know that sounds simple, but it underscores every decision we make, from how Giuliana talks about Bill when he's not

around, to what kind of flowers he sends her for her birthday (hydrangeas are her favorite). And though we both realize that we can't always know how to make the other person feel his or her best (we're not therapists or psychics), we do know marriage is a knowledge-seeking process, and couples have the ability to shape, bend, and learn in all kinds of ways if their relationship is supported by demonstrating their commitment.

What Bill's basketball coach used to call "stick-to-it-iveness"—a real determined sense of perseverance—we've also found can do wonders for a marriage. Because we talk about our relationship a lot in the media, we get tons of emails from husbands and wives who want to know the trick to marital happiness. Of course we're crazy about each other, but at the core of our happy union is also a certain stick-to-it-iveness about making it work. This might not sound very sexy, or modern-day Hollywood, but it's the truth. We've devoted ourselves to a great institution, established our expectations, and pledged ourselves to its success. That makes it easy for us to stay focused on our life as a fulfilled, supportive, and devoted couple.

But don't think for a second that figuring out how to stand by our commitment in a strong and satisfying way was an intuitive process from the start. In fact, we learned some hard lessons while we were still engaged—never mind on the air, more than once, for millions to hear. Here's the story of what we like to call, Radio Ca-Ca:

Giuliana: I've known Jamie Kennedy for ten years. I met him after he played Randy in *Scream* but way before he dated Jennifer Love Hewitt and her vajazzled yina-banina.

Bill: Her what?

Giuliana: How do I put it in classy layman terms? Her bedazzled pootang.

Bill: Oh, yeah. That's so much better. I get it. Her . . .

Giuliana: Yup, *that*! So anyway, Jamie was filling in on a small L.A. radio show and asked me to be his last-minute guest after someone backed out of an interview. I was happy to help a friend out.

Bill and I were only four months into our relationship, so Jamie used that as an easy jumping-off point for banter. I remember he asked if I was dating Bill Rancic from *The Apprentice* and wanted to know what a typical date was like with him. Jamie has such a wicked sense of humor that the pressure was on for me to be equally funny and follow his lead. So I told him that we stayed in a lot, because Bill's a really good cook, and that a hot night starts at Whole Foods, since Bill really likes ahi tuna steaks. Well, that's all Jamie needed to hear to start making fun of Bill's domestic side. He couldn't believe I was dating someone who liked to stay in since I usually went out to see-and-be-seen L.A. spots with friends and exes, and he swore our relationship would never last. Jamie joked his way through the broadcast, and I laughed alongside him as his loyal guest, but on the inside I flinched with every word. The truth is, I loved swinging by Whole Foods with Bill to grab a couple of fresh cuts of ahi tuna. I was thrilled with our date nights. I'd finally met a tall, dark, and handsome culinary whiz *and* business tycoon! But that's not what I told Jamie. I didn't try to save Bill from humiliation at all.

It's not like I added fuel to Jamie's fire by, say, comparing Bill to Ted Allen from *Queer Eye*. But because I didn't disagree with Jamie's quips, I essentially mocked Bill. I didn't think about how this might affect him at the time, because I was just trying to keep up with Jamie.

Bill: Kennedy thought I was a joke, and you were like, "Eh, I'll be done with him in a week."

Giuliana: Here's the method behind my madness: I didn't want to be that whiny girlfriend stereotype who says things like, "No, no Jamie! It's not what you think! Let me tell you all about our romantic nights!" I'm a tougher girl than that, and when I was single, I was very independent. I'd been single for a long time, and I felt good about it, and I didn't want to seem whipped. So I made the mistake of agreeing with Jamie about Bill's potential. I told him he was probably right. Who knew what would happen with us? And since we taped the broadcast in L.A., and Bill was in Chicago that week, I thought Bill would never hear the interview, and I could pretend the whole thing never happened. Man, was I wrong about that.

Bill: I first learned about that embarrassing interview months later—specifically, when I was on Adam Carolla's morning radio show in L.A. We'd just gotten engaged, and I was pretty excited to talk about our relationship when anyone asked about it. So after Adam congratulated me on the engagement and laid down some sweet talk about Giuliana, he threw me a zinger. The bastard played back the interview with Kennedy, and I was absolutely shocked.

Giuliana: After playing the tape, Adam and Bill called me while they were still on the air. Adam acted so innocent—he congratulated me and said what a great guy Bill was. I told him Bill was the best and we were so excited about being together. And then Adam was, like, *so then why did you say this?*—and played the audio again, on live radio. My heart started pounding out of my chest, and I began to feel a bit dizzy. I felt horrible and mortified for myself but more important, for Bill. Once the audio stopped, I told Adam and Bill they had it all wrong. I said I didn't mean a word of what I said (truly, the white lie meant nothing to me), and that I'd always had a hunch Bill and I would end up together. I felt ridiculous for selling out my fiancé for a joke.

Bill: Meanwhile, I felt like the biggest fool ever. I thought, *Did I just propose to this woman? Is it too late to get that ring back?* I managed to laugh it off with Carolla's mic in my face, but on the inside I was shocked, caught off guard, and hurt. It made me think twice about marrying Giuliana. From the way I acted, nobody on the show could tell I was floored, but my head was spinning.

Giuliana: Bill called when he left the station and hit the roof. "It's not what you said," he explained. "It's the fact that you talked badly about me behind my back. We're getting married, and I need to know that you are committed to me. If I can't trust you, who can I trust?"

When Bill first busted me, I didn't understand why he was so mad. I thought making fun of him was so innocent and dumb, and I assumed Bill would feel the same way. "I'm sorry," I said. "I love you, and I love your tuna. I was just trying to be clever and cute." This last part took balls for me to admit, since it implied that sometimes I try to be more "on" than I naturally am, but it didn't matter to Bill since I tried to be "on" at his expense. I felt like dirt.

Bill: I'm really big on loyalty and sincerity, and what she said on Jamie's show seemed like a huge red flag that Giuliana might not be the person I thought she was. I think a big part of committing your life to someone is being accountable for who you are and what you bring to the relationship. When Giuliana apologized, I told her it didn't matter that she loved me or didn't think I'd be listening to the show. I said to her: "Just know one thing. I will never, ever do that to you."

Giuliana: Like a knife to my heart! Not only was I disloyal, but I was also dishonest. What I said to Jamie that day wasn't exactly the truth, and as a result, I misrepresented our bond.

Bill's Famous Ahi Tuna Recipe

1 cup chopped green onions

1 cup chopped cilantro

2 tablespoons toasted sesame seeds

2 cloves garlic, crushed

1/2 cup soy sauce

1/4 cup honey

1/4 cup sesame oil

1 teaspoon hot sauce

3 pounds ahi tuna steak

Mix together the onions, cilantro, sesame seeds, and the garlic cloves in a small bowl. In a separate bowl, mix together the soy sauce, honey, sesame oil, and hot sauce. Next, combine the onion mixture and the soy mixture into one bowl. Place tuna steak in a shallow dish, and pour the marinade over to cover completely. Cover the dish and refrigerate overnight, or for at least eight hours. Grill to desired doneness.

Bill: Her duplicity really raised my hackles. I was reluctant to get married from the start, so this just rubbed me the wrong way—and only a few months before the wedding, no less. I was so cautious, and a little paranoid about choosing a wife; I didn't want to be yet another guy suckered into marrying a girl who takes him for his money and treats him badly.

When I confronted Giuliana, it was really important to me that we have realistic expectations of each other and of our relationship before we hopped on that plane to Italy to get hitched. I told her that I expected my wife to be loyal and sincere, and that she could expect the same from me in our commitment. I was direct and simple, just like that. It caught her by surprise. But since then, we haven't had a problem with this type of behavior. I like to establish expectations as soon as we face an impasse. It keeps surprising frustrations to a minimum.

Watch Your Mouth

Giuliana: When I talk about my commitment to Bill now—to friends, family, or even people who stop us on the street or want to say hi at a restaurant—I'm careful about the words that come out of my mouth to describe us. In fact, I tend to go on and on about how wonderful he is, and how I'm so lucky to have him. This might make me sound like I'm a publicist for my marriage, but it's not like that. Bill and I have chosen to put our marriage out there for the world to see and hopefully learn from (both the good and the bad), but we don't feel pressure to represent it in a disingenuous way. We're always careful to raise each other up, and describe the other person in a positive light because we mean it, but also because we know how much the other person will feel disappointed and duped if we don't. Moods change, but our commitment never will. We said our vows in September 2007, and we will stick to them like fondant roses on a wedding cake. Plus we really feel that when one partner is positive, the other one feels that good energy and expresses it, too. I think that back-and-forth is infectious and really healthy for a marriage.

Bill: We keep it very real. We don't go to wild, fancy parties to come across as a hip couple, and we don't pretend to be more lovey-dovey than we are. We're a normal couple, just like anyone else, and I think that's why people get us. We take walks.

We eat chocolate chip pancakes for brunch. We keep it real. At the end of the day, camera or no camera, Giuliana and I have each other—and if we're not happy with that, creating a false persona certainly isn't going to help.

The Jamie Kennedy incident was the first and last time either of us said something remotely snarky behind the other person's back. It's not in my nature to talk like that, and Giuliana learned a big lesson. I can't even think of a time I was tempted to make a joke at her expense and had to stop myself. I wouldn't treat her in a way that I wouldn't want to be treated myself—it sounds so elementary school, but it works really well in grown-up life, too. Once you go down that road, down a path of disrespect, it's hard to know the difference between what's acceptable and what's not because you become a little more permissive with your words each time you violate your commitment. I don't want us to encounter the point of no return.

Giuliana: You have to protect your marriage for the sacred commitment that it is. So many men and women, especially women, have a tendency to get together with friends and talk a little too openly about how their spouse frustrates them or pisses them off—they do it in the movies all the time, which makes newlyweds think it's OK. But I don't feel that type of chatter is helpful to anyone, since it can breed ugly rumors and unfounded judgments. You shouldn't paint your husband as a bad guy—he's your husband. Not only does a flip attitude make your guy look lame, it makes you look foolish for making a bad choice to marry him. And don't think for a second that what you say to your friends ends with them. Their husbands hear all about it, too. Unless you have something really bad going on, and you need advice from one close friend, keep your relationship quiet. Don't bitch to bitch—for sympathy, idle conversation, or otherwise. I'd never ask someone to wear a "Team Giuliana" T-shirt. No way.

Bill: What happens once you've asked people to take sides, then, is that your friends and their partners end up hating the supposedly evil spouse, and they can throw all the things you've said about the person back at you when you least expect it. Friends never forget the bad stuff, and here, the damn spouse wasn't even around to defend himself in the first place. And if you make up with your partner before your friends get the memo? Forget it. You're suddenly stuck going to dinner with someone you've spent all this time berating. They're kissing and holding hands, and you're like, "Wait, a week ago we just slammed him with you!"—and then we're the dummies.

Giuliana: Ragging on the person you care about is annoying and uncomfortable for everyone. A lot of women have trouble transitioning from being the single girl who gossiped about the men she dated to suddenly keeping their relationships with their husbands private—and I get that—but there should be a certain level of maturity and restraint that one maintains as a wife. When you take on that title, it comes with a lot of responsibility, including respect for your commitment.

Bill: Most of my friends have been married a lot longer than Giuliana's, so they're past the point of locker room talk, and if they think their wives are nags, they've already had that epiphany. Some of my friends who got married when they were very young didn't know what to look for in a wife or in a marriage. They built their mar-

Signs of the Hopelessly Devoted

- She tells you you're the love of her life and can't imagine living it without you.
- He plans for your retirement together.
- She thinks your hairy feet are hot.
- He thinks your belches are funny and perfectly ladylike.
- You put each other in your will.

riage on the wrong foundation—whether they were too young, they got married to make their families happy, whatever. Some of those friends air their dirty laundry, but they're the ones who could have a better marriage. I'll tell you when it gets really uncomfortable: when guys talk about their sex life. That's your *wife*, man. It was one thing to talk t and a when you were dating, but you shouldn't disrespect the mother of your kids that way.

Giuliana: We were recently out to dinner with four couples at Carmine's in Chicago. At one point, they dished about how often they fool around, and when it was our turn to share, Bill and I looked at each other and made this unspoken pact that we wouldn't spill the proverbial beans. "Eh, we travel so much . . ." Bill said, and shot me a look as if to say, *Say no more, DePandi* . . . All good here! I didn't want those girls at the table to have that visual of Bill, and he didn't want them to have that visual of me. Too bad we're stuck with the visual of everyone else!

Actions Speak as Loudly as Words

Giuliana: Commitment isn't just about guarding your tongue—you have to prove your allegiance with daily actions, too. For us, calling home when we're going to be late or ignoring a stranger's flirtation is no big challenge to our commitment. Making small sacrifices because they're important to our spouse, however, doesn't come without some effort, whether that means Bill has to kill a Sunday babysitting my sister Monica's kids or I have to watch *The Godfather: Part III* with him twice in one week. We're dedicated to each other's happiness and ensuring the other person feels special. Bill's really good at this—especially with making frequent little gestures that show how much he cares about my well-being.

Bill: For instance, when I pick Giuliana up from the airport, I always have a bottle of water, her favorite granola bar, and some sushi in the car. I know she's never satisfied by the small bag of mini-pretzels she has on the plane, so I want her to feel comfortable once she's home. You don't have to buy your spouse diamond rings or designer watches to let her know you care—even a gluten-free snack bar and Fiji water can make a woman feel exceptional.

Giuliana: I'm not as good at making these gestures as Bill is, but I did outdo myself when I set up Bill's iPad for him. I downloaded a bunch of cool apps without telling him about it, because he'd never know how to do that stuff without me. I'm the techie in our relationship.

Bill: Well, if we're gonna be honest: that's actually Giuliana's iPad that she set up. The one that she bought for me she didn't want to take out of the box, because she wanted to return it for the one with 3G. Giuliana likes to say she's doing me a favor, but in actuality, I sometimes think she's doing an end-around on me. She's giving me the outdated iPad, so she can get the new one for herself.

Giuliana: Whatev, I still knew he'd appreciate it, and that's what matters.

Commit to Your Commitment

Giuliana: For us, being committed means letting the other person know that divorce is not an option, that you'll always put him/her first, and that you'll try hard to be a good spouse. Sometimes you have to say these things to each other when you're feeling tense or need reassurance that you're not alone in a hard situation. When you do, it helps you begin to look more directly at what you bring to the relationship, what makes things work, and how you can improve in areas that don't. Sometimes I say to Bill, "I know I'm not the best wife in the world, but can you tell me something I've done lately that was good? And can you tell me something I've done lately that was not good so I can improve?" In marriage, I think it's important to leave your ego at the altar. You can't put yourself first in marriage.

Bill: Acknowledging your commitment is like renewing your vows without having to buy a new tux or spend tons of money on a venue.

Giuliana: It's funny, because when Bill and I got married in Italy, we told our priest, Father Mike, that we wanted to write our own vows. "No, no, no, no, no," he said. "I don't recom-

---

Commitment Commandments

1. Treat and talk to each other with respect. Turn on the sass, and you'll turn off your spouse.

2. Don't flirt with friends or strangers. It makes you look bad, and embarrasses your spouse.

3. Have a secret handshake or gesture that says "I love you." Bill squeezes Giuliana's hand three times to say "I love you," and she squeezes his back four times to say, "I love you, too." We've been doing this since we got married and it speaks volumes, especially in a crowded room or business setting.

mend that. You're going to get really nervous, and if you get jittery, you might let the whole beautiful experience of marriage get away from you. Let me say the vows so you don't forget them, and all you have to do is enjoy it and say, 'Si, si! Yes, I do!' " So we did that.

But while Father Mike spoke, as wonderful as his words were, they weren't things Bill and I would have said to each other. We ended up renewing our vows a year later for reasons unrelated to sentiment (a little legal mix-up which I'll get to later), and we were then able to say what we really felt—like that we promised to love each other forever and be best friends for life. Now, I feel like we recommit to each other every day, in our actions and words.

Bill: We're also planning to literally renew our vows every few years—not like Heidi Klum and Seal with costumes or themes, but we'll have a dinner with friends and family, maybe go to Vegas one year.

Giuliana: What I've found makes a commitment strong is marrying what you need versus what you want. I have a lot of friends who married their checklists. Does the guy have a nice car? Check! Does he have his own house? Check! Does he have good hair? Check, check, check! But these women didn't marry what they *need*: someone who empathizes with having divorced parents or knows how to deal with relationship baggage. It's important to marry for the right reasons. With Bill, I married a guy who can handle my hectic schedule, encourage my career every step of the way, and help me with trust issues. He goes out of his way to make me feel secure and confident in our relationship. Because of all that, he also makes my life easier.

Bill: Marriage shouldn't be hard, even if that loyalty and commitment is tested every day.

Giuliana: Case in point: The other day I was doing an interview with Ryan Seacrest, who is good friends with the heads of NBC. During the segment, I told him to get me the Miss USA hosting gig. We joked back and forth about this for a while, talking about how much I'd owe him if he got me this fab job. And then he pulled the kicker. "Who owns Miss USA?" he asked, and when I took the bait and told him Donald Trump, Ryan started taking digs at Bill. "Why isn't your husband getting you the job? Why can't he make the call?" I could have gone into a funny bit about how Bill didn't have the juice that Ryan does, but instead I treaded very carefully because I didn't want to say anything that would hurt Bill.

So I told Ryan that I didn't want Bill to have to play his Trump card (pun intended) on me and this occasion. And then I laid on the kind of mush I should have shown to Jamie Kennedy. I told Ryan that I didn't care if The Donald held a grudge against me if I wasn't up to snuff, but I sure as hell didn't want him to get upset with my wonderful, gorgeous, lovely husband. If only Bill had been listening.

TIPS FOR TWO: Keeping a Commitment Strong

- Be thoughtful when describing your marriage to others. If you can't say something nice, don't say anything at all.
- Talk about your spouse the way you'd want your spouse to talk about you.
- Commit to doing things that may be out of character for the sake of making your partner feel special.
- Surprise your spouse with small gestures to show you care.
- Stick to your vows, but recommit to each other in actions, words, and affection every day.

5 A Little Taste

We've always enjoyed the significant role that food manages to play in our relationship. We've learned that a decadent wedge of Camembert goes nicely with a quiet Napa Valley picnic, and a sloppy chilidog begs to be shared at a rowdy Cubs game. Consequent love handles aside, good food makes us happy in our stomachs and in our marriage. When done right, delicious treats can create warm and inviting memories worth revisiting, over and over again.

For us, the best culinary experiences blend exciting flavors with vivid reminders from our past that let us revel in the present. For instance, Giuliana is often tempted to make her mom's bubbling pot of tomato sauce for Bill, because it reminds her of animated family dinners, laughter, and that "no place like home" feeling. Bill, on the other hand, likes to drag Giuliana for gooey hot fudge sundaes at Ghirardelli Ice Cream and Chocolate Shop in Chicago because he knows she loves sweets, but also because the old-timey counter and checkered floor make him feel like a kid again. We find that sharing such sensory-rich experiences really deepens our relationship—and Bill, with his spoiled taste buds and sophisticated palate, often leads the way.

Even at home, Bill wears the chef's hat. For an hour or so before dinner, our modern kitchen turns into an oversized Food Network set, with Bill dressed in a red and white apron and poised behind his "prep station" of cutting boards and sharp knives. As the sweet master chef slaves over his hot stove—slicing, dicing, sautéing, and serving—Giuliana likes to think she makes an excellent sous chef and sommelier.

Although only one of us has any real skills in the kitchen, we agree that Giuliana doesn't need to cook well (or at all) to enjoy our time here together; it's enough to be with each other, while sharing an experience we're passionate about in different ways. Here's a look into our mouth-watering food adventures. We encourage you to eat up with your hubby or wife soon, too.

Bill: I cooked for Giuliana on our first real date in Chicago. We'd been dating for five weeks, but most of our time was spent in L.A. since her job was more hectic than usual. I couldn't wait to spend three days of nonstop togetherness with Giuliana in my hometown. It was time for a marathon weekend together—and for me to really show her what I was made of.

I picked Giuliana up from the airport around seven, and I expected her to be hungry for some dinner, since my girl is always up for some good chow. So when she walked in the door, I greeted Giuliana with a kiss and handed her a feast: shrimp cocktail for an appetizer, a grilled chicken and rigatoni dish for the main entrée, and a rich, dark and moist chocolate cake with buttercream icing from Ditka's, one of my favorite restaurants in Chicago, for dessert. Giuliana had never seen my condo, much less experienced how I live or eat at home, so

I wanted to pull out all the stops. I needed to make a good impression, and I'd hoped that a nice meal would set the mood.

Giuliana: After I landed, I was starving. So when I saw that Bill had prepared this beautiful meal, I thought, "What a romantic! He's such a keeper!" We had a wonderful night—dinner, candles, good conversation, and a crisp Sinatra coming from his speakers. It was really magical, and the whole evening made me feel special. Very few men have gone to such lengths to woo me like that. Bill really knew how to turn on the charm; admittedly, he had me at the kiss hello.

Cut to eight months after we'd been married. Bill and I went to dinner at Gibson's Steakhouse with our friends Mike and Janel, who had invited another couple, Grace and Jim, whom we hadn't met yet. They were full of questions: how did Bill and I meet, was it hard to have a long-distance marriage, that sort of thing. I gushed over the story about our first romantic date in Chicago: "I was so blown away," I told the table. "When I got to Bill's

> "As Bill cooks, I like to drink a glass of Tignanello and munch on hummus and wheat pita bread, mixed nuts, or Brie cheese and water crackers. As sous chef, I need to keep up my strength!"
> —Giuliana

house, there were candles, red wine . . . and he'd made this beautiful meal, with appetizers and everything." That's when Mike, one of Bill's best friends, interrupted: "How nice! Did he make the shrimp cocktail?"

So I said, "Yes! Shrimp cocktail!" And he said, "In a martini glass?" And I thought, *uh, yeah, it was in a martini glass . . . where is this going?* So then Mike laughs, "Did he make you pasta, with maybe some chicken in it? And let me guess: he served the chocolate cake from Ditka's?" Mike smirked, as if he knew something I didn't—and he couldn't wait to share.

"That son of a bitch," I said under my breath. I wouldn't be a girl if I didn't wonder if Bill made this meal for all of his hot dates. And if so, did that make ours any less unique or exceptional? I felt disappointed and embarrassed. I also felt my crazy Italian blood start to boil, and I was mad as hell that I thought he'd duped me into feeling like I was special.

"No, no," Mike said, reaching across the table to calm me down. "It's not what you think. That's the Rancic Special. I lived next door to him for five years. He used to make it for me, and when he'd make it for friends or family from out of town, I'd eat his leftovers."

I was so relieved. I'll take a one-trick pony over a spatula-wielding Casanova any day.

Food Is Family, Is Love

Bill: I'm the youngest of four, with three older sisters who were never home after school, so I was home alone a lot. My parents were both schoolteachers who stayed late for conferences and meetings, so I had the run of the house to myself after the age of ten or so. Since I came home from school each day to an empty house, I'd ride my bike and play ball with the neighborhood kids in Orland Park, where I lived, and I'd work up an appetite, so I taught myself how to cook. I liked to make macaroni and cheese with chopped salami for flavor, and vanilla sundaes with Oreos, crushed Cinnamon Toast Crunch cereal, and tons of whipped cream. Not bad for ten, right? I was no Emeril, but I sure made a mean after school snack.

No matter how busy we were, my family made it a point to have a delicious dinner together every night. It was mandatory to be home by six o'clock for my mom's beef brisket or meat loaf with a hearty side of green beans. We'd talk about the faulty tires on my ten-speed, my sister Karen's geometry homework, or my mom's latest overachieving student. Though mom's cooking was good, dinner hour was all about great conversation and family-time memories. But it wasn't until I moved back to Chicago after college that I began to really appreciate food as an art and develop a love for making, and eating, new and interesting dishes.

Now at the dinner table with Giuliana, I have the best of both worlds: good food and good company. It's an extension of the priorities my family instilled in me as a kid, and the taste buds I like to think I've refined as an adult.

Giuliana: My mom was a fantastic cook—to the point where she prepared meals, from her rather small kitchen, for lots of backyard bar mitzvahs in the D.C. area just to be nice (no catering truck needed). She fed seventy-five guests at a time, buffet style, with half a dozen homemade lasagnas, huge pans of sautéed rapini and mushrooms, meatballs, salads, veal limone . . . oh, and I almost forgot about the incredible tiramisu she made from scratch. I have the best memories of watching her make homemade marinara sauce with a sunken pork bone for flavor, and hot dogs with spicy peppers and onions on a crusty Italian roll. Our kitchen always smelled like the streets of Naples to me, with those old women in their housedresses hanging out on their balconies with wooden spoons in hand. Even when mom wasn't cooking, our kitchen smelled like fresh tomato sauce and basil.

Too bad olfactory was the only sense my mom allowed me to indulge. Every time I asked to help, or even watch, she refused. "No, no, no, no, no," she'd say. "Go talk on the phone or do your homework, and I'll have dinner ready soon." She always wanted me to be a kid, and she took great pride in cooking for our family. She never wanted my help, so I was never dying to learn. As a result, I never developed a knack for cooking, and I wasn't blessed with the gene.

You know how some people are just born with a golden

culinary touch? How any-
thing they make, even
baked potatoes, tastes like
they're hot out of a Viking
range? That's not me. If I
were to follow the same
recipe as Bill, we'd end up
with two different meals,
only one of which would
be edible. When I got my
first place, that's when I
first realized I didn't in-
herit my mother's cooking

> ### If We Could Hire Any Personal Chef, We'd Call . . .
>
> Gordon Ramsay
> Paula Deen
> Ina Garten, aka Barefoot
>   Contessa
> Anthony Bourdain
> Laurent Tourondel of BLT
>   restaurant fame

skills (which I'd gladly take over her large forehead, which she
did pass on). I was twenty-seven years old, had bought a condo
in Westwood, outside Beverly Hills, and couldn't wait to make
penne with (jarred) carbonara sauce in my new kitchen. So
grown up! After putting a pot of water on my new glass cook
top, pouring myself a little vino, and heading to my bedroom
to finish *The Secret* while waiting for the water to boil, I fell
asleep. Two hours later, I woke up to the piercing *beep-beep-
beep* of my smoke alarm! The water had evaporated, and the
empty pot had melted onto the stove where only a huge (and
permanent) hole remained. I haven't tried too hard to cook
since that day, when I became a walking cliché. I can just hear
my brother Pasquale telling my mother, "Giuliana can't even
boil water . . ." Ba-dum-bum.

So while food was always important to my family, it never
meant a lot to me beyond tasting it and enjoying what my
mom prepared. Like Bill, my family sat around the dinner
table every night—talking, laughing, and having fun for hours
(though we were such food lovers, so we probably focused on
the food and company in equal parts). Knowing how important dinner memories were to him, and how much of a role

food played in our families, it took me a few months into our marriage to confess that I didn't know how to cook. At one point, I offered to make dinner, just to see if I could, so I called my mom earlier that day to get the ingredients for her home-made sauce. But when we were at the store, I kept the list in my pocket because I felt like it was something I should innately know how to do. I wanted to seem like a natural, but I obviously wasn't. I fumbled around in the produce section, squeezing tomatoes and smelling bay leaves, before I confessed that I didn't know what I was doing, and was no longer in the mood to make Mom's recipe. Bill was happy to pick up where I left off, which is a nice metaphor for our partnership. Actually, I wouldn't be surprised if we went home with ahi tuna steaks that night.

Bill: Hey, I make other things beside tuna. I make good pastas, good sauces, I like to grill . . .

Giuliana: Mmm. And he seasons stuff; he puts it in a bag, shakes it up, marinates it . . .

Bill: I like to let a chicken breast or sirloin marinate for half a day before I grill it. I'm big on trying new marinades, too. I just discovered a new one called Tony Tah's. It's a sweet-and-sour sauce that balances tangy fruit flavors with Asian spices. I also like to make fettuccine with roasted chicken and broccoli rabe, and I top it off with red pepper flakes since both Giuliana and I love a fiery kick. When we're in the mood for seafood, my favorite new dish is grilled salmon with a sherry vinegar and honey glaze, and a spicy tomato relish. My buddy used to be the manager at Carlucci's in Downers Grove, about twenty minutes outside Chicago. I'd often go into the kitchen with him and learn to make the best rigatoni with grilled chicken breast, broccoli, red peppers, and roasted garlic cream sauce.

I know Giuliana felt bad that day she said she'd cook for me, but she brings a good palate to the table, I bring some mad knife skills, and that's a perfect match in my book. Besides, I'd be so fat if Giuliana were a good cook, since I don't have an off switch. It's obviously for the best.

Giuliana: Bill also takes such pride in his cooking that I suspect he likes being king of the kitchen, which works out because I like being his little assistant, his helpful sous chef. And by that, I mean I hand him the olive oil and drink a nice Chianti. It's fun for me to spend time with Bill as he does something he enjoys so much. I don't need to get my hands too dirty to get something out of it.

What doesn't work for Bill is when I don't participate in the cooking process at all—not even as his captive audience. Once, while he was making dinner, I was in my home office going over talking points for an interview with Julia Roberts about her movie *Duplicity*. After a half hour of what I'm sure was Bill's version of a very slow boil, he jokingly called from the other room: "Hey, DePandi! What am I, your bitch? Get in here and help me out"—which basically meant keeping him company while he plated spicy pork chops with a side of steamed asparagus. "I'm glad you can join me for dinner now," he said with a sarcastic smile, and I didn't realize until he gave me this mini-guilt trip that I'd taken his culinary contributions to our marriage for granted. Who could blame him, really?

Share, Share Alike

Bill: Since food's always been an important part of our past, we've managed to incorporate it into making new memories, too. I think a good meal can be a really intimate experience if you and your spouse have a similar appreciation for it. It's cool when we're in a restaurant and I see a guy cut off a piece of his steak for his date because he knows she'll want a bite. That's such a telling, intimate moment to me. Like that guy, there are times I'd rather give Giuliana a ribeye over roses, too.

You know, food played a big role when I proposed to Giuliana. It was the middle of December, and I'd been planning and rehearsing this moment in my head for weeks. That day, I sent a limo to pick her up at O'Hare. When she arrived at a private helicopter pad where I was waiting, I told her I was taking her to see the Christmas lights on Michigan Avenue in downtown Chicago the best way I knew how—from the sky. Just as we approached downtown, I asked her to marry me (I remember that she looked like a hot Christmas elf in her pink knee-high boots). During our helicopter tour, I pulled out her favorite deep-dish Chicago-style Giordano's pizza and a bottle of champagne—and back at the apartment, we gorged ourselves on Ditka's chocolate cake, since that's what I served her our first weekend in Chicago. The whole night was amazing, but the incredible food added a nice touch.

Date Night Delights

• *Italian.* Lady and the Tramp got it right. There's nothing more romantic than sharing a bottle of red and lobster linguini in a dimly lit trattoria.

• *Sushi.* Baked crab roles and ice-cold Sapporo. Need we say more?

• *Dinner at Houston's restaurant before a movie.* Spinach/artichoke dip, a cheeseburger with secret sauce, and a side of baked red cabbage. At the movies, dessert: Reese's Pieces dumped over a large bag of hot, buttered popcorn. We shake it up and dig for the melted candy. Yum!

Obviously not every food-related memory has to revolve around a big event, though. Some of our best talks about everyday nonsense like how our day went or something interesting we read in the paper have happened over a bottle of wine and roasted chicken. Meals—brunch, dinner, even an omelet and pancakes on the sidewalk of the Original Pancake House in the Gold Coast—give us a forum to slow down, connect, and talk about what's going on. We don't go out to eat with other couples as much as we'd like, so we tend to use meal time to wind down and talk about what we're going through. We've also turned the dinner table into our board table for work-related issues. If Giuliana has a fight with her boss during the day, or I need input about what to discuss at a conference in Indiana, I'll say, "Let's have dinner and map this out." We table the conversation, so to speak. Plus it's comfortable for us to talk business at dinner. In our world, some of the best deals are made over a good meal and a few rounds of martinis.

Giuliana: I think food compatibility is something that a lot of couples struggle with, but it's really important. I have a friend whose husband sometimes works late or on weekends, and when he does, he always stocks the fridge with cheese, wine, fruit, and fresh proscuitto. I think that's so sweet and thoughtful—and what she doesn't eat when he's not there, they share when he gets home from the office. Because they have the same taste in food, they travel well together, too—especially to foreign countries—and always have a new restaurant to explore, farmer's market to visit, recipe to dabble with. It's a common interest that's passionate and practical.

Bill: Think about it: eating happens at least three times a day, more for me. That's a big chunk of our time together, especially on weekends.

Giuliana: And when I'm sick, Bill always gets me my favorite matzo ball soup from Jerry's Deli in L.A., which I love because the broth is just right, the chicken is tender, and that big matzo ball is irresistible! The smell of that soup instantly makes me feel better. Some might say we're creatures of habit because we eat at a lot of the same places, but I like to think we're creatures of fond memories. When Bill and I renewed our vows, we had a big wedding on a boat and brought food from three of our favorite restaurants in Chicago: Carmine's, Gibsons, and Tavern on Rush. We had turkey sliders, grilled octopus and calamari, and sweet potato fries that all tasted so fresh and yummy, even though none of the food really worked together as one meal. But everyone left feeling full, blissful, and satisfied, which was the point of the day anyway.

Bill: For us, food is about shared experiences, not just fat and carbs. So on date nights . . . look out! One time we got hot dogs and cheese fries at this legendary Chicago-style hot dog stand called Wiener Circle that's open until five a.m. We went at two in the morning, pretty tipsy from the bar, and inhaled a bunch of hot dogs with mustard, onions, relish, tomatoes— the works. And the people who work there are hilarious. They're so pushy and crass, old-school Chicago style. We laugh about it now, and that's what makes food the stuff of great memories. There are times I have to twist DePandi's arm to enjoy a bacchanal for two because it's so fattening, but afterward she's always happy she went.

Giuliana: The good stuff always comes with a lot of calories! And it's one thing to gorge yourself when you're dating, because you see each other a few days a week and can be careful when you're not together, but when you're married, you're almost *always* together for meals and snacks. When we go out, Bill always wants me to try the cheeseburger from In-N-Out in

L.A. with pickles, grilled onions, and extra spread, or the fattening but super delicious penne with truffle sauce from Prosecco in Chicago. Or those greasy gyros from Five Fingers, Four Fingers . . .

Bill: Five Faces on Division Street! We pigged out that night.

Giuliana: See? I try to watch it, and then I feel bad because I think Bill just wants to share with me. Though I do get annoyed when we agree "no dessert," and then when the meal is over, instead of asking for the check, Bill asks for the damn dessert menu. The next thing I know, I'm twelve bites into a strawberry shortcake with extra whipped cream.

Bill: A little taste, a little taste.

Giuliana: That's what he always says, especially when he wants me to take a bite: "A little taste, a little taste." We walk out of a restaurant and within twenty minutes, he says, "I'm hungry." But we just ate dinner? "I know," he'll say. "I need a taste. I need a little taste of something."

Bill: I always need dessert. I try to be good, but I can't be good.

Giuliana: The first year of marriage is hard for a lot of women because men stock the house with fattening foods we would never have bought when we were single and living on our own. I have no willpower, so if there's random food in my kitchen, I will eat it—and potentially even mix it together (almonds and applesauce, pretzels and peanut butter . . .).

When I was single, I just didn't buy the chips or order the risotto like we do now that we're married. And the worst part is that I'd forgotten how delicious these things are because I'd never allowed myself to have them, so when I was reintroduced to them through Bill, I wanted them all the time! Cheese fries? Oh, how I missed you. Barbecue pork? OK, just a little bite. But all those bites add up. Men are constantly hungry, and I'm convinced Bill has a hole in his stomach because he's ravenous within half an hour of leaving a restaurant. No wonder he always cooked for himself as a child. His mom probably couldn't keep up with his insatiable appetite.

Bill: I like to eat, DePandi. I can't help it if I'm still a growing boy.

Giuliana: It's almost like Bill takes it personally when I turn down his culinary advances. At restaurants, Bill wants to split a pasta dish and dessert, and if I refuse and opt for the grilled salmon, he sulks. If I try to pass on stopping for a sundae at Ghirardelli, he sulks. If I don't order chocolate chip pancakes at Sunday-morning brunch, he sulks. But trust me, if I gained thirty pounds within the first few years of marriage, he might really sulk and think I'm one of those girls who gets married, eats like a piggy, and lives in sweatpants because nothing fits.

Bill: I don't *sulk*. I just don't like to eat alone. Eating alone is like going to a movie alone: It is a fine thing when you have no other option, but it's such a better time when you can share the experience with someone you care about, indulge in the moment, and then rehash it later.

Giuliana: You mean *regret* it later. So what I've learned is that instead of raining on Bill's gastronome parade by saying "No, I'm not going to come with you for the second banana pudding this week," or "I'm going to have a salad before the Cubs game and you can eat a hot dog alone," I just grin and bear it, and enjoy all this yummy food, within moderation, while I still have a fast metabolism. And then when we're apart, or I'm at work, I eat well. I save my calories for Bill.

Bill: She's so generous. But you know, if Giuliana doesn't want to join me on my tasty adventures, I can always replace her with Mike. His legs aren't as nice, but he's always been a compatible eating buddy. Something tells me he'd be happy to split the Rancic Special any time.

TIPS FOR TWO: Food for Thought

• Share food-driven experiences that allow you to have new and spontaneous adventures.

• Not every man wants his wife to be the Barefoot Contessa's doppelgänger, and not every woman dreams of marrying the Naked Chef. If you don't cook, play sous chef and hang out! Or bring a good pallet to the table.

• Don't try to replicate food-related memories from the past, because they may fall short of your expectations. Instead, create new ones.

• Experiment with fun ways to make culinary compatibility an intimate, sensory experience. For instance, a messy slice of deep-dish pizza makes us sentimental and gooey inside. . . .

• The next time you're in Chicago, swing by Ditka's for a slice of chocolate cake!

6 Our Jobs, Ourselves

Because we star in a reality show about our marriage, we bring a lot of our work home with us . . . literally. But regardless of whether you earn a paycheck by letting TV cameras follow you around, studies say that job satisfaction can have a huge impact on the way you feel about yourself and your romantic relationships. After all, careers affect your mood, self-esteem, free time, and other factors that hamper and uplift your bonds.

Because we're invested in each other's happiness, we're intent on helping the other person feel really good about his/her career aspirations. It's taken a few years, but we've finally learned how to walk the fine line between offering solid advice when it comes to work, and obnoxiously butting-in. What ultimately makes our professional meddling productive is that we trust that the other person has only the best intentions in mind. Career-related tips can be small and strategic, like when Giuliana helps Bill choose a jacket for his meeting so he feels handsome and confident—or large and complicated, like

when Bill tells Giuliana when to kindly tame her Twitter banter so she doesn't cause any unwanted drama (apologies to Billy Bush for that one). And because we look out for each other in our personal lives, it's only natural for us to want to help the one we love live up to his/her fullest potential as a professional.

Bill and I have managed to amass a crazy amount of *US Weekly* and *In Touch* clips throughout our careers, but they're certainly not our greatest accomplishments. Giuliana's gone from working at Domino's Pizza as a teenager to becoming an anchor for *E! News,* the most watched entertainment news show in the world; and Bill's journeyed from selling cigars out of a four-hundred-square foot Chicago apartment to impressing thirty million viewers when he was named Donald Trump's first apprentice on NBC. And while these are our individual achievements, we're very proud of how much we continue to inspire and encourage each other to do work that makes us feel fulfilled. We don't limit each other's professional aspirations for competitive or selfish reasons, instead we discover new ways to feed each other's enthusiasm for work and rescue the other person when they're knee-deep in a jam. Here's a story that illustrates how much we lean on each other's expertise, encouragement, and intuition when it comes to matters of the office.

Bill: I'm a self-made entrepreneur, so I pride myself on having sharp instincts, especially when it comes to making solid deals and getting things done in an efficient way. I'm also self-reliant, so I like to control a room. But Giuliana taught me a huge professional lesson that challenged the way I'm used to doing things—and at a time in our lives when our mutual careers mattered more than ever.

Giuliana: When Bill and I were first working with the crew of *Giuliana & Bill,* he kind of, how do I put this . . .

Bill: I rubbed people the wrong way. If I'm doing business with someone, and he's not operating up to speed, I usually say, "Listen, this is how it's got to get done." And when I do, changes are made. But I guess people who work in the entertainment business aren't always comfortable with such a direct approach, and when we began our show, Giuliana wondered, while nobody said anything outright, if a few members of the crew were interpreting my directness as abrasive.

Giuliana: Bill is such a good businessman. He's aggressive and strong, and he gets things done. He has a very East Coast/Chicago work mentality—a "big city" mentality. But when you come to Hollywood, it's a little different. There's a lot of schmoozing that helps you get your way, and people move a little slower in their decision making. West Coasters are also a little softer, especially those who work on TV shows, and they tend to be more sensitive, more creative, and take things more personally than the testosterone-driven tycoons that Bill's used to dealing with.

Bill: I'm very results-driven, and as a business owner, I directly attack problems a certain way: if A isn't working, I go to B, and if B isn't working, I go to C. But Giuliana and I noticed that whenever I'd make suggestions or offer solutions according to this formula, about a challenge or problem on the show, the crew was hesitant to change their game plan. I didn't get it.

Giuliana: I sensed that Bill's passion was being misinterpreted as aggression, and that nobody knew what to make of it or him. They were shutting off to his ideas.

Bill: At first, Giuliana noticed a few subtle clues that our peers were uncomfortable, like sideways glances from the crew on set or people shifting in their seats when I spoke.

Giuliana: So I started to carefully listen to Bill on conference calls, especially with the *Giuliana & Bill* team. I remember one meeting when Sarah and John, our network publicists, and a few of our marketing people were in the conference room at The Style Network studios to talk about the ad roll out for season two. We were all gossiping about Britney Spears's new boyfriend, sipping bottled water, and picking on leftover bagels from someone else's breakfast meeting. It was a very laid-back room, and I think we were even running a few minutes late. But when we called Bill in Chicago to conference him into the meeting, he was all business and had a let's-get-to-it attitude. It was obvious that he wasn't up for ice-breaking conversation and maybe a little annoyed that we were behind schedule. Because I know Bill, I interpreted his initial shortness and deep sighs better than anyone in the room, and knew they were harmless enough, but I could also sense that a few people were uneasy about his attitude and didn't see them the way I did.

"All right, let's jump right in," he said, taking command of the situation though he was thousands of miles away. Since Bill was on speakerphone, his voice sounded strong and powerful, two things I usually find attractive but realized might be off-putting to our co-workers. "I've made a list of things we need to get done in the next two weeks," he said, and he began to tick them off: *We need a better message board on our website so we can answer viewer questions; we shouldn't premiere in January since our younger viewers aren't in school yet and will miss our show; and we need to update the bonus show clips on the website since the ones on there now are old.* Those were all points, but I could tell Bill's direct approach scared the crew a little—and that they didn't realize Bill's advice and passion came from a good, and not a douchey, place.

Bill: Our reality show is fun to do, and we all want to have a positive impact on our viewers, but at the end of the day, it's a business, so that's how I handled it. In those meetings, I'm never out to make best friends, and in L.A., everyone's your best friend until you leave the room, so why bother? The call went on for at least a half hour, with me apparently force-feeding ideas, and I can only now imagine how the team

> ## Power Couples We Admire
>
> Tom Hanks and Rita Wilson
> Paul Newman and Joanne
>   Woodward
> Kurt Russell and Goldie
>   Hawn
> Bill and Melinda Gates
> George and Barbara Bush

elbowed each other and rolled their eyes when I spoke and when Giuliana wasn't looking. Looking back, this type of behavior makes me feel terrible. This was probably the third time I acted this way with our crew, so Giuliana wanted to nip it in the bud as soon as possible. I really appreciate that about her; like me, Giules likes to make sure the job gets done in the best way possible. My unintentionally abrasive style was at the heart of the impasse, but she knew how to get past it.

Giuliana: I didn't want to offend Bill or anything, but as his wife, I had to tell him that his great ideas weren't being heard, no matter how loud and strong his voice sounded. In his business world, that kind of domineering presence demands respect and tells everyone you're in control, which is a very positive thing. In Hollywood, not so much, because it's more about collaborative efforts and a kind of false modesty that lets everyone feel like they have a say in the process, even if we all know that there's one person steering the ship. So I called him right after the phone conference was over. "How do you think it went, honey?" he asked, as soft and gentle as can be. My heart sank. "Good, it went good," I said. "But I think we do need to talk about your approach. I agree with everything you said about the premiere date and the website, and I thought it was really on point because those things need to be addressed. But we should really discuss how your tone is being misinterpreted."

Bill: My inner ten-year-old braced for an "it's not what you said, but how you said it" lecture. I knew my ideas were being dismissed, but it never crossed my mind that this had to do with having an incompatible communication style with a team I appreciated and respected. I lean toward being a perfectionist, so if I'm not on the right track, I'll still pursue it the way a fat kid chases bacon until I'm told otherwise. Giuliana knows this about me, and she didn't want me to chase the wrong goal.

Giuliana: I simply suggested Bill get out of attack mode and adopt a gentler approach. "Maybe next time you can say something like 'I really like the pop quiz on the website' in a nicer tone, before you say what doesn't work, to help others be more receptive to your ideas."

I was nervous about how Bill might respond, but he's big on being pro-active, and this was the type of straight talk he likes. Bill and I are both driven people, but the way we demonstrate and execute our ambitions are very different, mostly because our industries speak opposite languages. I'm also lucky that we both believe criticism can help a couple as they move through life together, in work and otherwise, and advice doesn't need to feel like a slam when it's presented in a clear way and for a person's own good. I've learned that if I have good intentions, which I did at the time, and present my argument in a direct and honest way, I have the best chance of being heard by Bill. Teasing, being coy about an issue, or waiting for it to resolve itself can lead to a misunderstanding or even dismissing the situation altogether. Then nothing gets done.

I also didn't want to shove my opinion down Bill's throat. He's a grown man, and a very successful one at that. Neither of us needed for me to itemize his social deficits according to a bunch of flimsy Hollywood standards, but I did secretly hope he'd adopt some of my trademark moves for himself. For instance, I like to crack jokes, sometimes risqué ones, right off the bat when I'm in a meeting with a new producer or crew. It helps lighten the mood and also helps people to relax and open up. I've recently noticed that Bill's picked this up, but put his own spin on it when he tells a joke (of the cleaner kind) in a meeting.

Bill: I am who I am. But the whole experience showed me that different people have different standards of excellence. I take style points into account a little more now, with everyone really, which I didn't do before because I never had to. I still say what I want to say, and I'm not going to compromise my beliefs. But at the same time I'm careful about how I enter a room. I can either say, "Get out of my way, I'm here," or I say, "Hi, how are you?" with a smile and relaxed body language. And just be a little cooler about it. Admittedly, the latter is a nicer way to get projects done, too. The stress doesn't go away, but the whole atmosphere is more relaxed and friendly than when you talk in bullet points.

Giuliana: When I give Bill career advice, or he gives me career advice, we know it comes from such a good place that we usually don't fight it. We just take the advice and run with it.

Bill: The amazing thing about the way Giuliana works is that she's able to make professional friends and get stuff done at the same time. The girl was born to work a room, and she's helped me develop that part of myself more because it's as valuable a business skill as crunching numbers or knowing how to rock an Excel spreadsheet. I'm really thankful for that. I think a lot of men are tempted to shut out their wives when it comes to taking work-related advice, but it's not a smart way to go. I may not always want to hear what Giuliana has to say because I'm used to thinking I have all the answers about work, but marriage is all about opening yourself up to someone else's influence. Plus, my wife has the advantage of knowing my heart and intentions better than anyone.

If You Can Dish It, Be Ready to Take It

Giuliana: I'm not always the professional role model in our relationship—far from it. When Bill and I were on *The View* to participate in a panel discussion about couples dealing with infertility, and Whoopi Goldberg and I had a falling out over how I was supposed to gain weight to have a baby, Bill was ready with advice before I asked for it.

To catch up those whose lives don't revolve around tabloid reports: My Obgyn had suggested I gain five to ten pounds to help us have a baby at one point; this, mind you, was after a year of trying naturally and with various hormone treatments. I'd made the mistake of mentioning the weight gain suggestion to *The View*'s segment producer during a preinterview the week before the appearance.

As Bill and I sat on the panel, things were moving along smoothly as we told the hosts all about our very intimate and deeply personal struggle with infertility. With two minutes left until commercial break, the issue of weight came up out of the blue. I could easily have lied and told the audience that I'd gained ten pounds as my doctor suggested without hesitation, but instead, I was very honest and said that although I gained seven pounds, it wasn't something I enjoyed doing. Well, that did it. Before I could continue, the hosts flew at me, and I could hardly explain myself. Then Whoopi said that if I wasn't ready to gain weight, I sure wasn't ready to be a mom. Cue the media firestorm.

What I didn't get to explain to the press, because in their world life happens in quick sound bites, was that I know moms can safely gain up to thirty-five pounds to support the child's health once the baby is conceived. But it was hard for me to initially swallow a weight gain suggestion, since it was just one of many pieces of advice thrown at me about baby making during a very emotional and frustrating year, and I had my doubts. As anyone knows who's tried to have a baby and not immediately succeeded, subfertile women aren't sure what's going to work, and that's very stressful. For me, I needed to consider the effect that ten pounds would have on my professional life, too, since I'm in a business that demands I look a certain way, fit into teeny sample sizes, and uphold a certain image on-camera. I mean, I might as well be the Katherine Heigl character in *Knocked Up*. It also didn't help that viewers, co-workers, and friends had already congratu-lated me on being pregnant, though I was just pudgy from all of the hormone treatments. The thought of even more pound scrutiny made me feel vulnerable especially when I couldn't use exercise to help me feel balanced, focused, and upbeat.

As you can imagine, this would have been a hell of a lot to explain in a five-minute segment with four tough women and a husband who'd like to get a word in edgewise. I talk fast, but I can't work miracles. So when Perez Hilton, Huffington Post, and about 927 other bloggers and tabloid journalist asked for comments about the Whoopi fiasco, it seemed like I was the one who wouldn't let it go, when all I wanted to do was ex-plain myself each time the subject came up.

Bill: I thought that Giuliana gave the Whoopi situation too much airtime, and she's clearly still hurt by it. I let it go on for a while, but after two weeks, I had to let her know enough was enough. Giuliana was so entrenched in the mess that she couldn't see she was fueling the media's fire. One thing I'm good at is knowing when to walk away from a bad deal, and

Giuliana was in the middle of a raw one. She had to save herself or else this would just go on and on. I felt very protective of her happiness.

Giuliana: So one day, Bill talked to me about how the media was eating up my blabbermouth comments. "You know honey," he said, "you have every right to defend yourself, but maybe these writers and bloggers are taking the topic too far at this point, and now they're just trying to make you look bad. You've made your point, but I think you need to move on so that they can, too."

Bill couldn't have been more right, and I was thankful that he could point out what I was too frustrated to see on my own. Looking back, I think all those bloggers and press folks didn't even care about the so-called story; they just wanted to outtalk each other.

The funny thing is that ten people could have told me to walk away from the Whoopi mess, but until Bill gave me his perspective, I wouldn't have listened. Ironically, I'd just given Bill advice on how to navigate Hollywood's unconventional ways for our show, and here I was, stuck in my own TV-related fiasco. In the end, nobody wants me to do better in my career than Bill, and vice versa. We hold on to that notion for dear life.

We'll Know We "Have It All" When . . .

We purchase a house in Tuscany . . . Our kids grow up to love and respect us . . . We buy our parents vacation homes . . . We drive matching Aston Martins . . . We host a show together and can carpool to work . . . We retire under one roof and spend our days rocking on the front porch, while reminiscing about our extraordinary family, friends, and lives.

Build an Inspired Partnership

Bill: Even when our jobs have felt overwhelming in one way or another, I've always encouraged Giuliana to keep working, because I know it's important to her identity, self-esteem, and general sanity.

Giuliana: It's especially nice because Bill would secretly love nothing more than for me to move to Chicago and stay home with our yet-to-be-born babies, but he respects my need to work in L.A. for now.

Bill: Soon after we were married, Giuliana and I talked seriously about having her relocate to Chicago, and she came this close to pulling the trigger before I stopped her. "I can't let you do that," I told her. "I don't want you to ever resent me for suggesting you change directions for me. I have immense respect for what you do, and I'm not going to be a husband who denies you your passions."

Giuliana: Sometimes we talk about what we'd do if we won the lottery and didn't need to work anymore, and we always agree that we'd *still* work, because we love being stimulated every day. We also love having deadlines to meet and goals to strive for. It's healthy for our marriage. I think I'd drive Bill crazy if I stayed home all day and pounced on him at night like some of my married girlfriends, who don't work, do to their husbands. It's good for us to talk about our work day, what we've accomplished, and the frustrations we've faced.

Bill: Our careers are one more level to connect on, which is why we think the next best thing to being in the same city is working together as often as we can. And when it's for our reality show, the network picks up our airfare travel. I like that!

Giuliana: Our goal is to work together as much as possible, because we love to create things from the ground up. I think it's a testament to how we yin and yang our way through life; and if one of us gets down about a shared project, the other person lifts us up. I hear some husbands complain that it's hard to work with their wives on projects, especially those that require imagination, but we've found that the creative process is so rewarding when you indulge in it with someone you love. We actually started a production company called You & I Productions, because that's what it's about—just you and I—you know? It's kind of like that song, "You and Me Against the World." It's really nice knowing that all else could fail—your once-supportive friends could turn on you, your once-steady job could change on a dime—but your spouse will consistently support you and inspire you to be a better person. And then, of course, there's the fact that working together is a nice exercise in making decisions for the sake of the family money pot. Who knew our silly camaraderie would help pay the bills?

Bill: The challenge for us, especially when we work together, is to find that work-life balance. I feel that in life, it's very rare to have time and money. You either have a lot of time but no money, or you have a lot of money but no time because you're working so hard to make it. I think the key to finding a balance between these two things is to marry a supportive spouse who helps you discover what it means to you.

Giuliana: Trying to figure out a work-life priority forces me and Bill to make a lot of sacrifices, which are especially draining in a long-distance marriage. Our family and friends tease us about being such jet-setters, but when I'm flying back and forth from L.A. to Chicago so I can see my husband for the first time in three weeks because we've both been working so hard, there isn't anything glamorous about it. Bill and I spend so much time on planes that it would be very easy for one of us to say to the other, "Hey, you know what? I'm not coming to visit this weekend."

Bill: Giuliana's actually said those words before. That's not a hypothetical.

Giuliana: I have! I'd traveled four weekends in a row to visit Bill in Chicago while he was working there, nonstop, and I was at the point of collapse. All I wanted was to kick around in sunny L.A., get a pedicure, sit by the pool, grab a late-afternoon lunch at The Ivy, and hit the farmer's market in Santa Monica. (If you can't tell, I fantasize about this a lot. . . .) Instead, I had to haul ass to Chicago, where the forecast said it was going to be cold, rainy, and windy, which meant doing laundry, repacking, and buying myself a new umbrella because I'd left my old one in a cab. I'd have to rush out of work on Friday to catch a two p.m. flight and not even land in Chicago until ten p.m., where we could circle the airport thanks to weather delays.

So I said to Bill, "You know, maybe I won't come next weekend because you're coming to L.A. the weekend after. I've just been traveling so much, and I'd love to have some time off from flying." There was such a dead silence on the line that you'd have thought I'd asked Bill for a trial separation so I could go make greasy babies with Johnny Depp. "Honey," he said in his I-love-you-but-I-mean-business voice, "I was in eight planes in the past two days. I'm not doing that for fun. It's my career, it's our future, and it's what I signed up for—and you, too, as my wife." At that point, I felt a little selfish and made myself buy that damn umbrella. My pedicure would have to wait.

"If you don't want to come that's fine," he continued, "but I'd appreciate the sacrifice." Bill was right, and in the end, I went to Chicago. We both knew that the one weekend I'd miss would somehow make taking two weekends off OK, and then maybe three down the road . . . and that's where we'd start to dissolve as a team. And let's face it: I really miss Bill when our lives get too harried and individual, and we don't have time to connect because of work.

Bill: The importance of each of us liking our careers is one of our big life values—right up there with being good people, celebrating holidays with family, and teaching our kids to respect their elders. We believe in a hard day's work, feel it's necessary to personal satisfaction, enjoy when the other person achieves, and offer help when one of us faces a professional setback. It sounds old-fashioned, but these are all a big part of who we are. Although our work can be exhausting, it helps that we feel the same way about our careers because it shows we're on the same page and equally supportive of our mutual goals, and I don't think it will be a topic that causes conflict down the road. However, it's still important to keep an eye on how we're both faring at work, since having a family someday could change our priorities and throw off all that striving for a work-life balance. I think we understand each other's hopes, dreams, concerns, and disap-

> **Romantic Work Perks**
>
> • Date night means front row at the Emmys!
> • Bill's frequent-flier miles yield first-class upgrades to Rome, the Canary Islands, St. Tropez . . .
> • A work trip to New York doubles as a mini-vacay. Dinner and Broadway shows, here we come.
> • Filming our reality show, *Giuliana & Bill,* ensures we see each other more often than not.

pointments well enough to know we can handle any big change that comes our way—career or otherwise.

Giuliana: After all, our jobs are what brought us together in the first place. I just don't want to be one of those super-busy, über-driven couples whose lives zoom past at warp speed— and who one day pop their heads out from behind their computers and realize they've spent so much time building their lives that they never stopped to enjoy them. Bill and I are striving for no regrets, which is why we're gobbling up all we can while we still have the energy.

Bill: Eventually this old man's going to tire out, though. And while we know we're not saving the world one motivational speech and red carpet broadcast at a time, Giuliana and I care about what we do and the legacy we leave behind—and of course, who we share it all with.

TIPS FOR TWO: Working It Out

• If you want to offer your spouse work advice, do it in a kind but direct way. Cutesy teasing or waiting for the problem to fix itself can frustrate you and delay change.

• Respect your spouse's opinion, even if you don't always agree with it.

• Share professional struggles and victories. So much of a person's identity and self-satisfaction is intertwined with his/her work; make your partner a part of that.

• Work with your spouse to achieve a healthy work-life balance. It's tough, but doable!

• Never spend so much time gunning for the future that you miss out on the present.

7 Words to Love By

For a talkative couple like us, opening our mouths is synonymous with opening our hearts. Good communication is the foundation of our relationship—both the talking and listening parts—so we try to express our thoughts and feelings with care, and in ways our spouse understands. We also strive to stay positive when we connect, which is as much a feel-good priority as it is a physiological imperative. In studies related to stress and communication, research finds that negative talk like sarcasm and put-downs increase a husband's and wife's stress hormone levels, with a wife's hormones rising more sharply and staying up longer than her hubby's.

We're also grateful that words come easily to us. Giuliana is from a chatty Italian family, so effusive talks and storytelling are second nature to her; Bill is a born negotiator, so waxing poetic about how to make plans and progress is in his wheelhouse. When we connect, we've learned that good communication involves welcoming each other's perspectives and putting real energy into our dialogue. We like to initiate regu-

lar and productive "check ins," plus use soothing body language that says we're emotionally available. The hardest thing for Giuliana is to keep our communication from being one-sided. She's not proud of it, but she has a tendency to interrupt.

No matter how much one person likes to blab, or even overanalyze the relationship, we've found that it helps to know when to put a period at the end of a marital discussion. When Giuliana is keen on sharing fears and concerns, she needs an attentive audience, and rarely does Bill have the patience for an entire weekend of scrutinizing and rehashing. So if possible, we try to focus on topics that help us to recognize and appreciate the time we spend together, and apart. Because of our long-distance relationship, this is especially important. We've also found that cute nicknames and random compliments keep us going more than you know.

At the end of the day, sharing our thoughts, our shared goals, and even a bunch of silly nothings are essential to communicating with each other. So much of this book, and our lives, are an ode to communication. Here's a bit about how we've polished the art of good talk.

Giuliana: As early as our first date, Bill made sure that communication became a priority in our budding romance. It's common for men and women to play the occasional game in the beginning of a relationship, but Bill refused to let me get away with mine (looking back, this is no great surprise). We'd made a plan to have sushi on a Sunday at Nobu, which is in Malibu, about thirty minutes from my apartment in L.A. Our plans were set to go, but Bill being Bill, he sent me a text to confirm everything on Saturday. "Since it's a long drive, why don't I pick you up at five-thirty?" he asked. When I got the message, I poked my head outside and reasoned that if the next day were going to be half as sunny and beautiful as this one, I didn't want to be in the car for so long on a first date. I like to take advantage of dim lighting, smoky eyes and pale pink lips, and incredibly high heels—and who dresses this way for a five-thirty road trip to Malibu? So in the name of looking sexy and feeling my best, I decided I'd try to reschedule our date for a nine p.m. dinner during the week. I texted Bill: "Hey. So sorry. Something's come up :((Can we resched 4 another time?"

Bill: I was fly-fishing with my buddies in Utah, when I got Giuliana's text. We'd only met once when she interviewed me for a story on E!, but it was electric. So why did I suddenly sense cold feet from her now? "No matter what came up, canceling like this is ridiculous," said my friend Kevin, aka "Big Red" (he's tall, burly, and has red hair and cheeks). "If you ever date this girl for real, you need to let her know games don't fly." He was right, so I texted Giuliana back: "This week is not gonna work. Catch u nxt time I'm in town."

Giuliana: *Damn!* I thought. *Now I won't see him for a few weeks.* Considering the shortage of good, straight men in L.A., I was afraid that I'd just blown a prime opportunity.

Bill: Not a minute later, Giuliana texted me back . . .

Giuliana: It was an *hour* later.

Bill: OK, forty-five minutes later.

Giuliana: During that *hour,* I weighed my options: either I could suck-up my vanity issues, lose the heels, and opt for patent leather flats with Audrey Hepburn sunglasses . . . or I could choose to not see Bill for a few weeks and worry he might meet someone else. I didn't want to miss out on a good thing, so I swallowed my pride and typed. I texted Bill back and told him I was in for our sushi date after all, and I'm so glad I did, because we had a marvelous time. And yes, I wore the flats and sunglasses. But that wasn't the only time Bill lovingly layed down the law early on.

Bill: Giuliana was a textbook game player, and I didn't have the patience or time to deal with that. After the sushi incident, my antenna was up. And I immediately noticed that if I called her, she didn't call me back until the next day; and even though I suspected she was playing hard to get or whatever chicks think old-fashioned rudeness is, I wanted it to stop if we continued dating. During drinks on our third date, I said to her, "This whole not calling back until the next day shtick is baloney. G. Please call me back when I call you. To make a relationship work, we need to communicate with each other, and I don't want to play games." Sure enough, Giuliana agreed that she wasn't being entirely up-front with me all the time. Within our first three dates, we'd established that it was imperative to talk about issues as soon as they bugged us, so we could begin to make things better right away.

Open-Up and Say "Bla"

Giuliana: There was a lot of back and forth like this early in our dating life, which is why I think that it's been relatively simple for us to integrate good communication into our marriage. As a couple that's thrived as a long-distance duo before and after our nuptials, the glue that's held us together was talking about what worked, what didn't, and what we wanted out of our relationship.

Bill: I think our long-distance deal is particularly relatable to spouses who travel for business. When I travel or am on the road, away from Chicago or L.A., it would be so easy for Giuliana to worry about me if I weren't in regular contact. But if you're not in touch in a reliable way, the imagination wanders and flies to a worst-case scenario about where your spouse is, who he/she is with, and what that person is doing. When I'm away from either of our homes, Giuliana always has my cell and hotel numbers. I'm accessible to her 24/7, and it has to be that way because I never want her to think that something's happened when I haven't been in touch. She does the same for me, too.

Giuliana: I've dealt with a lack of communication in other relationships, but never with Bill. Part of a successful marriage is being available to the other person, emotionally and practically. I'm guilty of hitting the "ignore" button on other people's calls and shooting them to voice mail because I don't feel like talking to them, but I can't do this with my spouse. I always answer his calls, even if I'm napping or on the other line; or I call back immediately if I'm tied up on set. It's respectful. There's never a good reason to not be reachable.

Bill: And when you are in touch, a good communicator doesn't need to beat an issue to death. You don't need to talk too much about your relationship or concerns once they're resolved, because that wears out even the best husbands I know. G and I address an issue if one arises, but we don't rehash it a week later if we can help it. I like to always move forward. Each time you look back, you feed animosity by reminding each other of things that don't work, instead of things that do.

Giuliana: To make progress, I also need to ask Bill open-ended questions to keep our dialogue going (no husband of mine is squirming out of a talk with a simple "yes" or "no"). Since it can bug Bill to linger on the past, I make sure these questions focus on the future.

Bill: I rarely want to rehash a discussion from the night before, unless I feel it's not been resolved in an obvious or settling way. One of the worst times I can remember something eating at me the night of a fiasco, and then again in the morning, was when Giuliana bid on a $10,000 auction item at a charity event for the Mercy Home for Boys and Girls, a home for underprivileged youth in Chicago (we sit on the board of directors). It seemed like such a foolish move that I needed to talk about it twice to fully understand why she did it. She blew this money awhile ago when the economy tanked and the world seemed to be coming to an end, especially for those of us in real estate. Giuliana acted irresponsibly, and I was supposed to be cool with it because she'd had too much champagne.

Giuliana: I'd had *way* too much champagne.

Bill: So she bought a seven-night trip to Puerto Vallarta, in a villa, for five couples.

Giuliana: When I'm drinking, I rarely let a paddle come within inches of my right hand. . . .

Bill: But you did that night.

Giuliana: I'm usually so paranoid that someone will accidentally see me scratch my ear at a live auction, and then announce I'm the proud owner of a Cookie Monster portrait made with M&Ms, that I practically sit on my hands. And I'd never bid on anything at all if Bill were sitting next to me. But the villa bid happened when Bill had left to refill my drink and say hi to the mayor of Chicago, Richard Daley. He'd left me alone at the table with a few drunken girlfriends, so we started having way too much fun. I picked up my paddle in one hand

and Bill's paddle in the other, and began to outbid myself with both paddles. In the middle of my shenanigans, I looked at my husband who saw me and mouthed the words "Cut it out!" I knew I'd stop my personal bidding war before I actually owned the trip, but when I saw Bill say that to me, I waved to him with the paddle. You can guess what happened next: "Sold! For $10,000!" said the auctioneer—to me. Everyone clapped and thought I'd meant to make a very generous donation, so I couldn't explain or object. Plus, who doesn't love a little vacay to Mexico? Bill loves guacamole.

Bill: But not $10,000 worth of guacamole!

Giuliana: When we got home, Bill was bent out of shape. He tried to talk to me about what I'd done wrong, but I was still drunk, and he must not have been satisfied with how serious he thought I was taking the situation. So we revisited the incident the next morning. "Honey, this is a scary time for us to throw down ten grand on a charity donation," he said. "Try not to do it again."

Bill: I may have sounded a little like a parent, but I think you learn to communicate based on how your role models spoke to each other and to you, anyway. I never heard my

> **Talking Smack: Stuff You Should Never Say Behind Your Spouse's Back**
>
> "He's so cheap, it makes me sick."
> "She looks good tonight, but you should see her in the mornings."
> "He overcompensates for his teeny you-know-what."
> "It still bothers me that she slept with half her college football team."
> "I wear the pants in the family. He's my little bitch."

parents shout at each other, but they did talk things out in a sober way. Sometimes I'd overhear them late at night, in the kitchen or bedroom, talking about how my mom spent too much time at work or how my dad didn't discipline me for a bad grade. Their voices were serious, much like mine that night, but they never shouted.

Giuliana: My parents, on the other hand, yelled all the time. We're Italian, and that's what Italians do, but there was never any cruel intent. I remember my best friend Andrea came over a lot to play when we were kids, and when she'd hear the way my mom and dad shouted she'd freak out. "What are your parents fighting about?" she'd whimper. "Is everything OK? Should I go home?" She'd always give me a crazy look when I told her they were bickering over who ate the last mozzarella ball. This always confused me, because it was just how my parents talked. I never realized that other peoples' moms and dads didn't act the same way. My mom was especially bad. She'd yell at my dad about everything, like when an employee screwed up at his clothing store or about what to wear to a party—but again, she was never angry; just heated and overworked. As I got older, all that yelling seemed unnecessary to me. It's not like my mom caught my dad cheating on her; the shouting wasn't warranted. Because of my parents' dynamic, I'm desensitized to screamers, but I don't yell myself. I find it really annoying, to be honest.

Bill: There's a large Italian community in Chicago, so I know people who yell a lot, but their shouting matches diffuse quickly. I'm used to these interactions. I'll tell you this, though: Giuliana may not yell to get her point across, but she does have a fiery temper that flares up easily. I'm the sensible one, so when it's time to talk things out, we complement each other really well.

Giuliana: We have an open and honest dialogue, but I wasn't this expressive about my needs with other guys. I don't think I really knew how to be, before Bill and I figured it out together.

Bill: For me, I didn't want to be a good communicator with other women. If the relationship didn't have long-term potential, I didn't care as much about talking through problems.

Giuliana: I know a lot of married couples that still play games as if they're dating, and never talk about their issues. Even too much eye-rolling in front of your spouse or talking bad behind his/her back is a form of poor communication.

Bill: These are often the same people who are afraid of their spouses. They can't go out for dinner with the guys or play a Sunday-afternoon football game, because their wife is on their tail. It's no way I'd ever want to live.

Giuliana: Yeah, but the problem is that the guy we know who acts like this doesn't explain to his wife why it's important for him to spend time with friends, which is probably why his wife is always on his case. And the wife doesn't say that she resents the time he's away because she'd like a day off from the kids. The more she nags, the more he wants to be with his friends outside the house. Eventually, the cycle explodes—and all because they didn't speak up in the first place.

Talk Pretty to Me

Giuliana: Good communication shouldn't be a priority only when something goes wrong in your relationship; you should also communicate to make each other feel good. For instance, Bill and I compliment each other a lot—I'm a big fan of mush.

I also love to use nicknames to make him smile. One of my pet names for Bill is "Gorgeous." *Hey, Gorgeous. What's wrong, Gorgeous?* This way, he can't forget how hot I think he is, because I tell him ten times a day. I also like to call Bill "poo-poo head."

Bill: You also call me your "hot hubby."

Giuliana: My "hot hubby"—Bill likes that one. Compliments flow easily when you're dating, and we don't think this should stop or even slow down once you're married. Compliments also go a long way with me, but I think that's the case with a lot of women. The other morning, I was scrutinizing myself in the mirror the way girls do, and Bill gave me a reassuring smile. "You look better than ever," he said. "You look gorgeous, and your body is so sexy." It was sweet and unprompted. If your spouse doesn't make you feel good about the way you look, who will?

Bill: I have nicknames for Giuliana, too. Sometimes I call her "Paesano," because she's my little Italian.

Giuliana: He also calls me "baby doll."

Bill: "Cookie."

Giuliana: All of Bill's names for me are special, because they feel very insider-ish. Every morning, whether we're in the same bed or miles away, Bill turns to me or calls and says "Good morning, my beautiful wife" or "How did my beautiful wife sleep?" If it's early in L.A., Bill will text me: "Good morning, love of my life." Those terms of endearment mean the world to me, and when we have kids, we want our little ones to hear this so they always feel surrounded by love.

Bill: I have to admit, I like when Giuliana uses words that make me feel like she's still hot for me. "Gorgeous" is a powerful word. I like when she compliments my new jeans or a fresh haircut, too, but words that make me feel like she wants me are always appreciated.

Giuliana: You should see him when I say he's hot and gorgeous; Bill gets a huge burst of confidence. We also say "I love you" a lot—at least ten to fifteen times a day. Seriously. One day I asked Bill, "Do I say 'I love you' too much?" And he said, "No way. You can never say it enough."

Check In—with Each Other, Not the Four Seasons

Giuliana: After picking your spouse wisely, we think you need to work on the choices you make together to ensure everyone's happy. That's one of the reasons we randomly "check in" with each other, and though we urge friends to do it at least once a month, we like to do it a few times a month ourselves.

Bill: We check in when we're upset and when things are going well; checking in is like a nonjudgmental progress report, more than anything else. We also like to shut off the TV, turn off our phones, and unplug from the world when we do this. We only focus on each other.

Giuliana: I like that this is also a chance to make eye contact, hold hands, or rub the backs of each other's neck when we talk, too. All that touching makes it easier to open up. So for instance, we'll be in bed watching TV, and I'll look at Bill with one hand on his leg, and say, "Hey honey, I'm just checking in. Is everything OK? Are you happy? Are you sad? What's going on?" And at that point, he can say anything about our marriage—if he feels good about it, or if I've done anything to annoy him. This way, we both know that when we say "Checking in!" it can mean any of those things. It's this code that we understand immediately, and you don't need to work up to it, like you might with the usual (and intimidating) "we need to talk" conversation.

When I prompt him with "Checking in!" Bill might say nothing's bothering him or he might tell me about, say, how awkward he felt at dinner when I didn't explain to friends that we were trying to have a baby. Checking in is an opportunity to get things off our chests early, instead of letting them bottle up. What I also like about checking in is it's not negative—it's just candid.

Bill: It's always easy to find bad things to talk about, so I like when Giuliana uses this check-in time to tell me that she loves me a lot, has never been happier, and liked the flowers I bought her last week. It's also an opportunity to ask your husband or wife what's going on if you sense that something is off. After you're married, you develop this cool telepathic ability to read the other person's mind a little, like those couples on *How I Met Your Mother*.

I had this twenty-three-year-old female trainer stretch me the other day at the gym, and Giuliana couldn't take her eyes off the two of us. She was so jealous, but she didn't want to talk about it. So when we left the gym, I said, "Checking in! That trainer bothered you, didn't she?" This was Giuliana's time to talk about it; I didn't want her to let me know in a month, this was her chance to get it out in the open before it festered.

Checking in is a very pro-active idea—a good time to openly discuss your fears, guilt, any uncertainty you might have about revealing what's on your mind, and if you've been tempted to keep a secret, you can just spill it then, too. Sometimes, when one person asks for a check in, the other finds something equally intimate to share. There's a nice back-and-forth in that. We don't always agree with what the other person is saying, but it's important to hear him/her out.

Giuliana: There's something nice, too, about having this ritual in our lives. It's a constant reminder that nothing comes before the health of our marriage. As a woman, I can talk about the positives and negatives of our relationship until the cows come home, but Bill can only discuss our marriage for so long. Checking in suits both our needs; mine, to talk about my feelings and concerns, and Bill's, to come up with a solution to problems. Checking in, when you're lying in bed, can even lead to sex or making out. Once you get what you needed to off your chest, you feel so much closer to your spouse. It's like you're having make-up sex without the fighting!

Shut Up and Let Me Talk

Giuliana: Communication might come easily to us because I admittedly like to hear myself speak, and Bill finds it satisfying to make plans and follow through. If you squish those two dynamics together, you've got a couple who looks forward to regular talking dates, listens to what the other person has to say, and uses the conversation to make a change in their lives.

Unfortunately, I like yammering so much that I interrupt Bill a lot. Toward the end of our first year of marriage, we were at Topo Gigio in Chicago with our friends Jon and Allie, and on our drive home, Bill seemed lost in his own thoughts. I asked him what he was thinking about, and he was hesitant to open up at first. "Ah . . . I don't know," he said. So I pulled the checking in card, which always works. "I'm checking in, honey," I said. "Tell me what's bothering you." I couldn't believe my ears when Bill got honest. "Well, you interrupt me a lot," he said. "If I'm in the middle of a story, you like to finish it. I *can* finish a story." I told him I never thought of this as an interruption; I thought of it as just adding to our stories. "It doesn't feel that way," said Bill. "It feels like a blatant interruption."

Giuliana: I didn't want to believe it, but I agreed to stop to make Bill feel better. And then one day when I was watching the interstitials for an episode of our reality show *Giuliana & Bill,* I noticed that Bill couldn't utter more than two sentences before I "added" to his story. Bill was right; I interrupted him all the time! It irked me to watch myself, and I thought I looked really annoying. So I apologized to him, again, but on the inside I knew I meant it this time. "I'm sorry," I said. "I do interrupt you a lot, and I'm really going to make a conscious effort to stop." Bill was thankful that I apologized again, though I had to come to this sincerity on my own terms. Now when Bill tells a story, I wait for him to pause, and I pick up where he leaves off.

> ### A Boost a Day Keeps Divorce Away
>
> • "Bill, you don't need to ask for directions. You're a natural navigator."
> • "Giuliana, you make running clothes look sexy."
> • "Bill, I hope our kid gets your hairline."

Bill: Or at least she tries. Giuliana was careful for a while, but she started interrupting again when we did the talk-show circuit to promote our show that first season. She let me hold court when we did a local interview in, like, Kentucky. But the minute we'd do a national show like *The View* or *The Today Show,* I couldn't get a word in edgewise. It was really embarrassing for me, because I'd sit there like a mute, and I'm not that person. I consider myself to be a pretty sharp guy. And

I've done these talk shows a lot more than Giuliana has, so I'm an old pro at pacing myself for a five-minute segment, which is hard if you're not experienced. After a frustrating interview with one of the majors, I turned to her and compared us to, well, a flower. "There are two of us here who need to shine in order for this work," I said. "Our relationship is like a flower. If it doesn't get enough sun, then it dies. If one flower towers over another, neither will thrive."

Giuliana: Poor Bill needed some sun. He said this to me after we told the story of the first time I interviewed Bill for E!, which is how we met, over and over again to the morning shows. The problem was that I liked jumping to the punch line before Bill could get there. Bill is a more succinct storyteller by nature, so he runs right to the goal; I'm Italian, so I tell long-winded stories. This annoyed both of us. So when I noticed Bill approaching the story's finish line, I'd think, *Wait, slow down!* And then I'd rush to get the last word because I like my punch line better.

Bill: We'd created an unhealthy competition by going for the joke—who can get it out first?

Giuliana: Who tells the story better?

Bill: I began to notice, too, that our competitive edge even trickled over into work, in terms of who took credit for the projects we did. Instead of saying we had an idea, it was always "I" had this idea. We always tried to take individual credit rather than credit Team Us. Since so much of our work is our life, is our work, you can see why we needed to stop this. A related problem to this, of course, is that we also weren't listening to each other as much as we should have been. Listening to your spouse's feelings is just as important as expressing your own.

Giuliana: Our goal is to keep our communication positive and free-flowing, and a competitive spirit promotes anything but those things. I've never met a happy couple that didn't talk and listen to each other in a sincere way. And when we drive to Malibu for sushi now, I'm grateful that we've nailed down this repertoire. It's a long ride in heels and makeup, without it.

TIPS FOR TWO: More Than Words

• Never give your spouse's mind a chance to wander by being out of touch for too long. For us, this means always having each other's hotel numbers when we're traveling or in separate cities, and always answering the phone.

• Express your relationship needs to your spouse, but don't beat a dead horse. It makes men nuts.

• Endear yourself to your partner with nicknames to make you and your spouse feel desired.

• Check in with each other on a regular basis, to connect over good and bad things in your life.

• Try not to hog the conversation. Listening to your spouse is as important as being heard.

• If you're competitive, channel it into work or a 10K. It's an unhealthy trait to drag into marriage.

8 You Might Want a Kleenex for This

When there's a problem, we like to look to each other for support. But figuring out the right words, emotions, and how much ra-ra to give can be tricky, yet finding that balance is a must. In fact, a recent University of Iowa study shows that too much, or the wrong kind, of support can cause harm to couples in their first few years of marriage. For instance, study participants said that while they can't get enough of their partner's encouragement, providing too much unwanted advice is the most damaging type of support they receive. And yet most husbands and wives insist that they don't receive as much support, in general, as they crave! The lesson we took away from this is that couples expect the world from their spouses, but we can't expect our partners to be mind (or heart) readers. If we need support, we ask for it; and if we offer support, we ask how we can help. If we wanted to always overcome obstacles on our own, we'd still be single.

Our need for support happens almost daily, though sometimes it can seem so trivial that we don't even recognize it as such. Support doesn't need to seem like a big deal, like asking your spouse to sleep on the hospital floor after you've had surgery or discussing a dramatic fight with your in-laws on your behalf. It also includes the small stuff that affects our daily time, energy, and stress, like when Giuliana asks Bill to her find her a good accountant to review her taxes or Bill asks Giuliana to pick him up Zyrtec for his allergies on her way home from work. Support doesn't need to be a grand gesture, and in fact, we've found that the little requests impact our relationship a lot more than big deal issues, because they happen on a regular basis.

Support is about give-and-take, and to feel mutually supported, we often remind ourselves that throughout our marriage, we will always need different types of help at different times. This includes giving hugs and advice, listening and empathizing, brainstorming answers to problems, and cheering the other person on. After Bill's father died, it was hard for him to realize how and when to ask for support. He was afraid to be a burden, scared to appear vulnerable, and yet too upset to keep his feelings inside. Here's how we learned to give and receive support, especially when dealing with Bill's father's death.

Bill: I was twenty-eight when my dad died from renal cell carcinoma, a type of kidney cancer in which cancerous cells are found in the lining of small tubes (called tubules) in the kidney. He battled the disease for a year and a half before he died at age sixty-six. I was his only son and the youngest child in our family, so we were really close. My dad was my best friend and one of the greatest guys ever.

Dad was such a young man when he was diagnosed with cancer; he was full of life, in terrific shape, and one year into retirement. It was very difficult for me when it happened. I still can't believe he's gone. Not a day goes by that I don't think about him, and yet Giuliana was the first girl I'd ever told about my father, in terms of what his personality was like and the extent to which I still miss him. Other women I've dated might have known that my dad had died at one point, but I never shared much about his life, how my family suffered during his cancer battle, and how I wish he'd had a chance to see me as a husband and father someday.

I believe that in marriage, you've got to show the good, the bad, and the ugly. It's not always going to be about happy times. I think that when you lose a loved one, especially a parent, there's something about that loss that stays with you. It becomes a piece of you that you then have to share with the person you love. I think that in order for your spouse to understand you, or understand why sometimes you're sad or distant, you have to let him/her in. When you do that, you know you have a true partnership—you're husband and wife, becoming one, so to speak. I had to share this part of myself in order to make our marriage strong. As much as I wanted to be the tough guy, my dad's death was something that affected me more than I could have ever imagined.

Giuliana: On the night of our third date, we talked about a lot of important stuff, like details about our childhood and families, because I think we felt a chemistry with each other that we'd never felt with other people. We were very open, even then.

The dinner was at Ivy at the Shore, a very nice sushi spot in Santa Monica with dim lighting and lots of privacy. We talked and talked, even revealing what we'd want to name our first male child. I told Bill that I wanted to name my first son "Eddie" because my dad's name is Eduardo. And then Bill said, "Oh, my dad's name was Edward, too. I thought the same thing about naming my first boy Edward!" We both smiled as if fate just made a mental note, and I think that when Bill said his father's name to me, it helped him take that first step to talking about his dad in any way. Bill didn't elaborate about his dad and beyond using the word *was,* he didn't volunteer that his dad passed away or how. I never wanted to pry, because by avoiding the topic, it seemed clear to me that this death was a huge deal to him, a real life changer.

For a few months, we didn't bring Edward up again, but it wasn't essential for me to understand the nitty-gritty of what Bill was feeling, because there were some things I could sense. Like I knew Bill came from a great family, with three older sisters, so I could only imagine how happy his father must have been to finally have a son, which means they must have been close. And because Bill is such a great and successful guy, his dad must have been very proud—and I sensed that Bill knew that by the way he talked about him. I never wanted to ask Bill to elaborate beyond what he was comfortable saying to me, and I had to have faith that in due time, he'd trust me enough to really talk about his dad when he was ready.

Show and Tell

Bill: My dad got sick in August of 1998. Soon after, we flew him to Bethesda, Maryland, for treatment at the National Institutes of Health (NIH), one of the leading cancer hospitals in the world. A year and a half later, he knew he was dying and wanted to come home to Chicago. So I chartered a plane to bring him back; that was December 16, 1999. He died twelve hours after he got home.

Seven years later, on December 15, I asked Giuliana to marry me. I proposed on the near-anniversary of my father's death because I'd waited thirty-five years to ask a woman to marry me, and I wanted the date to have significance. I also wanted to include my father's memory in this special occasion. The day after our engagement, I asked Giuliana to join my family at the cemetery to honor my father as we do every year on the anniversary of his passing. I'd never brought a woman to his grave with me before, but since this was tradition and she was now part of my family, I explained to Giuliana that I wanted her to be there.

Giuliana: It was an emotional few days for us. First we had our engagement with the helicopter, food, and lights, which was magical, and then the next day we visited his father's grave, which was also special. It was a very raw, but necessary and beautiful, way to honor the start of our expanded family. At the cemetery, Bill's mom, sisters, their husbands, and everyone's children went around in a circle and told a story about Bill's dad. From those short anecdotes, I learned a lot about Edward—that he had been a superintendant of schools who cared so much about young people and wanted to make a difference in their lives, that he was a patient and kind man who loved his four kids and wife more than life itself, and that he cherished taking the family on adventures so he could expose them to new experiences while spending quality time together. The whole afternoon was very emotional, and I was too embarrassed to cry because I didn't even know Bill's father, but I couldn't help myself. I was moved by how close this amazing family was. I held Bill's hand really tight and wept like a baby.

Bill: It was a powerful afternoon. Being at the cemetery with Giuliana, who was now my fiancée, impacted me more than I expected. To this day, she gets very emotional when I talk about my dad, and I think involving her in such a moving experience had a real impact on her. Most people can understand how devastating it would be to lose a parent, and when you put yourself in the position of someone you love who's gone through that, it rocks you to the core.

Giuliana: For the next few months, I was careful not to push Bill to tell me too much more about his dad before he was

ready to go there again. I knew it would come up naturally before the wedding, anyway, because so many plans revolved
around the topic of our families—if they'd participate in the
ceremony, where they'd sit at the reception, who liked what
foods, who'd give what speech. I knew that at some point, Bill
would reference how he missed his dad or wish that he could
see us get married (sure enough, he told me a month before
the wedding that his father would be his "honorary best
man." We lit a candle near the altar as a tribute to him). We
were also having such a good time telling everyone about our
engagement and choosing dresses, rings, tuxes, cakes . . . that
I didn't want to force a super heavy subject on Bill that he
didn't plan to introduce on his own.

Bill: And then one random night, I was paying the bill at dinner about three months before the wedding, and when I pulled
out my wallet, Giuliana saw a picture I keep of my father. It's
on the Prayer card that we handed out at his funeral. My dad's
card has been with me since the wake, and I call it my "good-
luck charm." When Giuliana saw it wedged between a few
twenties, she asked me about it.

I shared everything. Memories and emotions I thought I'd
worked through just came pouring out. I told Giuliana about
how, when my dad was dying, I did everything to try to help
him and keep him alive. I researched clinical trials, reached
out to cancer diet experts about revamping his meal plan, and
met with his oncologist several times a week to discuss his
progress. Looking back, I realize now that I'd never really told
anyone about the whole traumatic experience until I opened
up to Giuliana. For years, I had bottled up the pain deep inside
me to keep it from surfacing, because the heartache of losing
my father, my best friend, was overwhelming. Right there at
the table, I broke down and cried. Of course, this made Giuliana cry, too, and it became a real tearfest as we discussed it

through dessert. We've never been so emotional while eating banana cream pie, but I'm glad I was able to share those details about my dad with Giuliana.

Giuliana: Bill told me a little more about his father as time went on—not every day, but when he was in the mood to share. Each time he did, I felt closer to him than I had before. The more experiences you have with someone, the more you can mentally track where their values and quirks come from—and with Bill, there'd always been a missing piece. Not a gaping hole, just a space that hadn't been colored in yet. I assumed that he got his drive and great speaking skills from his father who was a respected college professor, but he never told me that until now; I knew he was obsessed with chocolate chip pancakes, but I never knew that was influenced by memories of his dad taking him for pancake breakfasts on his way to school as a kid. It meant a lot to me that Bill was beginning to trust me more and more with his memories, but I was also grateful that I was learning a lot more about the depth of the man I was about to marry.

You Can Count on Me

Bill: About a year after we were husband and wife, I told Giuliana that I'd been involved with the Dean R. O'Neill Renal Cell Cancer Research Fund Foundation for NIH for eight years. NIH had done so much for my father that I wanted to give back in any way I could. So that year, I decided to participate in their Run for Life race in Maryland, a 10K that helps raise awareness and support kidney cancer research in the laboratory of tumor immunology that's headed-up by Dr. Richard Childs, my father's oncologist. I asked Giuliana to run the race with me, and she didn't hesitate for a second.

Challenges That Made Us Closer

Fertility issues: This struggle made us realize that if we weren't
able to have kids, we'd be more than content surrounded
by friends and extended family. Love makes a family, not
headcount.

Long-distance marriage: Living seventeen hundred miles
apart has been hard, but instead of griping about the
distance when we're together, we savor our time and leave
fights at the door.

Moving every six months: Moving is one of the most stressful
things a couple can do, but we don't let it get to us. We lean
on each other when our blood pressure shoots through the
roof—hey, we're grateful to have one over our heads.

Giuliana: There wasn't a question in my mind about whether
I should do it. I wanted to support Bill however I could. I was
always there to listen when he needed me, but I was thrilled
and even a little relieved that I could finally to do something
tangible for him—not to mention all the families dealing with
kidney cancer. It felt good to take a significant step toward
helping to find a cure for the disease that took his father's life,
with a man who loved him so much.

Bill: The day before the race, Giuliana arranged for us to have
lunch with Dr. Childs and then take a tour of the tumor immunology lab at NIH. I'm a kidney donor at the hospital, and
I've funded thousands of dollars in fellowships for research
doctors there, so we got the royal treatment. I was really interested to see where my money was going, and how they were
using it to help others. Dr. Childs led us through the lab and
showed us the most advanced equipment they use to explore

new and advanced detection and treatment techniques. We also saw the chemo room where my dad received monthly treatments at the end of his life. This was the first time I'd been among so many machines and frail patients since my father died, and revisiting it all was like a kick in the stomach for me. The chemical smells, the idle conversation between patients, the forced optimism of family and friends—it brought everything back. All of the details I'd tried so hard to forget just flooded back to me one hundred percent, almost in slow motion.

Giuliana: The whole afternoon at NIH was hard for us. My only role in the visit was to be there for Bill. I didn't want to be annoying and ask the doctor a million questions, like, "What's that machine? What does that one do?" I just wanted to be there for my husband, pat his hand, rub his back, and do or be whatever he needed. To be honest, I also didn't say a lot because I spent the afternoon choking back tears. I don't break down too often, but when Bill and I talk about his father, it just kills me. Knowing how much his death affects Bill, it hurts my heart.

We spent a lot of hours with Dr. Childs that day, since he'd spent so much time with Bill's father during his stay at NIH. It was poignant, too, when he later thanked me for bringing Bill to the hospital because he was so personally affected by Edward's sickness. It was endearing that Dr. Childs noticed all of Bill's efforts to make his dad better, and that Bill even made them to begin with. He added some wonderful details to the stories Bill had told me at dinner that night. My favorite part was when Dr. Childs explained how Bill made a list for the nurses, every night before he left, of everything they needed to get done—which is so Bill, it's not even funny. He'd post it at their station: *6 p.m.: take my dad for a walk; 7 p.m.: dinner, but no Jell-O; 8 p.m.: give my dad his pills and turn on the game.* Bill did everything he could to get his dad the best care possible. Even Dr. Childs said Bill was the best son a father could ask for. I believe that, too.

Bill: I did what I thought was right, and what was going to get my father better. I also did what my father would have wanted me to do. He was a list maker, too.

Giuliana: Bill even looks a lot like his dad! One night when we were at his parents' house—this was just before the wedding—he'd gone to bed, so his mom and I stayed up to look at photos from her wedding day. I couldn't get over the resemblance between Bill and Edward!

Anyway, the night of our NIH visit, we wanted to get a good night's sleep so we loaded up on pre-run carbs (Mama DePandi's delicious rigatoni with vodka cream sauce) and hit the sack. We said a prayer for Bill's dad, which felt more special than usual since he was on our mind every minute of that day. We then kissed each other good night and slept like two logs.

The next morning, Bill and I felt really refreshed and ready to kick some cancer butt at the 10K. I'd taken it upon myself to rally local and national PR machines to support Run for Life, and get behind the cause in a big way. But when we got to the event, the turnout was larger than I could have imagined. There were TV crews, newspaper reporters, and so many people who care about us—Bill's mom and sisters, my mom and dad, my brother and his family, friends of mine from high school, you name it. We also got to meet a lot of our fans and other runners who'd lost a family member or loved one to kidney cancer, or who knew someone suffering with it at the time. Bill was clearly faster than me, but when we got to the end of the race, he waited for me to catch up so he could give me a piggyback ride and cross the finish line together.

Bill: As I ran, I thought about my dad and how happy it would make him to see hundreds of people racing in the early-morning chill to help the fight against kidney cancer. I could almost feel him smiling down on me from heaven, and I would often look up at the sky with a smile as if to say, "I love you, too, Dad." The race was really cathartic, and running it with Giuliana was a pivotal moment for me and for our relationship.

Sharing Takes the Sad out of You

Giuliana: That trip was definitely a big bonding moment for us. I also realized something important after the race: Up until this point, Bill had left the door open for me to decide how much support I wanted to give, because he didn't want to be a burden on me. But all that time, I didn't ask that many questions about his dad because I wanted him to talk when he felt comfortable. If Bill and I weren't such naturally open people, we could have found ourselves stuck at a no-sharing impasse if we'd kept going like this. Gradually warming up to this topic ultimately worked for us—you get there how you get there—but realizing how long it took for us to connect about the subject encouraged me to be more forthright when gauging how he feels now. If I feel there is something Bill really wants to talk about—by the way he subtly repeats the same topic or gets lost in thought—I'll delicately probe a little deeper to see if he's in the mood to connect. "Honey, we should talk about things that upset you," I'll say to him. "I want to hear how you're feeling." I'm always careful not to say that I'm here to talk *if* he wants to, because then he can squirm out of the opportunity by saying that he doesn't. I let him know that it's a good thing for him to share his pain with me, since I'll always support him and have no ulterior motives.

Bill: I'm getting better at asking for support now, too, because I've realized that everyone needs their spouse to sustain them once in a while. I help Giuliana, when she needs advice about contract negotiations or how to talk to her girlfriend about a guy she's dating who isn't worthy of her time. Just because Giuliana doesn't need support in the same way I might doesn't make her needs less or more difficult, or important. Giuliana is also good at figuring out when I want to talk, and when to be my silent supporter. I'm not the easiest nut to crack, but we have an understanding. She can read a situation, and me, very well.

Giuliana: It's not that hard; you just have to know your audience. And I've done my homework so I can help Bill feel supported in all areas of his life. There's a lot of research that says when a man has a problem, the best way for a wife to support him is to give him advice that helps resolve the issue *with* him, versus *for* him. Men like when we listen to their problems and then react to how they're solving it, and I use this tidbit when I'm supporting Bill in matters unrelated to his father, for the most part. For instance, when he gets frustrated about how long it takes for a client to return his calls, it's enough for me to ask him how he plans to figure out the situation rather than try to empathize with him. (This is so unlike me, who'd be happier knowing Bill is on my side but doesn't expect me to do anything about my frustration right away.

Support or Torture? Giuliana Likes to . . .

• Slather Bill's face with night moisturizer and eye cream as he watches *UFC*.

• Pluck stray eyebrows against his will, while insisting it will save him from a unibrow.

• Replace his lost bedtime eye shades with silky bedazzled red ones from a gift bag.

I like when Bill comforts me and says he can relate, as I bitch until I'm out of breath.) Sometimes, he's such a closed book that I ask him what he needs from me, so I can give him the kind of support he wants. Other times, it's enough for me to just be there for him as he figures things out on his own.

I'm not perfect, though. I've been known to sense that Bill's upset and open the floodgates at the most awkward time, like when we're at a restaurant. I'll ask him to share what's wrong, we'll both start crying, and then everyone around us thinks we're arguing or breaking up. The waiter will come over, and here's Bill in tears, and you know the waiter's thinking, "Holy cow, this is bad if the man's crying. I'll bet they're getting a divorce. . . ." But it's not that *at all*. Sometimes all you need is a good cry. You have to really pay attention to what your spouse needs, because Bill rarely brings up on his own a subject that deeply upsets him, unless he wants to propose a plan to fix it; and with his dad, there's nothing to really "fix" when his feelings change from one day to the next. So I occasionally ask if he'd like to visit the cemetery or look at photos of his dad, if it's been awhile since we've done that together. But I never want to push Bill, because I don't live in his head. I could never really know how hard it is for him.

A Pocket Full of Kindness

Giuliana: About two years ago, I decided to get Bill a new wallet, because his old one was falling apart. So I went to Gucci to buy him a new one, but my main priority, more than color or leather, was its size. Bill's laminated Prayer card, the one I saw at dinner, had to fit in the wallet. It's the size of a BlackBerry.

The sales guy showed me five or six wallets, and no matter how cool or expensive they were, I kept saying, "No, that's

too small . . . that's not right, either . . ." I didn't tell the salesman why I needed a larger wallet, because I didn't think some
random person at Gucci needed to know. Finally, the salesman
looked me right in the eye with a tiny wallet in hand, and said
with a huff: "Trust me, guys like small wallets. Your husband
is not going to want a wallet bigger than this." To the salesman's credit, Bill's current wallet was relatively small, but his
dad's Prayer card hardly fit and was beginning to look a little
worse for wear. The card's also laminated, so I didn't want it
to slide out of any wallet that I'd buy for him. I decided to
dump the annoying salesman and look around on my own. I
found the perfect-sized wallet on the other side of the store
and asked a new salesperson to ring it up. "This is so pretty!"
she said, and I couldn't agree more.

On Christmas morning, I couldn't *wait* for Bill to open his
gift. When he tore off the ribbons and wrapping, he stared at
it for a while without saying anything. "Honey," I said. "I got
you a wallet that fits your most important possession: your
dad's picture!" I was so proud of myself.

Bill: It was a woman's wallet.

Giuliana: It was a *woman's* wallet! At first, I refused to believe
that I'd made such a lame mistake. "No, it's not," I said. But
Bill rolled his eyes. "It has a gold clasp and a coin purse," he
said. I looked at the wallet and felt so disappointed that I'd
missed these signs, but all I could think about in that damn
store was that I wanted the wallet to fit his dad's photo.

Bill: I didn't want to hurt Giuliana's feelings, so I tried to
carry the wallet around the house to see if it was realistic for
me to fit in my pants in public. I really wanted it to work.

Giuliana: He put the wallet in his back pocket, but there was
a huge lump where his tight ass used to be. I was like, "Oh

wow, now I understand why men's wallets are so little." Bill just laughed. "I love you," he said, "but I can't carry this around. I look like I'm playing for the other team. You should take it back."

Giuliana: But I didn't.

Bill: She didn't. It's her wallet now, and I still carry around my old wallet. It suits my lucky charm just fine. My dad always liked that old wallet anyway.

TIPS FOR TWO: Being There for Your Spouse

• Don't be afraid to ask your spouse for support. When you love someone, there are no burdens.
• When soliciting support, tell your spouse how you're feeling *and* how he/she can help you.
• When giving support, know your audience. Women prefer to give and receive emotional support. Men like to give and receive suggestions about how to fix a problem.
• Sometimes just being there is enough for either gender, if that's all your partner needs.
• Thank your spouse for his/her input, and always return the favor. You must give to receive.

9 Taking It 28 Days at a Time

Our most astonishing discovery about married life so far? Baby making is hard work, or at least it's been for us. We can't believe that we spent our entire adult life trying to avoid getting pregnant and when we finally wanted to, it seemed impossible. At least we found comfort in knowing that we aren't alone—some experts say that one in eight couples struggle with infertility. If we've learned anything at all, it's that a spouse's support, humor, and love are essential throughout this time, and that talking about our trials and tribs really helps.

Over the past two years, we've tried various natural means, as well as assisted reproductive technology treatments (ART), to expand our family of two. When our doctor told us after eight months of trying to conceive on our own that our fertility was hampered by factors both within and beyond our control, we were stunned to say the least. We come from large families with lots of kids (Giuliana has forty first cousins), so we always assumed we could have children when we wanted—

and if we didn't, that it would be *our* choice, not Mother Nature's. Having to struggle with what our friends and family seemed to achieve so easily was a confusing and painful process for us. And no matter how much we leaned on each other when our monthly pregnancy tests turned up negative, we didn't always share the same kinds of frustration and fears. This didn't make us feel less close, but it did make us realize that although a husband and wife might reach for the same things, each step can impact them in different ways.

Rather than feel sorry for ourselves or focus on our individual feelings, we devised a careful plan to overcome our fertility issues together. We're not the kind of couple that wanted to experiment with home remedies, drink herbs, or spend hours on blogs in search of a magic answer based on another person's diagnosis. While these options work for some couples, Bill and I realized that we're far too goal-oriented and impatient to dabble with the maybes that these solutions seemed to offer us. Instead, we leaned on the advice of esteemed fertility experts and followed our guts. Most recently, we decided to try IVF, and although it wasn't much fun, we're glad we chose to do it.

We clearly aren't doctors, so we're in no position to advocate certain treatments or give clinical advice on medical matters related to fertility or otherwise. What we will say is that we understand the emotional struggles that couples go through when trying to have a baby and want to help by sharing our story. There's something reassuring about knowing your wife isn't the first woman to cry on a toilet when she has yet another negative pregnancy test and your husband isn't the first man to feel like a lab rat when he masturbates into a cup for a semen analysis (even if your doc's office is BYOP, or bring your own porn). We're comforted to know that at least for us, these challenges have strengthened our marriage, not to mention shown us how much support we're capable of giving at a time when it would be so much easier to play the blame game. We've found that the process of figuring out what and how to have babies forced us to explore and share our most heartfelt priorities, plus the laughs and tears that come with them. We hope our baby-making journey inspires you to begin or continue your own.

Giuliana: I totally freaked out the first time we did it without a condom. . . .

Bill: Rode bareback . . .

Giuliana: Went au natural . . .

Bill: Pulled the goalie from the net . . .

Giuliana: Bill loves to use soccer terms.

Bill: It's a hockey term.

Giuliana: Oh. The point is, I'll never forget the first time Bill and I did it without a Trojan. It was Christmas 2008, and we'd spent the day with Bill's family in Chicago. There were kids, like, everywhere—running around in their festive holiday clothes, tugging on their parents' legs, showing off their new toys to anyone who'd pay attention. In our family, Bill is Uncle Bill and I'm Auntie Giuliana, and all day long, it was "Uncle Bill, will you play basketball with me?" and "Auntie Giuliana, can I have another pignoli cookie?" It was an exhausting day, but a good time. I was bummed that Santa had come and gone, because the more these kids played Ping-Pong and card games with Bill and ate up my Hollywood gossip, the more I thought, *I want some of those.*

So that night when Bill and I were in bed, we laughed and shook our heads at what a handful Bill's sisters' kids were. The rug rats were so cute, but they were at an age where they just wanted our attention all the time, and loved testing our patience. "What little devils," I said to Bill. "When we're parents, we'll have the best children in town." I realize that everyone thinks this way, and it's easy for us to gallop in on our high horses with this opinion; after all, our parenting insight is limited to babysitting other peoples' kids for a few hours at a stretch, and even then we coax them into submission with pizza and Taylor Swift videos. But there was something about our family's little ones on Christmas, covered in hot cocoa stains with wrapping paper bows in their stringy hair, that nudged me to have a baby talk with Bill. "We've been married a year," I said. "So we know this is the real deal. I've been thinking lately that it's kind of the perfect time to get pregnant." Bill looked shocked at first, but his wide eyes slowly softened and introduced a sly little grin. "You know, I wouldn't mind having a baby with the love of my life, DePandi . . ." he said, and leaned in for a kiss. With that, we pulled the goalie from the net . . .

Bill: We don't need to get into that last part.

Giuliana: Oh please, fine, when we did it that night without a jimmy cap . . .

Bill: Come on.

Giuliana: That's the street term for condom!

Bill: Let's just not . . . come on.

Pull and Pray...for a Baby

Giuliana: After we got it on Christmas night, I was totally and utterly convinced that we were pregnant before we even put our pajamas back on. You know when you hear all those smug first-time parents who say stuff like, *We just knew right away that we'd made a baby,* as if some magical instinct clues you in to one of the most fragile, intricate, and confounding processes the human body is capable of handling? Well, I swore the same thing had happened to us. "Oh my God," I told Bill. "Our lives are changing, Bill. Bill! Nine months from now, we're going to have a baby! We need to start planning, like, now. Where will we live: Chicago or L.A.? What are we going to do about child care? Are we baby nurse and nanny people? How much time would we want to take off? Should we make an appointment with our money manager to make a budget?"

Bill: If Uncle Bill wasn't so damn tired, Giuliana's freak-out might have made him nervous. I knew our lives would change if we had a child, but I wasn't ready to think about how we'd have less freedom, more financial responsibilities, less sleep . . . I told Giuliana to relax and that we'd have ten months to figure everything out, if this were our lucky month.

Giuliana: Bill's reaction was a real role-reversal for us, because I'm usually the one who's more laid back in our relationship. And for the next two weeks while Bill patiently waited for me to take an official pregnancy test, I'd swear that even the most benign nausea, weird food craving, or moody outburst was a sure sign that I had an embryo in my belly. *Oh my God.* I'd think. *This is it.*

Two days before I expected my period to come, I ran to the drugstore to buy a box of pregnancy tests. The instructions said two lines meant Bill and I were going to be parents; one line, better luck next time. So I peed on the stick, waited five minutes, and was beyond stunned to see one pink line staring back at me. "Oh no!" I yelled to Bill from the toilet, to which he replied, "Nothing? Shit."

This became our call and response for the next seven months. Each cycle, we'd have as much sex as we could, insist we were preggers, learn we weren't . . . and do it all over again. In my frustrated and anxious mind, that single pink line began to look more like a middle finger staring back at me; I felt like my uterus was flipping me off. What began as a bummer, soon turned disturbing, and then into a real dread that something could be wrong with me or Bill. We had no idea if our timing was off, if one of us had an undetected health issue, or if the right sperm just hadn't met the right egg yet. Bill and I did OK in sex ed back in high school, but we wondered why those kids on *16 and Pregnant* managed what we couldn't.

Once in a while I'd notice funny things going on with my body that I'd otherwise overlook—an eye twitch or a fluttering in my belly—and I'd wonder if these could be more subtle early pregnancy signs than the obvious sore nipples and morning sickness you hear so much about. So I'd hit the Internet, and sure enough, there was always at least one other person on Yahoo! Answers, Ask.com, or a pregnancy message board with the same question I had, and a few other people chiming in that yes, I *was* experiencing a sign, congratulations! But then I'd get my period—which, incidentally, these boards also tell you are possible if you're pregnant—and feel hugely disappointed. It took me a few cycles of having weird "symptoms" and then seeing that one pink line to realize that most women trying to conceive can become desperate for any clue to buoy their hopes, and that even a minor cramp or sneeze has meant something to someone, somewhere. In fact, if you plug almost any bodily function into Google next to the words "sign of pregnancy," women will fill you in on their theories. Brittle nails, funny pee smell, bad breath . . . you name it. I plan to turn this into a drinking game once Bill and I make it out the other end of this ordeal.

The truth is, I rarely read blogs, unless I'm trolling for

celebrity dirt or looking for tech reviews, so I didn't feel comfortable joining an online community to talk about our fertility issues. I realize that a lot of women find mommy-to-be groups encouraging during such a maddening time, but for me, the chipper but conflicting voices and opinions made me anxious. I found that a lot of the advice was either anecdotal or a secondhand tip based on a doctor's prognosis, but it really comes down to a woman's body, her medical history, diet, stress level, and lots of factors. So I leaned on Bill as much as I could and kept the rest to myself. I've heard stories about women whose obsession with getting pregnant damaged their marriages, and I didn't want to be one of them. I tried to manage my feelings, on my own, as best as I could. It helped to bury myself in work.

Bill: I have to admit that I think Giuliana was a lot more nervous and strained during that first year of trying than I was—and rightfully so. Baby making has affected both of our lives in a profound way, but Giuliana was the one who had to take the pregnancy test every month and experience the first hit of distress before talking to me about it. So I did my best to be supportive of her and the process in ways that I knew how: I surprised Giuliana with weekend getaways to Laguna Beach, booked a couple's massage for us at her favorite spa, even sat bored to death while she got a mani/pedi once a week. She was going through so much for the both of us, the least I could do was try to make the roller coaster as pleasant as it could be.

After a year of not getting pregnant, I told Giuliana that we needed to change our game plan and start taking the baby-making process more seriously than having sex whenever we could and letting God handle the rest. This started with slowing down our schedules, which were really brutal. There were months when either Giuliana was on the road, or I was on the road, and when we got together, all we'd do is sleep. Who knows if the times that we chose napping over having sex coincided with when she was ovulating? Our schedules made perfecting the process very difficult, as did our stress levels.

> ### Lessons We'll Teach Our Tots
>
> • *Always* say "Please" and "Thank you."
> • The only thing in life that's free, is true love.
> • Respect yourself and your body. Take good care of both.
> • Don't sweat the Pythagorean theorem. You'll never use geometry.

Anxiety can really hamper the fertility process—not only because it kills your sex drive, but because it can have a negative medical effect as well. Some say that lowering stress levels can regulate hormones like cortisol and increase blood flow to the uterus, both of which are necessary during conception, and that lower stress enhances proteins in the uterine lining that are involved in implantation.

"We've got to slow this train down if we're going to do this thing the right way," I told Giuliana, "or it's never going to happen." So I accepted fewer speaking engagements and Giuliana took a few days off from work, here and there, when she felt her stress level climbing. I remember that award season was especially tough on Giuliana. She had hours of rehearsal, eight hours of live TV, post-show interviews, and hours of prep for hosting *Fashion Police* the next day—all in addition to her daily *E! News* schedule. The poor girl's stress level was through the roof, and it didn't help that she doesn't like to show people when she's taxed; instead, she bottles it up inside and stays cool as a cucumber. Ordinarily, this would be an admirable feat, but as a woman trying to conceive, she wasn't in good form.

The next thing Giuliana and I did was speak to an Obgyn. My sister Karen recommended that we talk to her doctor, Elias Sabbagha, who's based in Chicago. After we met with him and expressed our concerns, Dr. Sabbagha ran some basic tests on Giuliana to make sure her anatomy, hormone levels, and eggs were in good shape. He also did a semen analysis to test my sperm count, plus their shape, movement, the whole thing. When all of our tests came back, we learned that the quantity and quality of Giuliana's eggs were slightly compromised by her age and that her uterus was misaligned. He also said my sperm might have been affected by stress, age, and even having sex with Giuliana too many days in a row. When you're trying to conceive, some experts say to have sex every other day to give a guy's sperm count enough time to build up. But when Giuliana and I were together only a few days a week, sometimes we'd do it a lot more in a short period of time—and apparently, all this sex might have worked against us.

Giuliana: Dr. Sabbagha suggested a colonic because he suspected that my colon was pushing my uterus to one side—and sure enough, an ultrasound confirmed this. He also prescribed hormone shots that caused my body to produce more follicles, and subsequent eggs, than anyone's body could naturally make on its own. After the shots, the doctor then told us which day, and at what hour, we needed to have sex to achieve maximum results. When two months of this MO didn't work, Bill and I moved onto two attempts at intrauterine inseminations, or IUIs. Here, I gave myself more hormone shots to increase the number of follicles in my ovaries and received a different shot to induce ovulation; the doctor then

> **Baby Names That Didn't Make the Cut**
>
> Juliette
> Sophia
> Lincoln
> Allegra
> Cole
> Argenta
> Easton
> Clementine
> Wilson

inserted Bill's washed sperm (washing it ensures that only the healthiest sperm is used during the procedure) through a catheter, directly into my uterus. The IUI goal was to increase the number of sperm that could reach my fallopian tubes and increase our chances of fertilization. In street terms, the point of an IUI is to get the sperm "all up in there." The IUIs didn't hurt me (it felt like a Pap smear), but they were a more clinical approach to making a baby than our prior go with hormones and timed sex. That said, all of the hormones came with a slew of side effects—bloating, cramps, weight gain, moodiness, hot flashes, night sweats, breast pain—and yet none of the treatments worked for us.

Bill: It was a difficult process for us, because our doctors had us on a very tightly timed schedule of blood tests, sex, sonograms, ejaculation appointments in cold, tiny rooms with old porn from the eighties . . . and we were working really hard toward an important and challenging goal. But when our hard work didn't pay off, it was upsetting. Giuliana and I began to get down on ourselves and feel like we were somehow failing each other. We're goal-oriented people, and that comes with feeling that you're in control of a situation's outcome—"If I work hard, then I will see results." But when you're trying to get pregnant, you can only influence the ending so much. I can see why so many attempts at trying and falling short is rough on couples. I mean, if you were to feel this disappointed, this often, about anything else—a job, a diet, a relationship, you name it—you might cut your losses and move on to a new job or diet that would guarantee success, or at least a more pleasant process. But that wasn't an option here. Giuliana and I told ourselves that we're not quitters, and decided that if one way of getting pregnant didn't work, we'd move on to another. And we'd keep doing this until we exhausted our options or each other.

Shortly after seeing Dr. Sabbagha, we did some research.

We were shocked to learn that according to Resolve, the National Infertility Association, one in eight couples have fertility problems and that female fertility dramatically declines after age thirty-five; some doctors even say that among women in their mid-thirties, almost one in four have impaired fertility. That's twenty-five percent!

Giuliana: For me, the age issue was the biggest surprise of all. I had no idea that thirty-five was such a turning point for female fertility. I always knew that it was easiest to have kids before thirty, but I didn't get married until I was thirty-two, so I didn't beat myself up for missing this window. Plus, I know plenty of pregnant women in their forties, so I figured *some* doctor must have figured out how to repair the disconnect between biology and a society of women marrying later. I'd just see him.

In Hollywood, I'm surrounded by actresses who work their asses off until they're well past their fertile prime—and then, voila!, pop out a pair of squishy twins. When I'd interview these women on the red carpet, I'd exclaim, "Twins! What an amazing surprise!" and they'd tell me all about how twins ran in the family. Though I didn't realize it at the time, these celebs were probably lying to me, since most women today can thank fertility treatments, not genetics, for their double blessing. I didn't fully realize all the doctors, shots, costs, and health concerns related to having kids later in life. Had I known, maybe we would have started trying on our honeymoon.

Then again, my whole life, I thought I'd be as fertile as my Italian relatives are. I have forty first cousins, my mother is one of six kids, my dad's one of six kids—and none of my aunts, my sister, my cousins, no one that I know of has ever had to use fertility treatments to have a child. I always told Bill: "The problem can't be with me, because I have amazing Italian eggs." And he'd say, "First of all, just because your eggs are Italian . . . wait, what the hell does that mean?" And I'd tell him my eggs were fiery and strong, and that I came from tough stock. Even though I know it takes two to tango, I always secretly feared that I was the one letting Bill down by bringing defective girl parts to the table. I felt I'd somehow mislead him by showing off my huge family.

To lighten the mood, Bill and I decided to share the "blame" by calling each other Old Eggs and Old Sperm—O.E. and O.S., for short. We knew the situation was more complex than that, so the nicknames added some humor to an otherwise bleak situation. We were tired of feeling depressed and disappointed. I'm such a sucker for romance, and it upset me, too, that we'd gone from making love to making babies in the most uninspired, methodical ways. Sex was now a means to an end, not an experience for us to relish and share—or at least not every time.

Bill: For a while, Giuliana was using ovulation sticks and her doctor's orders to tell us the best days to have sex, her assistant at the time was tracking it all on a calendar, and we had to balance all of this stuff with our busy travel schedules and long-distance relationship. It was so unnatural. Sex began to feel like a job, and it took us longer to get in the mood than usual. But that's life. Not everything goes the way you think it should. One night Giuliana waited for me with chocolate body paint, hot pink lingerie, and half of a turtle cake. She lit candles and everything, but my delayed flight made me get in later than I expected. She was sound asleep when I got home, and though we had fun sex when I woke her up, the whole evening was less than ideal.

Giuliana: We tried our best to keep things romantic, but it was difficult. One thing I didn't do was make Bill rush home from work to have sex when I'd get a smiley face on my ovulation stick.

Bill: No, no, no, no, no.

Giuliana: I didn't want to be that person for my nerves, and I didn't want to drive Bill nuts. The doctor might have told me to do it at three p.m., but if it was more fun and less stressful to have sex around nine p.m. after a fun dinner, that's how it went down.

Hit Me with Your Best Shot

Bill: While we were expressing our frustration to Dr. Sabbagha about all those failed shots and IUIs, he suggested we meet with Dr. Bryan Kaplan, a reproductive endocrinologist (aka fertility specialist) and pioneer in his field, who operates out of IFC, Infertility Centers of Chicago, one of the top infertility clinics in the country. Since the least invasive fertility treatments didn't work for us, we decided it was time to explore the motherload of assisted reproductive technology: in vitro fertilization. IVF is a complex and invasive procedure, not to mention a serious time and financial commitment. Some IVF doctors don't accept insurance, and the procedure runs between $12,000 and $15,000 per cycle. Depending on the couple's problems, age, and treatment goals, it can cost a lot more. These prices rarely include fertility drug costs, ultrasounds and monitoring charges, and blood work, among other customized needs.

Dr. Kaplan explained that an IVF procedure, from start to finish, can take up to two months from your first shot to the day you're finally allowed to take a pregnancy test. There are five main steps involved, and each one sounded more scientific and intricate to us than the next. Here's what happens: First, the doctor prescribes fertility medications to regulate a woman's menstrual cycle and stimulate the development and number of high-quality eggs (you want to have as many eggs as possible to be fertilized later). Next, the eggs are retrieved during a minor surgical procedure that involves guiding a small hollow needle through the woman's pelvic cavity; this needle removes the eggs from the ovaries. You're out cold for this, which is something Giuliana was not happy about.

Giuliana: I have a very serious fear of dying while being under general anesthesia, so the thought of enduring this in the near future was not a welcome one.

Bill: Once the eggs are retrieved, the doctor then uses the man's sperm to inseminate the eggs in a laboratory dish that supports and nourishes the fertilized eggs; they're also monitored very closely by lab technicians during this time. Within about seventy-two hours after fertilization, the embryos are transferred into the woman's uterus using a catheter. In a nutshell, it's a pretty invasive procedure and has a reputation for being emotionally and physically grueling on most women.

Giuliana: Armed with this information, Bill and I had to make a decision about whether we were ready to take this step. There are a lot of pros to IVF, like a higher-than-natural pregnancy rate and the ability to only fertilize the best embryos to fend-off early miscarriage (which is very common in first-time pregnancies in older women). But there are also a lot of negatives, like the fact that the shots affect you mentally and physically, and your ovaries painfully plump up from the size of a dime to the size of a golf ball. Without a doubt, it was one of the scariest decisions we've had to make since we've been married. From the start, Bill's been supportive about whether or not we should take fertility measures to have children. And ultimately, he said it was my decision to make, as to whether we should pull the trigger on treatments like IUI and IVF.

A lot of women I know like to complain that they have to

do all the work during fertility treatments and/or pregnancy, and then childbearing, while the man sits around for however many months and shows up on the delivery day to scream "push harder!" While there's some truth to this, I made the decision that whatever route we took, I'd refute this way of thinking. While yes, it's true that I'll do all the work in the beginning, Bill would certainly have his work cut out for him once the baby was born. From that day forward, we'd be equal partners, 50/50, and I felt that if I was super cool and cooperative during our fertility trials, plus the nine months of pregnancy, then my good behavior would rub off on Bill and be a good start to our parenting partnership.

Bill: We're in this together. The way I thought about it was that we're either going to be a great married couple with kids or we're going to be a great married couple without kids. Family means a lot to me, but I told Giuliana that our marriage isn't based on bringing someone else into the world. Even if we're never able to have kids, she'd never stop being my wife. I never wanted Giuliana's mind to wander and think, "What if we can't have kids? Will he leave me?" I'm in it forever. That's the promise I made in front of God, and that's the vow I'm going to stick with. If we have babies, it's a bonus. I told her that if we decided not to have kids, we'd still have a rich life together. We'd travel, have different hobbies, make new friends, learn new languages, and fill our life in other ways.

Giuliana: I was also worried that if we went through with IVF, and it didn't work for us or God forbid I miscarried after a few months, the experience would make Bill realize that he *did* want kids more than he thought, and then he'd feel twice as disappointed that we couldn't have them.

Bill: I'll tell you what she was nervous about: she thought I'd trade her in for a younger model.

Giuliana: A younger model who was more fertile and who'd steal all his money, but at least he'd get a baby out of it.

Bill: Either way, Giuliana decided to go through with the IVF procedure, which made me really happy.

Giuliana: Bill might say IVF was my decision, but it was totally something we decided together; he gave me unlimited support and conviction in my ability to make a sound decision for our family, and that meant the world to me. He told me he'd be by my side every second of the process and support me however I needed him to. I wasn't surprised when Bill stood by his word.

A One-Man Support Group

Bill: Supporting each other was essential at every point of baby making, even in the beginning but especially when we did IVF. So it was hard for us to figure out who to tell and how much to say, and when. There's also a certain level of privacy that an expecting couple wants to maintain until they know that if the woman does get pregnant, that her baby's healthy until that second trimester starts. Many couples average about a three-month wait before they share news with friends and family.

Giuliana: Early on, we had a decision to make when we were trying to have a baby in quiet: We could either lie about this part of our lives and not film it, or we could do what we said we were always going to do with *Giuliana & Bill*, which is let people know what our life is like with the hope that they might learn something from our journey.

Bill: Honestly, we didn't know if we could keep doing the show *without* talking about fertility, because it's been what so much of our relationship's been about for the last two years. We felt that if we didn't discuss this part, it wasn't a true "reality" show, and we would either have to pull the plug on the next season or film a bunch of lies. We opted to talk about our journey.

Giuliana: It was interesting to see how many people really cared about the process, especially when we announced that we tried IVF. I'd be on an airplane, and the flight attendant would ask, "Would you like something to drink? And did the IVF work?" It was a little weird to let strangers into something that's allowed to be private for so many couples but not for us. Then again, that's what we signed up for, so I just smiled graciously and told everyone, "Hopefully you'll hear some good news soon!"

The thing is, too, it was really important to us to lift the veil off the Hollywood ruse of how a lot of older women become pregnant, have twins, and even hide their miscarriages. Everyone is entitled to their privacy, even famous actresses, so we respect that women in the spotlight would want to remain quiet during such a hard time. But for us, Bill and I just felt that the whole subject of how difficult it is for one in eight couples to have a baby is

> ### Lessons from Bill's Dad That We Plan to Pass Down
>
> • Taking the high road will always take you to the right destination.
> • There's no substitute for hard work. Working hard pays off; doing nothing pays nothing.
> • Don't seek revenge. The bad guy will always get his.
> • Balance is crucial in life. Work hard, but know how to turn it off at the end of the day.

one we wanted to expose. Not only did we want it to help people who were going through this ordeal, but we wanted others to understand and feel more sympathetic toward friends and loved ones who were experiencing pregnancy challenges, too. The most refreshing thing about being so public about our fertility problems is that it's helped a lot of viewers. We probably get about fifty-plus emails a day thanking us for talking about our fertility problems. We feel that couples who want to have a baby—whether it's achieved naturally, through IUI or IVF, or through a surrogate, egg donor, or adoption—should be proud to talk about their journey and embrace whatever method they need to use to bless them with a child. How these parents get there isn't the issue; the only thing that matters is having a beautiful baby to hold and love for the rest of their lives.

Bill: It sounds like a cliché, so I wouldn't say this if we didn't mean it with every ounce of our being, but if we help one other family get through a fertility ordeal, we've done our jobs. We're lucky to be in a position to do that, too. When our show first launched, some critics didn't think *Giuliana & Bill* would succeed because our story lines seemed too clean and wholesome (versus dirty and scandalous like most reality shows). But our goal was to show a loving and fun relationship and make marriage look "cool" again. In the process, we've tackled issues that a lot of American couples address on a daily basis, like infertility, and other shows won't touch. We're proud of that.

Giuliana: You know what was hard to show? Bill giving me hormone injections. I was so scared.

Bill: But I was better at it than I thought I would be.

Giuliana: He was really good at it. He's like my Dr. Mc . . . Rancic. (Hmm, McRancic doesn't quite have the ring of McSteamy or McDreamy, so I'll have to work on that.) Anyway, when we did IVF, Bill had to travel for a few days, so I had to give myself the shots, and I hate needles, like a lot of people do. Bill knows that, so he would call me when it was time for the injection and give me a sweet pep talk. "Put me on speaker," he'd say. "I'll talk you through it." I'd stand in front of the mirror with the shot in my hand and say, "All right, here I go. Here I go . . ." and I'd never do it. "All right honey," he'd try again. "On the count of three, you're going to just do it, and then you'll climb into bed, and we'll be that much closer to this being over."

A scary thing happened, though, when we were in Aspen together for two of the shots. On the first night, I hadn't acclimated to the 9,000 foot altitude. After Bill gave me the shot in the bathroom, I began walking to the bed and felt so incredibly dizzy, I fell to the floor. Bill went into crazy, hot, ambulance guy mode.

Bill: I was like an EMT!

Giuliana: Oh my God! McEMT! Nah, still no good. So Bill carried me to the bed, put pillows under my legs to elevate them, gave me a cold towel for my face—it was so scary for us. We called Dr. Kaplan, and he said I'd had a reaction to the altitude change, which was a relief. But Bill took good care of me during IVF. I definitely couldn't have done it without him.

I will say the side effects were rough, though. You get really, really bloated and feel very unattractive. You put on a lot of weight and can't work out for more than two months since your ovaries are very swollen and delicate. This was hard for me, since I love running and consider myself an athlete. Working out for me is like knitting or gardening or reading a good book for other women. I do it to look good, but more important, I do it to feel good and elevate my energy and mood. So taking away my favorite daily hobby was hard, even though I knew it was going to be worth it in the end. Bill was great with all of this, and he never made me feel like the bloated wood tick I was. It was hard, too, because I was going to work, and though I'd announced that we were doing IVF to the press, nobody knew where we were in the process. So I'd head to the studio every day, and I wouldn't be able to wear a dress that I'd worn a few weeks prior because my stomach was so badly pronounced, since my ovaries were huge. Dr. Kaplan even said that since my ovaries were so enlarged, I had to be very careful to avoid twisting or turning a certain way that might strain them; he said that if I did, there was a chance that I could damage them so badly that I could kiss good-bye my chances of ever having a baby. What's more, on my already slender frame, people at work suspected that my weight gain meant I was already a few months pregnant. They jumped to conclusions when they saw me looking bloated in my normal clothes, and then really became suspicious when I wore loose-fitting baby-doll dresses and oversized tops. I even began to get an increased number of viewer emails saying, "Congratulations! How many months along are you?" No woman wants to be mistaken for pregnant when she's not! All I wanted to do was run on my treadmill.

Bill: Run? She'd be doubled over from cramps because she walked too fast across the street to make a light. . . .

Giuliana: Yes, I was *walking* too fast. And my ovaries were so big that even stepping too hard on the pavement made me yell "Ouch!" The stabbing pain is really horrible. And once you're done with your hormone shots, your ovaries stay inflated for another two months—at least they did for me. So I didn't feel like myself at all and my body just ached. But more than usual, Bill went out of his way to make me feel like a million bucks. A few times he caught me looking at my inflated stomach or boobs in the mirror, and he'd tell me I never looked better. That meant a lot and always brought tears to my eyes because I felt like I'd never looked worse.

Bill: I think I always try to make her feel beautiful. But let's be honest: There were some cranky and moody moments when Giuliana got a little crazy, like when we had dinner at Roy's Chicago, which is this amazing Hawaiian fusion restaurant in the Gold Coast. I'd already eaten one order of a Maine lobster dim sum with cream sauce as an appetizer, and I wanted another.

Giuliana: The lobster was swimming in sauce with white truffle emulsion, and the first order was so rich. For some reason, the thought of watching Bill eat a second order made me feel totally grossed out. "Trust me, you're not going to want a second," I told him. "You're going to be sick." I was irritable and puffy from the drugs, and I felt irrationally jealous that Bill could eat two orders of a creamy fish appetizer without gaining weight or wanting to gag.

Bill: So I jokingly said to Giuliana, "Hey, don't tell me what I can and can't eat! Not in my house, girl!" And then all of a sudden, it was as if I'd been making out with her best friend in the booth right next to her. Giuliana *freaked.* "How can you talk to me that way?" she asked. "That's so disrespectful!" I was shocked and explained that I was just kidding, but it didn't matter.

Giuliana: "Fine, I'll never talk again!" I said. "Is that what you want? I'll be a subservient wife. Yes, Master. Whatever you want to order, Master." It was ugly.

Bill: And then, of course, she calmed down as quickly as she blew up. It was like one of those Florida storms that come out of nowhere, rain down real hard, and then pass as quickly as it came. And of course when the lobster arrived, Giuliana ate eighty percent of it because her hormones made her so hungry all the time. It was hilarious and frightening all at once.

Giuliana: If Bill has the patience to handle me, something tells me a few kids will be a cakewalk for him. Parenthood, here we come.

TIPS FOR TWO: When Your Baby Wants
a Baby . . .

• If you and your spouse know that you want to have kids, you may want to see a doctor in the early stages of marriage to make sure you're in prime baby-making shape *before* you potentially run into problems later.

• If you face fertility challenges, set a goal and research experts who can help you achieve it.

• Don't overwhelm yourself with too many options. Focus your energy on one remedy at a time.

• Remember to honor your own needs during the baby-making process. Before your husband was just a penis and your wife was just a womb, you were a married couple who loved each other a lot.

• Provide your spouse with a never-ending stream of support. Experts say baby making can put a big strain on a marriage, and some feel that stress can physiologically impede the process.

10 Who, Me? Jealous?

A jealous spouse is a miserable spouse—there are no two ways around it. There's also a decent reason for this: gnawing suspicions eat away at the very principles that contribute to successful and happy marriages. These include deep trust, commitment, loyalty, respect, security, open communication, and sexual confidence to name a few. And while researchers at the University of British Columbia and University of Iowa find that married couples are less likely than dating couples to argue about jealousy, they say it's much more destructive when they do. This may be because marriage has higher levels of relationship commitment and joint investments (children, financial assets, friendships), so there is more for a spouse to lose if envy harms the relationship or leads to betrayal. We think it sucks no matter what.

We rarely struggle with jealousy, but during the few times we've come face-to-face with the green-eyed monster, it hasn't been pretty. Jealousy can lead to distrust, and the only thing worse than not trusting your spouse is feeling like you're not

trusted *by* your spouse. What's interesting about jealousy, too, is that so much of it is based on the baggage you bring into your current relationship, whether you like it or not. For instance, Giuliana never considered herself to be a jealous person until one of her exes betrayed her in a hurtful and public way. The ex's insecurities wreaked havoc on their relationship, and when it ended, the situation left an uneasy impression on Giuliana, who then brought it into our marriage. As for Bill's hot button topics, money and family catalysts can make him feel envious at times.

We've found that one of the best defenses against jealousy is to refrain from comparing ourselves to people in our pasts, or even strangers on the street. There will always be someone more attractive, successful, sexual, or confident than we are, but that's not what matters. Our chemistry, differences, and even flaws mix to create a unique and valuable bond that strengthens our marriage every day. Read on to find out what happened during the times that jealousy nipped at our relationship's heels.

Bill: About six months after we were married, Giuliana and I went to Maryland for the weekend to stay at her brother Pasquale's house in Potomac. We'd had a low-key weekend with her family, and on Sunday morning, Pasquale's wife, Nikki, woke us up with a loud buzz on their in-home intercom. "Come down, guys!" she said. "I have a surprise for you in the kitchen!" I wasn't dressed, but Giuliana suggested I throw on sweats, which is what she said she was wearing.

Giuliana: I put on a Juicy velour hoodie and matching pants, so I was totally presentable. This was 2007, when that outfit was the bomb.

Bill: "You're part of the family now," Giuliana told me. "You don't need a shower. They probably have breakfast on the table already, so let's just hurry up." I didn't want to keep Giuliana's family waiting, so I threw on a T-shirt and basketball shorts. I ran my hand through my hair and ignored the pillow lines still carved in my face. I brushed my teeth, but it was admittedly a last-minute decision. I didn't even put on shoes.

When we showed up in the kitchen, we expected the "big surprise" to be our first names spelled out in whipped cream on a stack of waffles or something. Instead, I saw Giuliana's ex-boyfriend Chris, and his entire family, seated around the breakfast table. They'd apparently "dropped by," and Pasquale asked them to stay for brunch. As we all said a friendly "Good morning!" I felt incredibly self-conscious. Chris was wearing a Brooks Brothers suit, and his whole family—mom, sister, and niece—looked like they'd sailed in from the Newport Regatta. I gave Pasquale the stink eye, as if to say, *What the hell, dude?* I felt like Greg "Gaylord" Focker in *Meet the Parents*—and this Chris guy was Owen Wilson to my Ben Stiller. To make matters worse, before I came along, Giuliana's family all but coined Chris "the ex who got away."

Giuliana: My dad is a tailor, and he owns a men's clothing store just outside Washington, D.C. My ex-boyfriend Chris, his mother, brother, sisters, and their father shopped at my dad's store for years before Chris and I even met. One afternoon when I was eighteen, Chris was getting a suit fit with my father and I happened to drop by after school. We hit it off. Later that day, he called my dad and said, "I hope this isn't inappropriate, but can I take your daughter on a date?" Died! My family was instantly charmed. So I met Chris through my dad, and our families became close friends, as a result. Chris and I dated for three years before we finally broke up, though my family had always hoped we'd live happily ever after. Poor Bill's heard his share of stories.

Bill: Giuliana's parents love him because he's so rich. Let's just say Chris owns a chain of car washes, and they do very well.

Giuliana: They own, like, thirty of those "car washes."

Bill: No, not *that* many.

Giuliana: Bill calls Chris a used-car salesman, a lube man . . .

Bill: I do.

Giuliana: But he *owns* the car washes. It's a respectable and very profitable business. Anyway, when I first saw Chris in the kitchen, I was shocked to hell. And I was scared, too, that Bill would say something he'd regret. I also wanted to avoid one-on-one conversations with Chris, so we couldn't share any weird moments. After all, the reason my brother and sister-in-law invited the family over was because Chris's niece Jessica, who I knew as a baby, is my niece Olivia's friend from school. So Jessica wanted to see me again, and when Chris heard they were coming over, he invited himself along. I don't think he considered whether Bill would be there, but when the two locked eyes over their initial handshake, it was the most awkward situation ever.

> **Bill knows Giuliana's jealous when:** *"She purses her lips tightly and doesn't say a word. After an hour or so, she grants one word answers. She only reveals she's mad after Bill has spent a few hours trying to get it out of her."* **Bill's jealousy shows when he:** *"Asks lots of questions, and follows up answers with 'Uh-huh . . . I see . . . uh-huh . . . I see.'"*

Bill: To start, Chris and his family were a little condescending. Chris gave me the third degree, and grilled me with inane questions like "So Bill, what is it that you do?" as if he didn't know I worked for Trump or won *The Apprentice*. I mean, thirty million people saw that season finale, and even if you weren't one of them, you'd have certainly heard about it, especially if your ex had just married the winner.

Giuliana: It took me a half hour to figure out what my role in this scenario should be. Should I make Bill feel comfortable? Buffer Chris's remarks? Rip my brother a new one? I chose to ride out the conversation, with one hand on Bill's leg for assurance.

Bill: Giuliana's brother likes to jab me, so I think he enjoyed watching me sweat. Pasquale made jokes about Chris in the past, which didn't help me feel so hot in the situation now. For instance, Pasquale likes to tell Giuliana that she could be retired by now if she'd stuck with Chris.

Giuliana: Come on. I'd be selling bulk car-wash packages during the week, and helping Girl Scouts make signs out of posterboard for their annual car wash on weekends.

Bill: I can see it now: "Excuse me sir, can I interest you in the Turtle Wax?" Even though I was the one who married Giuliana, I still felt jealous in that moment. I'd only heard about him until now, and if I had my way, I would have liked some time to prepare a solid first impression. Instead, I was envious of his clothes, of the established relationship he had with my new family, and with the history he shared with Giuliana. None of these feelings were rational, but envy rarely is. I'm a secure guy, but everything about this situation threw me off my game.

Giuliana: Chris went on to talk about how well his business was doing, and how he'd opened ten new shops. The only time he took his eyes off me was to gauge Bill's reaction to his remarks. The final straw came when Chris turned to me and asked: "Are you happy?" His tone was dripping with sarcasm and doubt. "Of course, I'm happy!" I exclaimed. What was this guy thinking? My husband was sitting right next to me, and we were practically still tan from our fabulous honeymoon in the Grand Cayman Islands! Bill had steam coming out of his ears. Chris's underlying message was clear: "Had you married me, you'd be living large with the shiniest Audi in town." I think Chris was trying to be a cad. He's a salesman, a talker. He knows how to push peoples' buttons and then play it off in a suave way.

Bill: I felt like I should produce financial statements to Giuliana's family to prove I wasn't destitute. No joke, I was ready to show them my goddamn tax returns. The problem was that I was so far at a disadvantage, in so many ways, that I knew there was no way to fight my way back on top. I was knocked down on the mat bleeding. If I wasn't so raw, I might have thought it was cute when Chris's mother, Julie, reminisced about the time they all bought matching Christmas sweaters.

Giuliana: Those sweaters were hilarious! Before I met Bill, my parents always compared the men I dated to Chris. I could be with a perfectly sweet and successful man, and my family would always find a way to sneak Chris into the conversation. "He seems nice," they'd tell me. "But remember when you were dating *Chris*? Does your new boyfriend have a nice family like *Chris* does?" And I always thought, "Shut up, already!" Sometimes I'd come home for the weekend, and the first thing they'd tell me is, "Guess who was at the store buying suits? Chris!" And when I'd say I was sorry to have just missed him, they'd correct me: "Oh, no, he was in two weeks ago." It was so weird. I'd think, *So why are you bringing him up?* They must like saying his name. My family has mentionitis like a jilted ex.

When Chris and his family left, Bill asked if I'd known about Chris's "impromptu visit." He found it hard to believe an entire family would just show up at someone's house on a Sunday morning, dressed in their finest, and he thought I might have been too nervous to tell him about it ahead of time. After all, I *was* wearing my cutest sweats. But our families aren't that formal with each other. We pop in, and then we pop out—no big deal. "I swear on my life that their visit was a surprise," I told Bill. Then I pulled my sister-in-law aside to reiterate that they really did drop by for Olivia's friend, since they'd heard I'd be in town. She said it never dawned on them that it might create an awkward triangle, since we're all happily married. Had I known about Chris, I assured Bill that I would have warned him or stopped it from happening. I'd never want to put him in a situation where he feels out of control.

That's the hardest thing about jealousy: there's very little you can do to keep it from surfacing. You can create ways to manage it, but it bubbles up on its own. And once you know what it feels like or what your spouse's triggers are, you need to do whatever it takes to get rid of it.

Bill: If Giuliana could have stopped that train wreck from occurring, I know she would have. There's no reason for a loving spouse to test her partner's jealousy. It's a painful, horrible feeling.

Fighting the Green-Eyed Monster

Giuliana: I can't fault Bill for how he felt about the Chris situation, because I'm hardly immune to jealousy. Bill's friend Jezebel ruffled my feathers shortly after we were married. She was in Chicago for a short time, and she asked Bill to dinner while I was still in L.A. I'd never met Jezebel before, so I didn't know if they had history. I didn't know what this chick's story was, and besides, who has a friend named Jezebel? That seemed like a sign to me.

Bill: Jezebel's story is that she's a lifelong friend who's married with kids.

Giuliana: I didn't know that at the time, but why does that matter anyway? A lot of people fall in love with their high school friends all over again on Facebook. I trust Bill, but it's the other women I don't have faith in. I know how chicks operate, and I'm often nervous that they'll try to seduce him with alcohol or push their boobs in his face. Jezebel could have slipped him a roofie and stolen his Rolex! Or, you know, she could have slept with him. I wasn't used to Bill going out with close girlfriends. I mean, he has girlfriends who are the wives of his buddies, and there are a few others that I don't consider to be a threat. But this one was supposedly attractive, and a mystery to boot. Sometimes that's all it takes.

Bill: When I told Giuliana that my old friend and I were going to grab a bite, I never imagined that she'd feel so uncomfortable; in my mind, I didn't have bad intentions, so I wasn't sure why Giuliana would think so. I knew in my heart that nothing would ever go wrong.

Giuliana: When Bill told me his plans on the phone, I gave him the silent treatment, refused to explain myself, and then hung up. A few minutes later, I called back with a lame excuse about flight times to Chicago and tacked on a seemingly innocent question: "So, where are you and this friend of yours going for dinner?" I refused to say the woman's name. Bill told me he'd made a reservation to sit outside at a sushi joint called

Tsunami, which sounded benign enough, but I was possessed by jealousy. I called Bill back a second time. "I've been thinking about it," I told him, "and I really don't think it's a good idea for you to go to dinner with that married-with-children lady." We'd had a lot of press at the time, since we were newly married, so I used this to my advantage. "Friends or paparazzi might see you together and think you're having an affair. They'll think you're a cheater and a bad guy!" Bill was confused. "But I'm not having an affair," he said. "Honey, I think you're being a little ridiculous." Before I hung up, I went in for the kill. "Bill, I'm doing this for *you*," I said. Unfortunately, Bill just laughed and said he'd call me after dinner.

After stewing for ten minutes, I called Bill back one last time. I was as direct as I could be. "I've been thinking about this, and I know it's OK for you to have girls who are friends, but if people start to think you're cheating on me, I will be so hurt and embarrassed. I'd rather you don't go at all. I know I said that this is good for you, but I need you to do this for me." I was dead serious.

Bill: I didn't understand why Giuliana was so upset, but I also didn't want to cancel on Jezebel, so I came up with a solution to make everyone happy. I called Giuliana back again. "I really can't cancel on this girl," I said. "This is her first visit to Chicago in the two years since she and her husband moved to South Africa, but I've come up with a great solution: I'll bring a friend." After a little back-and-forth, Giuliana was fine with the idea. So I called all my old buddies—Carson, Kyle, Tom—and nobody was around. And then out of the blue, I got a text from Skip, an old friend—literally, old. He's pushing seventy and looks like my grandfather. I asked him to join us for dinner, and he was happy to accommodate and catch up.

Giuliana: It was awesome! I couldn't have cast a better friend for this role myself.

Bill: Well, it fixed the problem. I got to see Jezebel and Skip, which was a nice bonus. I was able to make Giuliana happy, have a nice dinner, and bring peace to the family. Some guys might have said, "Screw her," or "I'm going to show my wife she can't boss me around"—and then make the situation worse than it needed to be. But there was nothing for me to gain from that kind of rebellion, and if the roles were reversed and I had an inexplicable fear, I'd have hoped Giuliana would do the same for me.

At the time, I didn't think to ask Giuliana what the real cause of all this jealousy and tabloid talk could be. I just assumed that she'd had a bad day, and that's all it takes to eat away at your confidence in a long-distance relationship sometimes. To ease her nerves, I called Giuliana the minute I left for dinner, during dinner, and the minute I got home.

Giuliana: When he called me during dinner, he put me on the phone with J-Rizzle so I could play nice. "How are the kids? You must miss them and want to get home soon," I said. I was terrible.

Where'd You Get That Baggage?

Giuliana: Everyone has baggage, and the most I brought to my relationship with Bill fell into the jealousy category. What's important is that Bill and I understand where these traces of jealousy come from, and that Bill and I do everything we can to calm them when they bubble up to the surface of our relationship. I feel lucky that I've always had amazing relationships before I met Bill, with the exception of one man who I dated and trusted immensely, and who eventually deceived me. Nothing about Bill is misleading, but it only takes one lousy incident to impact your head the way my ex's lying did mine. I'd never go as far as to say this guy "ruined me" for other men, but he did throw me off course for a few years.

Bill: This is Giuliana's story, so I'm going to step out for a minute.

Giuliana: I met an actor, let's call him Tom, at a party at the W hotel during Super Bowl weekend in 2004. He approached me in the lobby and made a big scene. "Oh my God!" he said. "You're that hot chick from E!" He gushed that he loved watching me on TV and was dying to go out with me, and I was flattered from the start. He was intent on making me feel like the only girl in the room. "This is so cool," I thought. "It's fate." We went out right away and had a very fun relationship. We were inseparable, and it wasn't long before he talked about getting engaged and having babies. So I never had any reason to suspect Tom might deceive me because we were always, and very publicly, together. But about six months into our relationship, things started to change.

I began to see a very jealous streak appear. Tom has an extreme personality—happy one minute and really down the next. He could be the best boyfriend ever, and then the most jealous, mean man I'd ever met; he also seemed jolly and exuberant on the outside, though I always felt he hid a more fragile core. I started to feel like I was dating Dr. Jekyll and Mr. Hyde. He began to question me about everything I did. If I didn't answer the phone immediately, he'd say, "What are you doing? Where were you?" I'll never forget when I went to the *Gigli* premier to interview Jennifer Lopez and Ben Affleck. It was an afternoon premiere on a Sunday, no less, and we were running behind because J-Lo hadn't arrived yet—she's notoriously late for these things. So for a good hour after I'd told Tom that the premiere would be over, he kept texting me. "Where are you?" he wanted to know. "When am I going to see you?" I told him to relax and said I'd call when I could. But at one point, I couldn't respond to my texts anymore, because Jennifer was about to arrive. I put my phone in my bag and figured I'd call Tom after the interview.

Just when I was about to ask J-Lo who designed her dress, I noticed a tall, frazzled guy standing alone at the gas station across from the movie theater. *Is that Tom?* I thought for a second, but I couldn't give it much thought since I had work to do. When J-Lo stepped off the podium, I quickly glanced toward the gas station a second time—and now, I realized it was Tom, since he was waving like a maniac and giving me the universal hand signal for "call me!" So I gave him the universal hand sign for "one minute," and then called him right away on his cell.

"Are you OK?" I asked. "Is there an emergency?" I couldn't imagine why he'd be outside my event unless his condo was on fire or my parents were in the hospital. Instead, Tom was as calm as can be. "Hey, home girl. What's up?" he said, all blasé. "I just wanted to make sure you're OK . . ." I paused for a few seconds and told him of course I was fine, and that I had to get back to the premiere. "OK, well I'll just wait here until you're done," he said.

Looking back, this was pretty creepy behavior for a grown man in his thirties. But at the time I thought the attention was sort of cute—a sign that Tom loved me so much. And it wasn't too different from when he'd invite himself out for drinks with my girlfriends or call every twenty minutes when I was on deadline. If nothing else, at least Tom was consistent. Once in a while, I'd ask Tom, "Why do you need to know everything?" and he'd tell me it was because he felt nothing but love and always missed me. *Wow,* I'd think. *Nobody's ever treated me like this before. He must be the real deal.*

There were a few situations, however, when Tom's jealousy became so ugly that it made me question our relationship. I'll never forget the time my parents, my sister Monica, and her husband, B.Z., took me and Tom to dinner at Giorgio's in Santa Monica to celebrate a promotion I received at work. My brother-in-law is a ballbuster; so we like to needle each other, much like blood siblings. During drinks, he proposed a toast in my honor: "To Giules, who's moving up in the world! I'm proud of you, kiddo"—and gave me a pat on my lower back. I didn't think anything of it; nobody did. But after dinner, Tom gave me the silent treatment while driving home. When I finally got him to crack, he sounded disgusted. "Have you ever slept with your brother-in-law?" he asked. "The way he patted you, I saw that."

I was speechless. Was he serious? "*Everyone* saw that, you nut job," I told him. "What is wrong with you?" I had never been accused of such an unthinkable and disgusting thing in my life. To say my blood was boiling is a gross understatement. "You've been jealous before, Tom, but this is the strangest I've ever seen you. Drop me off immediately. I don't want to hear another word from your mouth, and I will not even *dignify* your question with a response." Tom's accusation offended me to the depths of offense. I called my friends when I got home, and they all agreed that he'd crossed the line. I told Monica, too, and she was appalled. "You have to get rid of him," she said. "You need to end this."

Tom called a million times, and when I didn't return his messages, I came home after work the next day to find him waiting in my lobby. When he saw me, he dropped to his knees. "Please, please, please," Tom pleaded. "Talk to me. Talk to me. Talk to me." People were watching us, and I was embarrassed, so I told him he could come upstairs for a minute. In my apartment, Tom dropped to his knees a second time. "I am so sorry," he said. "I love you so much. I can't believe I said that about your family." This was the kind of stuff that happened in our relationship, even when things were going well. To this day, I still feel sick when I remember that story. Monica and B.Z. erased Tom's name from their vocabulary and never spoke to him again.

When It's More Than a Hunch

About a year and a half into our relationship, Tom and I were a pretty hot item. We went to black tie events together, appeared in magazines together, we'd mention each other on the air—Tom and I were in love, and everyone knew it. Rumors swirled about an engagement, and it never happened, though the subject came up a lot and all signs pointed to an impending proposal. When I made the Maxim Hot 100 list because some poor blind editor felt sorry for me, I flew out to Las Vegas for the issue's launch party. I wish I could say I made their top ten, but I was ranked number 94—and I don't know what's worse: not making the list at all or appearing at the bottom of the barrel at 94. E! wanted me to cover the red carpet in Vegas, and of course, I knew Tom would be there to support me. "Want to come to this Hot 100 party with me?" I asked. "There'll be ninety-three other girls there who are hotter than me." He told me I was the sexiest girl on the list and even called his friend at *Maxim* to tell him they should have bumped me up. If that's not a good boyfriend, what is?

The event was awkward from beginning to end. When I wasn't working the red carpet, I was being interviewed on the red carpet. At one point, I grabbed the mic and interviewed Tom about who the most smokin' girl at the event was, and of course he said it was me. We were always good for shtick. And all the while, I noticed a certain famous model/actress (or "mattress" as Tom would jokingly call that combo) had arrived on the red carpet and was about to approach the E! mic for an interview. Let's call her something generic, like "Lisa." At the time, "Lisa" had just broken up with her husband, so when she passed us, Tom noticed her and joked that he'd let me go so I could interview real famous people, meaning Lisa. I decided I'd rather go into the party with Tom, so I handed the mic back to my producer who spoke with her instead.

Once inside, I was pulled away for photos—and during that time, Tom and Lisa met.

The next day I was having my hair done with some other girls from the *Maxim* party. Tom called to check in, as usual, and asked who else was there. I named names, including Lisa's. Tom showed up five minutes later. I noticed him smile and wave at her, but I didn't think much of it. "Do you guys know each other?" I asked. "Not really," he told me. "I kind of met her at the party for a second." So I blew it off. The next weekend he planned a guy's trip to Vegas with some of his college friends. "Should I grab some girlfriends, and we'll go?" I volunteered. Tom grasped for words. "Actually, it's a guy thing and probably not the best idea . . ." he rambled. There was no reason not to believe or trust him; he'd never lied to me before.

After that Vegas trip, our relationship went downhill. Almost overnight, it plummeted from a consistent and reliable ten to a sudden three. I knew something was up—I'm not a complete idiot—but I couldn't peg Tom's behavior to any event, other than that trip to Vegas, which he insisted was harmless dude fun. He began to pick fights and avoid my calls and texts for up to five hours when he used to reply within five minutes. A few times, I even said to him, "Tom, if something's going on or you're seeing someone else, tell me." But that made him defensive. "How could you say that?" he'd insist. "Are you crazy? What are *you* doing to make you ask me such a question?" He'd turn the whole fight around on me, until I didn't know which way was up.

Coming Clean

After a week of this push/pull, which was utterly crazy-making, I did what any suspicious girl might do to a boyfriend who isn't forthcoming: I invited him over for coffee to talk about our feelings. Ha! As if? I listened to his voice mail. I already had Tom's email passwords and voice mail codes on hand, in case I had to use them someday. (If you don't have anything to hide, what's the big deal about sharing these?) When I listened to Tom's messages, I heard one from Lisa. She was really casual with him, as if this wasn't the first time they'd talked. She didn't say anything that might implicate him or suggest they were fooling around, but I did think: *What on earth is Lisa doing on my boyfriend's voice mail?* When I told my friend Colet, she said she'd read an article in the *New York Post* about how Lisa was dating an entrepreneur in Vegas the weekend Tom was there. "See, she's with someone!" Colet said. The alibi made me feel better.

> ### Giuliana's Long-Distance Trust Tips
>
> • *Answer the phone.* We take each other's calls, no matter what. We're always a phone call away.
> • *Use Skype as a verb.* We Skype for a few minutes before bed to say good night.
> • *Send pics on our camera phones.* Silly snapshots make us feel like we're there.

I laid low for the next three weeks, just in case I was the nutty one prone to overreacting. But Tom continued to act fishy—for instance, he'd tell me he was going out of town for work, and I'd later find out he was in L.A. (and I imagine, with Lisa). It was very hard for me to discern truth from fiction from assumptions, since Tom was always open, and all my girlfriends who knew him and our relationship thought there was no way he'd cheat on me since he talked about love and marriage so much. He had everyone fooled. I'd tell friends and even family that I had to break up with Tom, and they'd suggest I think twice. They didn't think I was jumping to conclusions; they just protected him because they genuinely believed in our relationship.

Finally, Tom and I went to the movies, and he seemed distracted. Before the film started, I asked him to open up. "What's going on? You're so distant," I said. "If you're seeing someone else, tell me so I can be free and move on with my life. Let's break up, or at least take some time off from each other." But Tom said no, he was simply preoccupied by things going on with his family, and during the movie, my gut kept telling me that we needed to end our relationship. As the credits rolled, Tom gave me his best puppy dog eyes. "You know what? I'm going to be better," he said, with sincerity. "I'm going to be a better boyfriend. I'm so sorry. I've just been going through a lot lately." So I forgave him (again). I'm not one to chase a man or force him to love me, but I think Tom was torn. I think he loved me but had met someone he'd fallen for, too.

The next day at work I received a phone call from Ken Baker, who now works for E! but at the time was an executive editor at *US Weekly*. We were friendly, but we didn't ring each other up for fun, so my stomach nervously fluttered when I heard his voice. "Hey, it's Ken Baker from *US Weekly*," he said, and I knew something wasn't right. "I'm going to put this right out there, Giuliana. Is your boyfriend dating Lisa?" I felt like I'd been kicked in the stomach. "We have a lot of sources who've seen them together," he said. "A lot." Despite what I suspected, I was stunned, and even more upset that a tabloid reporter would be the one to validate my suspicions. I tried to hide my surprise, because I didn't want to look like an idiot, so I told him Tom and I weren't dating anymore. "So you guys broke up?" he asked. "Yeah, we broke up a month ago," I told him. "We've just been hanging out as friends for the past month."

I put Ken on hold, and shut my office door. I cried a little harder than I'd like to admit. All I wanted to do was bolt

home and bury myself under my sheets, but I had to tape *E!*
News in less than an hour. The comfort of knowing I'd be in
bed within a few hours helped me out. Once I composed myself, I asked Ken where his sources had seen Tom and Lisa.
"The first spotting was in Vegas," he told me, and said that
she'd been shooting an indie documentary—and I put it together that this was the weekend he'd flown out with his college friends. I wanted to kill my boyfriend. I hung up with
Ken, called Tom, and told him that I'd just informed *US*
Weekly that we'd already broken up because he made me look
foolish to friends, family, and anyone else who cared.

"I can't believe you," I said. "I gave you a month to get out
of this, and instead you went behind my back. First, it's someone famous, and that's bad enough. But then you lied about it,
too? What did I ever do to you to make you treat me this way
and put me in such a mortifying position?" Tom was speechless.
"There's nothing I can say," he said. "There's nothing I can do.
I'm sorry." And that was basically it. Tom went from being
Boyfriend of the Year to a complete piece of garbage, and all
over some former B-list actress. It was pathetic, sneaky, and exceptionally hurtful. I suspect that all those times he acted jealous and insecure during our relationship were triggered by
knowing he was capable of deception himself. I also think his
identity was so wrapped up in our relationship that he was un-
necessarily, and unfairly, suspicious of anything I did or said
outside of him and us.

Since then, of course, Lisa's gone on record with the *New*
York Post and other media sources that she met Tom poolside
at the Hard Rock Hotel in Vegas after splitting with her husband.

To this day, Lisa will not speak to me on or off the red carpet; she and Tom will, however, do interviews with other E!
correspondents. The funny thing is, when the producers look
at the list of stars attending an event, the producers get to her
name and say to me, "That's probably a pass for you, right?"

And I'll say, "No, if they're willing to talk, I'm more than happy to speak to them on *live* television." But it's been four years, and they've denied all requests.

Two years ago, as I was reviewing my notes on the red carpet at the Emmys, I felt a tug on the back of my dress, turned around, and it was Tom. "What's up home girl?" he asked. "How are you?" I told him I was great and asked him how he was. "I'm good," he said. "I've got to say, you look beautiful." I wanted to vomit. He congratulated me on my marriage, and I returned the salutation to be cordial. And the thing is, I didn't need a word of it. I wouldn't even say that being in love with Bill is the best revenge I could get; it's more like, being with Bill makes me realize how much less of a man Tom is—and how exceptionally fortunate I was to dodge that bullet.

When Your Past Catches Up with You

Giuliana: I tell this story because I think it helps shed some light on why I was so testy about Bill's dinner with Jezebel, and my fear that the tabloids might suspect he was having an affair, though he clearly wasn't. Bill knows that Tom's cheating still haunts me, so he's careful to do whatever he can to resolve a similarly distressing situation before it happens. And let's face it: We have the kinds of jobs that could make the other person feel the occasional pang of jealousy, more often than not.

Bill: Yeah, this one likes to speak Italian with Clooney on the red carpet.

Giuliana: Hello? Bill was a judge in the Miss Universe pageant! If that couldn't make a girl's head explode, I don't know what could.

Bill: I think the key to avoiding jealousy is to unload your baggage early in your relationship or marriage. I told Giuliana before we were engaged that I wasn't an angel before she came along, and she was open about Tom and how that affected her. Our backgrounds did not complement each other that way. If we didn't discuss our pasts early on, they could have caused major conflicts down the road. I also didn't want my friends to tiptoe around her when we talked about the old days—or for her to jump to conclusions that upset her.

Giuliana: Bill and I have realized that who we were before we met each other only matters when it impacts the way we act when we're together. We can't help that we have baggage from complicated relationships in our past, but the process of moving on from that has been really freeing. Some of the best conversations Bill and I have had are about our prior relationships, and that's helped us become clear on how we want our future to be with each other. It makes us feel closer.

Bill: Even when we walk down the street, I can predict what will set Giuliana off because we've covered similar territory during our talks and check ins about envy.

Giuliana: Bill's a good-looking guy, so I expect other women to look at him. But he's also so thoughtful, because when a hot girl walks down the street and I see her, I'll look at Bill's eyes to see if he notices, too. I don't know whether he does it on purpose, but he'll quickly glance and then look away—not like some piggish men I know.

Bill: I always look away. Of course, I do that on purpose.

Giuliana: He does! And I like it. He's not the guy who'd look a woman up and down; that would be so rude. I do the same if I see a really attractive guy walking down the street, too.

Bill: It's about respect.

Giuliana: I don't even like to joke and say, "Look, there's your girlfriend!" I'm a huge believer in the law of attraction (I've read *The Secret* eight times) that says you attract into your life whatever you think about; if you put a message into the universe often enough, it will occur in some form or other. So we want to respect and protect the sanctity of our marriage. I know it sounds über conservative and traditional, but these days, so many couples have lost that reverence. By making loaded jokes about other people, it puts bad energy out there.

And if Bill ever *did* make a jealous remark about a good-looking guy walking down the street, something like "There goes my replacement," I'd come up with a million reasons why I think Bill is the hottest guy in the world or how the guy probably has a low IQ or smells bad in the morning. I also try to take some time each day to make Bill feel good about himself—and he does the same for me. We don't have time to feel insecure when we're busy loving each other up.

Bill: You always want to build up your spouse. You want to remind your number one person why you married him or her and what makes your partner so special that you can't live without each other. As I like to say to Giuliana, "Trust me, honey. I married you, didn't I?"

TIPS FOR TWO: Taming a Jealous Streak

• Discuss your baggage early in your relationship. Talking about the past frees you to live in the present and plan for the future.

• Once you know why you have pangs of envy, come up with ways to feel good about yourself. Fear and insecurity don't stand a chance against self-confidence bolstered by your spouse.

• Don't compare yourself to people in your spouse's past—or even strangers on the street.

• Remember that your spouse's past matters most in how it affects your current relationship.

• Don't tease your spouse about having other crushes. The Law of Attraction may respond!

11 The Power of the "F" Word

A lot of marriages get stuck between a rut and a hard place. On the one hand, sinking into a comfortable routine with your spouse can make you feel safe and at-home. Yet experts say that when married couples don't color their relationships with new and surprising experiences, their love lives can become a matter of habit, which makes them feel stuck, bored, and disconnected. It should come as no surprise, then, that a study done by researchers at Stony Brook University and University of Michigan found that couples who regularly fell into ruts were significantly less close and reported less marital satisfaction than their novelty-seeking counterparts.

Getting stuck in a rut is a lot like ordering "the usual" at your favorite restaurant every night of the week. At first, it feels good knowing that after a hard day, you can retreat to a cozy place where someone appreciates what you want before you ask for it. But after a while, the experience gets old and your pallet craves spicy, bold, and original flavors. Similarly, your relationship needs more than "the usual" to thrive; new, fun, and challenging encounters allow it to function at its best. The tough part for most couples is figuring out when and how often it's OK to lean on familiar habits without completely dulling the senses. Comfort food is great once in a while, but an entire diet of mac-and-cheese can make you sedentary and miserable.

We're definitely prone to ruts. If we didn't force ourselves to refresh our routine for the sake of our marriage, we'd behave like gerbils on a wheel: We'd hang out at the same bars, stay at the same hotels on vacation, and go running on the same path every morning. Routines often feel like a safe haven from the daily hustle, but it's hard not to let our love for security interrupt our need for novel ways to enjoy each other. So we rely on road trips and weekend getaways to wake up our relationship, and creative date nights to keep us feeling close. Changing up our actual dates keeps things fresh, too, and while it's fine for us to go on a lot of hikes and see a lot of theater, because we love to do these things, we take a different trail and alternate between musicals and plays each time we go. The point is for us to enjoy each other and take small risks in the process. Here's how we got past the first real rut in our wedlock, thanks to the help of an unassuming friend and Bill's big plan to make the most of the "F" word.

Bill: One Saturday afternoon about a year after we were married, a buddy of mine—we'll call him Jimmy—called to say hi. Jimmy's great, but he's a playboy who likes to live large. To put it in perspective, he was cast on foreign television as *The Bachelor,* and he loves freedom, women, stiff drinks, and reckless abandonment. But I can't really fault him for any of it. To an outsider, Jimmy's life looks like a good time. So when I asked him what he'd been up to lately, I should have known he'd give me an earful. "I just got back from Mexico, where I met the most incredible girl," he said. "And Bill, we had a wild time. We went parasailing, drank tequila, danced all night, and ate the freshest ceviche with lime . . . you would have loved it." I'd put Jimmy on speaker so Giuliana and I could both talk to him, but as he went on and on about his latest adventure, we both started to get bummed out. I couldn't help but think, *I wish I could have been in Mexico having a blast,* and when I looked over at Giuliana, she had a faraway look in her eyes, too. "So," Jimmy asked, coming up for a breath. "What did *you* do today?"

Giuliana: "Oh, we got up, went to Equinox. . . ."

Bill: "Had brunch at the Original Pancake House. They have the best turkey bacon!"

Giuliana: "Went to Ace Hardware, ran some errands. We'll probably have dinner at Carmine's, Gibson's, or Tavern tonight . . . you know, the usual spots. . . ."

Bill: And in my head, I thought: *then we'll come home, go to bed, and do it all over again tomorrow.* We sounded so lame. It was like Groundhog Day at the Rancic house. The thought of following this stale routine for another fifty years scared me, and judging by the look on Giuliana's face, she wasn't inspired by our agenda, either. I guess one person's rut can be another person's dream day, but doing the same thing over and over was not the lifestyle we wanted.

What's in a Rut?

Bill: There's an old saying that the difference between a rut and a grave is how deep it is and how long you're in it. That sounds about right to me. The thing with me and Giuliana, though, is that our rut snuck up on us; we didn't realize we were buried six feet under until Jimmy's anecdote helped point it out. In fact, my reaction to his story was a complete surprise to me. More than anything else, I thought we were just feeling comfortable with each other. That's usually a good thing, right?

Giuliana: And yet if we took a closer look at our lives, all signs pointed to feeling stuck: We romanticized trips we'd taken while we were still dating, felt antsy while watching a week's worth of TiVo on Sunday afternoons, and were totally disappointed when our go-to restaurant was booked for the night (after already eating there twice in one week). I think the biggest clue that we weren't making the most of our down-time together was that we both felt embarrassed about it when Jimmy called. If you feel bad about any plans, then your activities can't be very healthy. I think it's normal to fall into a humdrum routine when you're married, but the trick is to get out of it before it becomes something that's a part of your relationship instead of just a fluke. Bill and I didn't need to fight three days a week or only have sex once a month for us to realize that we needed to give our bond a little more TLC. And we didn't want to become one of those couples that ignore the early signs of a rut, and let their busy lives get in the way of repairing it. The deeper an emotional ditch becomes over the years, the more difficult it is to climb out of it.

Bill: The weird thing about ruts is that they're not always the result of doing the same recreational things over and over (or doing nothing at all). They can also happen when you're so in-sync about working toward the same goals that you don't take a minute to connect. Giuliana and I are both guilty of burning our candle at both ends. We're a well-oiled machine when it comes to running a lot of errands in a few hours, working to pay off our mortgage, and hosting dinners for friends. But while we might get a lot done when we're focused on the end-goal, our paths don't always cross in the process—and we emotionally fall out of step. It's easy to take each other for granted.

Giuliana: Sometimes I have to remind Bill to slow down and smell my Chanel N°5. My friend once read somewhere that couples in ruts should spend time appreciating each other's nuances, which means I should pay more attention to what ties Bill wears to work and he might want to notice what color I've painted my toenails. This helps us stop, take a breath, and recognize something new about the other person—and who doesn't love to feel noticed? Ruts dull the senses, and this helps refresh them. This type of exercise can also introduce new conversation ("Hey, you're wearing the tie I stole from E! wardrobe. Why do you like that look?"). Bill and I have no interest in slogging through life, so if we tweak our daily routines and recognize small changes in the other person, the eye-opening experience can do wonders for our dull routines.

How to "F" Things Up

Giuliana: Instead of Googling "Hot Ways to Reignite My Marriage," Bill and I just had an open and honest conversation about how to get ourselves out of our uncharacteristic slump. I wasn't miserable in our routine, but I knew that if I felt a little ho-hum, then Bill probably felt it, too. So I started with the positive: "You know what's so great about being married? We're so comfortable with each other. And we have this amazing bond that's not going anywhere. But with that, we've lost some passion. Let's pull out of this rut and give our relationship some oomph, a little *jeuge*."

Bill: She never said "jeuge."

Giuliana: I like the word *jeuge*!

Bill: Anyway, I completely agreed with Giuliana. So I suggested we formulate a plan.

Giuliana: Of course he did.

Bill: I started by visiting my buddy Jerry's parents, who have an amazing marriage and have been together for more than thirty years. They travel a lot—from spending summers on Manhattan Beach to touring Italy by train in the spring—but they seem just as happy puttering around the yard together on a sunny afternoon. So I asked soon-to-be role models, "What's the secret to a happy marriage?" That's when Jerry's mom said, "The 'F' word."

At first, I was like "Euch, gross." I've known these two since I was fourteen years old; I never wanted to think about them *that* way. I must have really flinched though, because Jerry's dad jumped in to squash the nasty image in my head. "No no, Bill. It's not what you think," he said. "When we say the 'F' word,' we mean *fun*. It keeps things fresh in our marriage." He told me about how they have monthly Scotch nights and go wine-tasting by bike in Napa Valley. Their lives sounded so cool to me that I almost asked them if they wanted to double date with us.

> "Recently, I made Bill come to a kickboxing class in Chicago instead of doing our usual workout together. He was afraid he'd be the only guy there and look like a tool—and you know what? He was, and he did. But watching this alpha male do roundhouse kicks to 'Single Ladies' made us laugh until our cheeks hurt." —**Giuliana**

Giuliana: I knew we had to spice up our life a little, because I didn't want our relationship to go dull. But to be honest, my biggest concern was that I didn't want *Bill* to start roaming. The last thing I needed was for him to wander off with some saucy Mexican whore who'd feed him ceviche in the moonlight. So my first instinct was to do something like take a dance class together or go on a scavenger hunt. I'm obsessed with scavenger hunts for some reason; I must have seen them in a movie as a child and thought they looked cool to do.

Bill: Before Giuliana could download a treasure map off the Internet, I took charge of the situation. "Here's the deal," I said. "Our plan is to have *no plan*." I think I blew her mind.

Giuliana: I love flying by the seat of my APC jeans, so I was really into this nonplan plan.

Bill: Our plan kicked off with a surprise road trip, since I think road trips are the best rut-busters out there. You're in the car with your spouse for hours, so you have a captive audience who'll talk to you and laugh at your jokes. Great, right? You can also stop the minute something catches your eye or pull over if you're feeling horny. On our trip, we rented a fun car, a Mini-Cooper convertible, and drove it from L.A. to San Francisco along the coast. We stopped in Big Sur, and we got an awesome hotel room where there was no TV, no phone. It was really off the grid.

Giuliana: We stayed at a motel outside Pizmo Beach where the bathrooms were in the hall, so let's just say I filled my "new and exciting" quota every time I had to pee. And the funky love seats looked like they were straight out of an Austin Powers movie, though I'd never want to shine a black light on them. It would have been so easy to drive five minutes down the road to a luxury hotel, where our robes would be personalized and our soap would smell like lavender. But this hotel's quirks kept things interesting, and we'll remember that place more than if we stayed at the Ritz.

Bill: Giuliana was scared to fall asleep that night, so she set a booby trap by the door in case someone busted in. To do this, she wedged a chair under the doorknob, like they do in the movies. I couldn't blame her; the locks looked like the latches you find in a public bathroom. They were so flimsy. Someone could have given it a little kick and terrorized us.

Giuliana: Laugh all you want, Rancic. That place gave us some good stories to tell afterward.

This Ain't Your Parents' Date Night

Bill: The spontaneous no-plan plan was fun for a while, but we couldn't sustain it; relying on the other person to come up with so many surprises, as our primary means of fun became high pressure and tiresome. So Giuliana and I decided to set aside three evenings a month for date nights (yes, married couples can still date, but only each other); these were a nice constant that we could look forward to on a regular basis. When I was single, I used to laugh at my married friends who'd designate a date night with their spouses; I didn't understand why they had to put a label on spending time with someone they loved. But now I get it. I was thinking the other day: if meetings and conferences are important enough for me to put on a calendar or in my BlackBerry, so is regular quality time with Giuliana. What's nice is that as much as I think I know my wife, she's always changing in small ways; so for me, going on dates with her feels like when we first met. We come up with a fun plan, get dressed up, have a few drinks, and see where the night goes. Date night also shows us that we don't need to do something big, like take a road trip, to reboot our marriage. It can be enough to get out of the house, sit face-to-face, and have a conversation about the waiter's ridiculous handlebar mustache. It's all about being playful but still feeling secure in your marriage. Giuliana's parents still hold hands, and my dad always planned ski trips and weekends at our summerhouse for our whole family, which let him and my mom to have fun together but in a new environment. Our parents set the right tone for our relationship.

Giuliana: You also need new experiences to act as conversation starters. If you're constantly going to the same restaurant, taking the same walk, going to the same gym, and seeing movies at the same theater every weekend, you're going to fall headfirst into a rut because you have no mind-stimulating fodder. Good conversation gives you a chance to really listen to your spouse and focus on being together. There's no Twitter to follow, no blogs to update, no basketball scores to check online. When Bill and I are away from distractions, we can just let ourselves go.

Bill: Even doing something simple like changing our running course gives us something new to talk about. We always ran north on the beach in Chicago, but lately we've been running south a lot. We're always like, "Hey, I never knew that restaurant was there. Let's try it next week."

Giuliana: The other night, we went to this cozy little restaurant called A Votre Sante in Brentwood that came up during one of our runs, and I did something kind of cool: I insisted on ordering the entire meal for both me and Bill. And then, I deliberately ordered things Bill never would have gotten in a million years, but I've always wanted him to try. You know how when you go to dinner, you always want your spouse to try your food? And it gets boring when he or she orders the same thing?

Bill: Giuliana ordered me the Mediterranean Platter with hummus, tabouleh, eggplant dip, baba ghanoush . . .

Giuliana: It was so good. When we usually order the Mediterranean platter, Bill will say to the waiter: "All hummus." And
I'll say, "But what about the baba ghanoush, tabouleh, and
eggplant?" And he'll be like, "No, no, no, no. All hummus"—
and yet he's never even tried the rest of the dish! So when we
were at this restaurant, I said, "Listen, we're switching things
up. I'm ordering. Just go with it." Sure enough, Bill ate the entire platter minus the tabouleh. Then I ordered a vegetable
stir-fry for me, with all these weird vegetables, and everything
was swimming in a spinach sauce that wasn't part of the original dish, but I thought might be fun to taste. I ordered Bill a
chicken curry wrap with veggies, rice, and hummus, but he actually ended-up picking off my vegetable plate that he initially
thought sounded unappetizing. And that sparked this talk
about how his family thought it was weird that he liked vegetables as a kid, something I'd never known before.

Love Was Made for Me and You

Giuliana: I remember when Bill and I first fell in love: the tension of getting to know each other, all those late-night
calls. . . .

Bill: We used to fall asleep on the phone together when we
were first dating, because we'd be in different cities and talk
until late at night. The getting-to-know-you part was so exciting. . . .

Giuliana: In the beginning, we were so nervous around each
other because everything was unknown. Our life was full of
firsts—our first vacation, our first Christmas, the first time I
met his family . . . It was exhilarating and nerve-racking at

the same time. There's actually NIH research that shows married couples experience two different types of love: the first kind happens when you're falling in love, and the second, when you feel more like friends after a few years. In the beginning, it's very passionate. And once you're married for a while, it's not worse, but it's different—more predictable and secure, and much more sustaining for the long term. Some experts tell couples to find ways to rediscover or even relive that original feeling of passionate love, but I think it's hard to recreate a milestone. Instead, I think you have to recognize your relationship for what it is: progressing in stages, with each one more important and special than the one before it. But it's up to me and Bill to keep things moving forward in a positive way.

Speaking of milestones, I remember the first time we kissed. We were in Bill's condo in Chicago, and I was there for Memorial Day weekend. We were drinking pinot noir and dancing to Sinatra by candlelight. At one point, I laughed so hard that I spilled my red wine all over Bill's brand-new white carpet! He wasn't mad at all—and that, my friends, is dating. The next morning, Bill and I spent a good hour scrubbing the carpet and joking about what a klutz I am. We ruined that poor rug, but it was so worth it; back then, even the worst situation was crazy fun because we were together and our relationship was still new. Cut to now, and if Bill and I ever danced to Sinatra by candlelight, it would feel forced; and if I spilled wine on our carpet, Bill would have my head! So instead of trying to find creative ways to trick each other into revisiting the old days, Bill and I feel grateful that we've added stability and comfort to our emotional repertoire, but try not to get lost in it. When you're dating, you look so hard for a person to become your rock, and when you get it, you shouldn't take advantage of it. We just need to regularly check in with each other to make sure we're not tiptoeing into rut territory. It's something we have to be aware of.

Bill: Sparking passion all goes back to surprise for us. If you can surprise me, I'm all yours—and Giuliana is the same way. I remember one night, she came home from work and the house smelled like caramelized onions. I said to her, "We have a surprise guest coming for dinner!" It was her best friend Pam, and we spent hours talking about the new guy in her life and giving her advice on how to handle the relationship. Another time, I thought Giuliana and I were going on a date night, but when I got in the car (I was driving), she revealed where we were headed next on a need-to-know basis. We ended up in Newport Coast at a hotel and spa I'd been wanting to try. The best part of this was that I'd been dying to get away, and Giuliana took the wheel.

Giuliana: There's something, too, about choosing activities that feel new but make your spouse feel known at the same time. It's a nice mix. For instance, if Bill were to mention that he misses bumming around Rome and eating pasta, and we'd already been to Italy a few times, I might pick another place like Greece or Madrid that has a similar Mediterranean feel. I'd think, "What does Bill love about Italy? Well, he loves the food, he loves that people are out on the street late at night in the piazzas, he loves watching strangers walk arm in arm while smoking cigars and eating gelato. So that doesn't just happen in Italy . . ." Thinking this way opens us up to new experi-

Romantic Road Trip Essentials

- Three CDs you've never heard before
- Books on tape
- Flip-flops
- Two large bottles of water
- Picnic basket full of goodies for an impromptu side-of-the-road lunch
- Condoms in the glove compartment

ences and shows we're making an effort that's informed by our past experiences.

Bill: At the end of the day, I think that breaking out of a rut relies heavily on taking risks, whether that means booking a trip to Greece or meeting your spouse for a picnic in the middle of the day. Sure, it might be a gamble as to whether your husband or wife appreciates the specific gesture, but it's even riskier not to take a chance at all and opt for a potentially monotonous relationship. Everyone needs to feel stimulated, and without an element of mystery or danger to do that, relationships can go south. And the only time you want to go south in a relationship, is when you've booked a private yacht to the Caribbean for a week of decadent island hopping.

Giuliana: Sign me up! Take that, Jimmy.

TIPS FOR TWO: How to Bust a Rut

• The difference between a comfortable routine and a rut is how it makes you feel.

• The best time to fix a rut is before it becomes part of your marriage.

• Slowing down your pace, introducing novelty and fun into your routine, and noticing small things about your spouse can help your marriage climb out of a rut.

• Mix big surprises with regular date nights to keep your relationship and conversation fresh.

• Take risks with your partner. Sign up for a class together, swap errand duties, or invite a surprise guest to dinner. The goal is to put the "F" word back in your marriage to take it in a new direction.

12 Hogs and Hiking Vests

Some of our best memories have been made while simply hanging out together. We've found that feeling passionate about a shared activity is a testament to our compatibility, as is our willingness to try new things that the other person likes. What's crucial to making this last one work for most couples is a genuine desire to participate in a spouse's favorite thing. A recent study published in the *Journal of Marriage and Family* found that among wives who do activities that their guys like but they don't, the women who engaged in this stuff most often were less likely to be happily married. That's a real disappointment, but it makes sense to us. Joining your spouse for eighteen holes of golf or a boating trip off Maine is only fulfilling and entertaining if you want to be there. If not, resentment builds, fights erupt, and a wife can feel more alienated than when she didn't participate at all.

We're always learning something new about each other, and we've found that one of the best ways to do this is to dive into activities that interest our spouse to see if they're something we can enjoy together. Early in our relationship, Bill was wild about riding his motorcycle and wanted to share his passion for the sport with Giuliana. It was a revealing adventure, to say the least. Same deal for Bill, who found ways to make the most of daylong hikes—treks he'd never have done without Giuliana's push. We also maintain our separate interests, but not to the extent that we forget how much we like being with each other and what brought us together in the first place. It also stands to reason that the more intertwined our life is, the more incentive we have to stay together, long term. Developing common interests is an investment in our future.

What matters most is how all this quality time influences our dynamic. Bill always says that marriage is the result of how much effort we put into it, and the grand prize of so much together time is a true best friend. Love that. Here's how our free time has fed our connection.

Giuliana: I always swore I'd never get on a motorcycle—mostly because I promised this to my dad, who had a bad accident when he was a teenager in Naples, Italy. He was on his motorcycle heading to a friend's house in the mountains, when he crashed and broke two bones in his left leg. But when I met Bill, he told me that riding his shiny black Honda Rune was one of his all-time favorite hobbies. I never got over my crush on Danny Zuko from *Grease* as a kid, so Bill was the next best thing in my grown-up mind. When he suggested we go for a ride, I decided to suck up my fears and never tell my dad. Zipping in and out of traffic on two wheels wasn't my idea of a good time, but I wanted to learn more about what revved Bill's engine, and I wanted to spend time with him. Both meant learning to try something Bill enjoys.

I decided to join Bill on his speed machine over a long Memorial Day weekend, the first time I'd been to Chicago after dating Bill for a few months. I'd never visited his city, and Bill made me feel right at home. He picked me up from the airport with snacks in hand and drove me to my hotel in the Gold Coast, which is the best location because it's near museums, good restaurants, and of course, fantastic shopping on Michigan Avenue. In my room, I found a welcome basket from Bill that he'd put together himself with the best of everything from Chicago: Garrett's famous popcorn, a map of the city, a book on Chicago history and hot spots, Chicago postcards, and a Cubs T-shirt and hat because—surprise!—we were hitting a Cubs game that weekend. There was also a note from Bill that said, "Welcome to my town. Can't wait to show you around!" It was written on stationery with his name "Bill Rancic" inscribed in a stately font. This guy was already something.

Bill: I basically buttered her up, so she'd be more agreeable to go for a ride with me.

Giuliana: I don't doubt it. Bill made my first motorcycle experience as Giuliana-friendly as he could. That meant driving to the North Shore, a beautiful suburb of Chicago with relatively traffic-free streets. And when it started to storm, he pulled over at an outdoor mall. We went into a Crate and Barrel to shop and kill time . . .

Bill: No, we initially went in to buy towels because we were soaking wet! Then we browsed for dishes and sofas while we waited for it to pass; when the sun came out again, we had a picnic at a nearby park. It was very romantic, actually. Giuliana was the first girlfriend to ever ride with me on my bike. She wasn't a natural, but I liked that she went outside her comfort zone for me.

Giuliana: Bill has a really nice bike. It goes fast, and I was scared. Bill's friend Chris likes to ride, too, and I like his wife, Tricia. So when we were at Crate and Barrel, I thought, "OK,

---

Giuliana's Perfect Solo Day

❑ Wake up early and hit the gym for an hour of cardio
❑ Grab a fresh-squeezed veggie juice on the way home
❑ Shower and change into a comfy sweat suit and tennies
❑ Run errands that Bill never wants to do—like spend an hour choosing frames for wall art or walk up and down the drugstore aisles reading the backs of vitamin bottles and face creams
❑ Get a mani/pedi: light colors on fingers, dark colors on toes
❑ Sneak large fro-yos into a tear-jerking chick flick with friends

---

I can do this. The guys could go for a ride, leave the ladies to have lunch and shop at the mall . . . This could work." I can see the merits of riding a motorcycle if shopping, socializing, and snacks are involved.

Bill: Once, we went north along the Pacific Coast Highway in California. It's one of the most scenic routes in the U.S. We rode through Santa Monica and Malibu, just past the Ventura County line to Neptune's Net, a biker bar with a menu full of artery-clogging foods. We hung out with some hard-core bikers, and ate deep-fried shrimp, oysters, and clams. It was incredible.

Giuliana: That trip was the first time I wore a helmet in front of Bill, since California has a motorcycle helmet law. Too bad I have a giant head, and nothing fits on this massive dome. I didn't want to call attention to it so soon in my relationship!

Bill: The man at the Harley shop gave Giuliana an extra large female . . .

Giuliana: And lo and behold, it didn't fit. It sat on my lollipop head all lopsided, and I pretended it worked to draw less attention to myself. "Is your head in there?" Bill asked, as he tried to jimmy it onto my oversized skull. "Yes, yes, let's get going," I told him, and the whole time we were on the road, I had one arm around Bill's waist and the other on my noggin to hold that helmet on because it was so tight on the inside that it just rested on top of my head.

Bill: Giuliana couldn't see anything because it was falling in her eyes.

Giuliana: It fit like a little beret. It was a half helmet, like Clooney wears.

Bill: Clooney and the military.

Giuliana: Riding on that motorcycle was not made any less scary by that helmet.

Bill: But now she loves riding!

Bill's Perfect Solo Day

❏ Sleep in and watch the news in bed for an hour
❏ Hit the gym with one or two of my best friends
❏ Grab some turkey burgers after a good workout
❏ Take a half-hour nap
❏ Hit an afternoon Cubs or Bears game
❏ End the day at a neighborhood pub for steak, Scotch on the rocks, and cigars with the guys

Giuliana: I tell Bill I love it. It's terrifying. I'd rather be in a car with airbags. But Bill feels free and invigorated when he's flying through the streets, and he says he loves the feeling of having me behind him, so I've learned to enjoy it as much as I can. "Hold on," he tells me, "and put your arms around my waist, honey"—because sometimes I'll put them on his shoulders. "No, no," he'll correct me. "Put them around my waist so you don't fall off." I know he really does this because he likes the feeling of a chick with her arms around his waist.

Bill: Mmmhmm.

Giuliana: I told you.

Bill: It's safer, too.

Giuliana: The only thing is that his bike seat is so uncomfortable, because it's made for one.

Bill: It's not designed for girls with big bottoms, let's just say that.

Giuliana: Is he saying I have a big badonkadonk? Cripes, Rancic. Anyway, it's really stiff and has no padding. And every time we get to a red light, every twenty minutes or so, I have to get up and stretch. I stand up off the bike in traffic, and stretch and bend over, because it hurts my butt bone so bad. But it's OK; I do it because my husband loves it. I don't force myself, because then I'd get bitter. But it's something we can do together, and God knows I wouldn't do it with anyone else. Riding is definitely a thrill, I'll give it that much. And it's a visceral reminder that I married a man who's a risk-taker and loves a good rush. I forget this sometimes, especially when Bill bombards me with spreadsheets, budgets, and plans for our future. The contradiction is a real turn-on for me.

Climb Every Canyon

Giuliana: I've introduced Bill to plenty of hobbies, too. I love to hike through the great outdoors, and Bill's gradually come to enjoy it. He's a real bench-pressing, gym kind of guy, so it took longer for him to come around to hiking than it did for me to appreciate his greased lightning.

Bill: Well, yeah. Hiking wasn't necessarily my forte, or something I would have done on my own. I like skiing, snowboarding, water skiing. I like more active, fast-paced sports. I didn't think an activity that encourages you to wear a fanny pack would be my thing.

Giuliana: When I brought Bill hiking for the first time at the Topanga Canyon in Malibu, he couldn't wrap his head around the idea of moderately walking up dirt paths for fun. We were engaged at the time, which is why I think he initially agreed to join me.

Bill: We were only on the trail for ten minutes when I got bored.

Giuliana: "Why don't we start running, honey?" he said. Only Bill would want to turn hiking into an adrenaline sport. "Well, the walk is uphill," I said. "It's serious stuff." Bill didn't buy it and hit me with questions like a kid on a road trip: Where is this hill going? What's at the top? Are we there yet? What's the point, again? "It's exercise," I said. "Just shut up, and trust me."

Halfway up the hill, Bill proposed a race. "This hill isn't bad," he said. "Let's run it." "Dude, everyone else is walking," I said. But I never turn down a challenge, and we blew our wad after thirty seconds—the hill was too steep. When we got to

Our Best Sunday Together

❏ Watch *CBS Sunday Morning* in bed, and maybe even a little
   preaching by Joel Osteen
❏ Eat fluffy egg-white omelets with a side of buckwheat
   pancakes at A Votre Sante in Brentwood or Original
   Pancake House in Chicago
❏ Take in a Cubs game, chow on hot dogs and pretzels, and
   wash it all back with tall beers
❏ Get buzzed and dance to live reggae at Wild Hare in
   Chicago

the top, we sat on a bench to soak up the view, but even that
didn't impress Bill. "I can see views from our apartment window," he said.

The next day, Bill could hardly move. "My legs and butt
never hurt this bad," he griped. The poor guy was in pain for
days, but that sold him on hiking. He needed to feel the burn.

Bill: I hike for the exercise; is that so wrong? But I also like to
mock Giuliana when she dresses like she's on her way to
Mount Everest.

Giuliana: Bill wears all Nike gear, because to him, hiking is an
intense workout. But I put an entire jungle outfit together. I
have this cute khaki vest that has a lot of pockets that I stash
with Ziploc bags full of nuts and dried fruit. I'm one of those
weird people who need to be ready in case we get lost and have
to survive for a week. When Bill got to the top of that Malibu
overlook and said he was hungry, who do you think had a
sandwich, granola bar, and nuts waiting in her many pockets?
I wear a hat, SPF, and glasses, too. I also have hard-core Mer-
rell hiking boots, but I only bought them because they were
the prettiest combination of orange and gray. I recently went

to Sports Authority and bought a Camelbak hydration pack, one of those backpacks you can fill with water—and you drink it through a long straw. Bill thinks it's the funniest thing.

The other day we were running in Central Park during a business trip for Bill, and after a mile in the heat, I was dying of thirst. "I need water. I need water," I panted. "Where's the water fountain?" Bill pointed to a stone fountain ten yards away, but I told him I couldn't make it that far. "Let's go, De-Pandi," he said. "Next time we'll bring your Camelbak." Bill makes fun of me, but I don't care. I like having a straw on my back at all times, so I can just pull it over my shoulder and drink.

Bill: She's such a drama queen. We'd just had a liter of Trump Ice in the hotel room, were five minutes into the run at best, and you'd have thought she went days without fluid.

Giuliana: Bill's gangster about hydrating. He'll walk a whole hour through the woods while holding a big bottle of water. Not me. I need my hands free at all times.

Bill: Once we were married, all the pockets in the world couldn't help Giuliana when we went hiking at Camelback Mountain in Paradise Valley, Arizona. We'd taken the Cholla Trail, which is almost a mile and a half long. It's a strenuous and steep hike, and the incline goes up about twelve hundred feet! There's all this dirt, gravel, and boulders, so it's hard to find your footing. We made it to the top OK, but as we started to make our way back, it began to rain.

Giuliana wouldn't let the weather slow her down, but I was nervous. It's a complicated climb, and we were scaling rock faces. I checked in to see how Giuliana was doing. "Step aside. I'm a hiker," she said. "I do this. This is my thing, *beotch*." Just as she said the "B" word, she slipped and both feet flew out from under her. Slam, right on her ass. "I have rods in my back! I have rods in my back!" she yelled. I was pet-rified. I was ready to call for an air ambulance, because I thought we'd need to get Giuliana air-vac'ed out of there. She's screaming, crying on the ground.

Giuliana: When I was in college, I had two metal rods surgi-cally attached to my spine because I had scoliosis. They're still in there. And when I hit the ground hard, all I felt was pain in my backside, but once I focused, I realized that my tailbone, and not my back, had hit the rock. But I started crying any-way, and then I became embarrassed that I was crying over a sore butt, so I told Bill I thought I'd hurt my back. "My rods!" I cried. "My rods are broken!" I was fine, but Bill went into hot EMT mode because he was so concerned. "Stand back," he told the gathering crowd. "I've got it. It's OK." He gently laid me down. "Don't move your head," he said.

Bill: That's what they say in the movies: "Don't move your head or your feet." I wanted to keep her stabilized in case she needed to be slid onto a board, like when a dog gets hit by a car.

Giuliana: Did he just call me a dog? He thought I was going to be paralyzed, and I, on the other hand, just liked the atten-tion.

BFFs for Life

Giuliana: Bill and I feel very strongly about doing hobbies as a couple; we're not big believers in having too many separate hobbies. That was something our grandparents did. They were part of that *Mad Men* generation that celebrated a real split between the sexes and their gender differences. Husbands played golf or caroused with their friends, while women played bridge and hosted lunches with the ladies from the Junior League. But that's not how we roll. Bill and I believe one of the keys to a good marriage is being part of each other's free time as much as possible. Yes, there's a time to have martinis with your girls, and for guys to hit a baseball game, but this kind of division shouldn't last a whole weekend. Over time, that can pull a couple apart.

Bill: My dad didn't play golf for eight hours on a Saturday; he worked around the house, and my mom helped. My parents were busy raising four kids on a limited budget, but they did it as a team. Our family was together all the time, whether it was in the evenings after we had dinner or driving from Illinois to Colorado on vacation. For my parents, I think raising us was their hobby.

Giuliana: My mom and dad also do everything together and always have. I think it's important to differentiate, too, that there's nothing codependent or pathetic about wanting to spend most of your free time with your spouse. It's not like I want to be with Bill so he can't spend time with someone else, or because it makes me feel uncomfortable to be alone. Or that I don't feel entirely whole if I'm not with him—please. I want to be with Bill because there is no one else I'd rather spend my time with. And Bill feels the same way.

Bill: Because of this, though, it's also important to encourage your spouse to be social outside your marriage. It's not our natural inclination, so a well-intentioned nudge can be necessary.

Giuliana: If Bill has tickets, say, to a Blackhawks hockey game, I might tell him that I'd love to go but if he wants to invite one of his guy friends instead, I'm happy to stay home. He rarely chooses to take a friend when I give him the option,

> *"We love a couple's Thai massage at Siri Thai Therapy in Westwood, California. It's only $45 an hour, and the first time Giuliana took me, I thought the vice squad was going to kick down the door. The joint is seedy, but the ladies give one hell of a massage—without the happy ending."* —**Bill**

but I don't want to force my husband to spend time with me. That's sad.

Bill: We weave in and out of each other's hobbies, social circles, and families in a seamless way. We're passionate about each other, but we also have our own interests. Sometimes we invite the other person to be part of them, or maybe we do them alone—it ebbs and flows in a natural way. It's true that spending time together can be more trying since we live in separate cities, but we're with each other a couple days a week and on weekends; we want to make the most of that quality time.

Giuliana: For instance, we used to do different workouts and now we collaborate on them.

Bill: I like to spot Giuliana when she works with weights, and if we have something important to discuss, we'll have that talk at the gym. When we were negotiating our most recent house, we StairMaster-ed next to each other, so we could talk about how we'd finance renovations and decorating. Giuliana hates the StairMaster, but she climbed stairs in place for a half hour so we could talk and work out that great ass of hers at the same time.

Giuliana: Then again, there are some hobbies Bill will never like to do with me. When we were in New York recently, we spent the day on a long walk together. At one point, I noticed that my shirt was see-through and asked Bill if we could run into the Gap to get me a new one. Bill didn't mind, and even offered to go in the store with me. *Excellent!* I thought. *I get to do my walk with Bill and we get to shop together.* Inside, it seemed like Bill was browsing, but just as I said, "Hey Bill, look at that cute plaid shirt for guys"—he made it clear he was looking for help, not for fun. He wanted to get the hell out of the Gap. "She needs a T-shirt," he said to a saleswoman. "Where can she get a T-shirt?" We followed the woman upstairs to a table piled with tees, and in one smooth motion like a basketball player who goes for the shot, Bill grabbed a shirt, ripped-off the tag, threw me the top, and handed the tag back to the woman at the cash register. "Where's the shirt?" the saleswoman asked. "You can just scan the tag," said Bill. I put on my tee, and we left. So much for my walking/shopping friend!

Bill: I like to browse in Ace Hardware for new tools, go to car dealerships to check out the latest models, and drop by the cigar shop to stock up on my favorites, but I don't need Giuliana to join me for any of this. In fact, I like doing these things without her because I know she'd be bored senseless if she were with me, which would make me feel annoyed and rushed. I think that's normal, not to mention, healthy. There are limits to what you can expect your best friend to do.

Giuliana: To us, "husband and wife" is synonymous with "best friend."

Bill: I think it's a chicken and egg thing: you become best friends in your marriage by having common interests and hobbies. Your marriage is the product of the effort you put into it. You have that best friend relationship by making time for your spouse and trying things you wouldn't ordinarily try. Like me hiking, or Giuliana riding on the back of my motorcycle.

Giuliana: Think about what makes a close friendship work: best friends are trustworthy, safe, understanding, reliable, loving, accepting, loyal, forgiving, and respectful. Who wouldn't want to discover and nurture those qualities with the love of their life?

TIPS FOR TWO: Sharing Interests with Your Spouse

• Join your spouse at his/her favorite hobby to remind you what makes that person smile.

• While making time for shared hobbies, don't compromise your own interests for your marriage. You won't gain anything from learning to ski if adrenaline sports make you resentful.

• Save a few hobbies for you to enjoy alone or with friends.

• Encourage your spouse to discover new interests with friends and family outside your marriage.

• Recognize the qualities you look for in a best friend, and use these to become a better spouse.

13 Can't We All Just Get Along?

Come holidays or Saturday nights, we often feel as if we spend as much time keeping our friends and family happy as we do nurturing our own relationship. These connections were always our top priorities when we were single, so it was important to us that we invest ongoing energy and thought into helping everyone enjoy their roles in our married lives. The alternative? More stress than we're equipped to handle. Issues with in-laws, in particular, can put real strain on a couple's relationship if they're not in good shape, especially when they're between a mother-in-law and daughter-in-law. In one study, nearly two-thirds of female participants admitted to suffering long-term stress and unhappiness due to friction with their husband's mom.

We can't tell you how relieved we both were when we realized that we liked each other's family and friends. Have there been tense moments? Of course, but we don't let them interfere with our marriage. With family especially, we made an effort right from the start to deter nagging and bickering over

trivial matters by having dinner with in-laws, planning holidays well in advance, and joining our families for Little League games and the occasional Mass—often by our suggestion. We've shown our families that they have no reason to fear we'll neglect them or morph into someone they won't recognize, and so far, it's worked. We also go out of our way to demonstrate that our new and extended family is much more fun because our spouse is now part of it. When it comes to our friends, we've followed a similar route. Bill has a few buddies who disappeared once they were married because their wives didn't like their spouse's friends, and as a result, it was important to Bill that he not take the same path.

Not every couple has easy relationships with their collective friends and families, but we've noticed that there are things you can do to delicately improve this that involve, first, cutting yourself a break and, then, talking to your partner about establishing boundaries, expectations, and patience. After all, relationships with your spouse's friends and family were thrust upon you, and if the best you can do is muster up some respect for your new circle, we say you've done your job. Here's how we make the most of our time with each other's loved ones, and the challenges we've faced along the way.

Bill: My thorniest encounter with Giuliana's family happened when I asked her father, Eduardo, for his permission to marry her. Wait, scratch that. I had to ask Giuliana's dad *and* Giuliana's brother Pasquale for their blessing. It's always a family affair with those friggin' Italians.

Giuliana and I had only been together for eight months, so I don't think anyone saw my proposal coming. We were at her sister Monica's house for Thanksgiving, and Giuliana's whole family was there. I needed to pull Eduardo aside in private, and I wanted to bypass Monica's husband, B.Z; he's a nosy guy. I was also afraid that if I got too comfortable with her female relatives, I'd slip about the proposal. So I laid low with a glass of wine and plate of antipasti, glued to the Macy's Thanksgiving Day parade, until I could make my move.

Giuliana was in the kitchen with her sister, mom, and the rest of the ladies. They were putting the finishing touches on two twelve-pound turkeys and clucking about who knows what. Meanwhile, B.Z. and the other husbands were preoccupied with the kids. I knew I had to take advantage of this rare lull in activity—they don't come often during holidays with the in-laws. I approached Giuliana's father with as much confidence as I could summon. Too bad I was scared to death.

"Want to go outside and smoke a cigar?" I asked Eduardo. Pasquale overheard us and elbowed his way into the powwow. "*We'd* love to," he said. I knew I wouldn't be able to shake Pasquale—he's almost as nosy as B.Z.—so I grabbed a few extra Cubans and headed out to the patio. I took a few puffs from my Artruro Fuente Hemingway and poured my heart out to these men. "Giuliana makes me very happy," I said. "We're really in love and I'm planning to, you know, take this to the next level."

Giuliana's dad doesn't speak fluent English, so it wasn't clear to him that I was talking about marrying his daughter. "What do you mean-a?" Eduardo asked in his thick Neapolitan accent. "What is this take-a to the next-a level?" He looked at Pasquale for help and then back to me with raised eyebrows. Pasquale didn't utter a word. "You know," I stammered. "I'd, uh, like to ask her to marry me."

Eduardo and Pasquale were quiet for a moment, and then Pasquale began pelting me with one question after the next. I suddenly felt bad for his daughter Olivia, whose fiancé is in for a real treat when she's old enough to get married. "Do you have the means to take care of my sister? Where will you two live? Have you ever been married?" I began to sweat. Pasquale took another puff from his cigar. Giuliana's brother and I get along great, but we also like to rib each other, so I couldn't tell how serious he was about all this. What I did suspect is that if I assured him that his sister would be financially taken care of, he'd leave me alone. "Neither of you have to worry," I said, in my best competent husband voice. "I just purchased another building, my speaking business is busier than ever, my investments are booming . . ."

Pasquale smiled, and Eduardo waved his hand as if to say "Enough." Then my future father-in-law went in for a hug. "Billy," he said, patting my back. "You-ah make-ah my-ah Giuliana ah-very, very happy." It was a nice moment with Eduardo and yes, even Pasquale, the patron saint of ball busting. And believe it or not, they kept my secret right up until I proposed.

The Gang's All Here

Giuliana: My parents were very accepting of Bill from the start. And apart from the Chris incident, I never put him in a situation that felt like a sneak attack.

Bill: Giuliana's trying to say that when she first met *my* family, I fed her to the wolves. It was very early in our dating relationship, and I'd decided to have dinner with my mom, all my sisters, and all of my friends. We sat outside . . .

Giuliana: That's not how it went. Let me tell this. The first time I came to Chicago—we'd only been dating a couple of months—Bill asked to take me out for tapas. I thought it sounded like an awesome plan until he told me that the reservations were for six p.m. "We're going that early?" I asked. "Can't we go a little later? Take a nap first?" And that's when he added, real casual, "I actually have some people joining us. I want you to meet my sister Karen and a few friends." I had

Tips for Auditioning Couple Friends

1. If they mention the words *swingers, hedonism,* or *open marriage,* grab your spouse and run to the nearest exit— without them.

2. If they think having affairs is "inevitable" in marriage, comply with escape route from Tip 1.

3. If they badmouth and spill secrets about their other married friends, cut them off. They will do the same to you.

4. If they share your morals and goals in life, plan a couple's trip to Cabo and call it a night.

no choice but to be cordial, since I didn't want to sound too demanding so early in our relationship. I also knew Bill's friends and family meant a lot to him.

Well, when we showed up, the welcoming committee was out in full force: his three (yes, three!) sisters, a couple of their husbands, his mother, three of his best friends, and two of his nieces—all of whom couldn't wait to meet me. We were a table of thirteen! It was very intimidating. His entire network was there to size me up.

Bill: It was a social thing. Nobody was sizing her up.

Giuliana: Oh, come on. Bill doesn't like to make a reservation without asking everyone but the mailman for his opinion; I'm not surprised that he wanted to invite the neighborhood to meet his newest girlfriend. Anyway, I naturally felt like I had to be "on." Even if everyone else was having their own conversations, all eyes were on me. I felt like the new panda at the zoo. If I made a comment to his sister Karen, it was as if someone turned down the volume on all conversation because they were trying to hear what I had to say to her. And if I talked to his friend Janel, who he's known for years, forget it. Let's just say a man's female friends can be more judgmental than his buddies. But it was fine, because each person was nicer than the next. His friends and family are so warm.

Bill: Giuliana's always made an effort with my family. I think that's why they love her so much.

Breaking the In-Law Code

Giuliana: Once I met Bill's family and friends, there were things I did to keep from having that all-too-common tug-of-war with them over their son/brother/friend. For starters, I found that being kind, generous, and accommodating can really throw everyone off guard. When parents and siblings, especially, can tell that you're marriage material, it's common for their needy instincts to kick in. They're scared of being neglected or lost in the shuffle, and can feel threatened by your influence on the person they know and love. So one thing I did, and still do, with Bill's circle was never say "no"—which is easy for me, because they're such great people. But I've never denied Bill's parents a dinner invite, or siblings an afternoon of our time. In fact, sometimes I'll even say to Bill, "Call your sister Karen, and see if she wants us to pick up a few pizzas and pasta. Let's hang out with the boys and have dinner at her house." Karen's always

> "We like to make a secret game out of annoying things our in-laws say. For example, every time Bill's cousin Mickey talks about his great golf game, we sip our drink. We're the only ones in on the game, which makes family dinners much more enjoyable." —Giuliana

surprised but thrilled. We don't have to stay all night, but the gesture means a lot to everyone. I also figure that these types of efforts will score us a free pass, should we ever need to get out of a barbecue or christening because we've made other plans. If you put in time with family and friends to show that you enjoy being part of their world, I've found that they won't feel grabby and offended when you do your own thing. I learned a long time ago with my own parents that a little effort—like driving my mom to a doctor's appointment or joining my father for dinner at his diner—goes a long way. Parents are just in-laws in training, so I cut my chops at home.

Bill: Nobody likes to think that someone is going to change a family dynamic they've spent so many years cultivating and relying on. So when a new influence like your spouse enters the picture, the best thing this outsider can do is reassure everyone that he/she will enhance, not subtract from, the life that your family is used to. This promotes trust and helps everyone let down their guards. We do this, and our families never bug us to spend time together—if anything, we bug them.

Giuliana: We bug Karen all the time! And the other day, Bill's mom asked us to join her for church on a Saturday, though we usually like to go to Mass on Sundays. I had a headache and would rather have watched reruns of *Keeping Up with the Kardashians,* but I thought it would be the nice thing to do and make Bill's mom feel like I'm all about family. It's worth noting that Bill's mom didn't push at all, she just asked. So we went to church, and I realized during the sermon that I did this as much for Bill, as I did for his mom. Like a lot of men, Bill was very worried about how his life would change when we got married, and I want him to always know that he doesn't need to worry about my family values.

Bill: Family is important to me, and I didn't want to marry a woman who tried to harm those relationships.

Giuliana: In a similar vein, I'm careful to always make the first move when we're making holiday plans. Splitting this time is difficult for a lot of newlyweds, so whether it's Thanksgiving, Christmas, or Bill's birthday, I always call his family to ask if *they'd* like to join *us* for the occasion, and express how happy we'd be if they did. I don't even ask Bill about this first; I take the initiative, and it sets a precedent that it's safe to do the same. I think that if you begin your marriage as a good wife or husband, then extended family and friends have nothing to criticize or be afraid of. There's no reason for their minds to wander: "She must not like me. I wonder if it's OK to call? I'm not going to make an effort if she doesn't." It blows to be on either side of that conversation. We never want our in-laws to feel like spending time with us is an imposition. If anything, they're adding to our life in wonderful ways. Bill and I do this a lot by playing along with our families' efforts to connect. Bill's mom likes to show me "new features" on Facebook that I've secretly used before, and Bill acts surprised when my father tells him about a new cigar he's "discovered."

Bill: You know what I think helps ingratiate me with Giuliana's family? The small stuff, like when Giuliana's parents travel, I make sure to get their flight information so I can upgrade them with my miles. I fly so much for work that it's nothing for me to do this, and yet they really appreciate it. Or if her family flies into Chicago for a family weekend, and Giuliana hasn't arrived yet, I'll spend the day with them before she gets there—I'll show them around, take them to Little Italy for a cannoli. I love Giuliana's family, but more than anything, I do these things for her.

Giuliana: Now I realize that we got lucky, because I adore Bill's family, and he really likes mine. But I'm aware that not everyone has such fortunate relationships with their in-laws, and that it can be hard on a couple. I don't know the stress of a needy mother-in-law who hounds me to take her to lunch twice a week or suggests better ways to cook for her son; and Bill's never experienced a father-in-law who demeans his job or makes fun of his Midwestern upbringing. These are annoying qualities in any people, much less those who call themselves "family" just because you chose to marry their child. I get that, but it helps to find ways to deal with infuriating interactions or else they'll just fester and wreak havoc on your marriage.

From what friends who've been through this ordeal tell me, in-law conflicts can cause disagreements about how to build your own marriage and establish values and routines that work for your household, which may operate differently from the one you or your spouse grew up in. (Nobody likes an in-law who butts in on how to decorate your living room, take care of your health, or raise your little ones.) Underlying concerns about "stealing" or "changing" a spouse, like Bill mentioned earlier, are also big in-law complaints. These and other things come up, especially when a couple is newly married and families are finding their sea legs, which makes that first year dramatic to say the least. The ironic thing is that when a spouse doesn't get along with an in-law for any reason, the ensuing argument can put as much stress on the marriage as the original disconnect does. So it's worth putting in the work to figure out how to iron out these kinds of wrinkles.

When you're uncomfortable around in-laws, I think you need to establish boundaries. What a lot of new spouses don't get is that you can be close to your families but also keep aspects of your marriage from them. You have to preserve your marriage first, and resist the urge to say that one person's family is "better" or acting like you want your honey all to yourself.

If you can take the emotion out of it, being good to your in-laws is about being decent to people who'll be in your life forever. Like it or not, in-laws come with marriage, so if you can't enjoy them, then you should just try to grin and bear it. I think dealing with in-laws can be a lot like going to the dentist. Nobody like the visit, but if you want teeth, you have to endure the occasional scraping, drilling, and bloody mouth.

Bill: I think you need to treat your spouse's family the way you want them to treat yours (even if you don't get along with yours, you don't want other people to treat them badly). You can't change your spouse's family, so you need to change how you handle them. And if things get ugly, your spouse can always step in to help. He/she has had years of practice at handling their fickle ways, so talking to them on your behalf or interjecting during arguments can help.

Worst-case scenario? Just be polite. If you can accept that your relationship isn't going to be the same as a mother/daughter or father/son bond, it's easier to deal.

Giuliana: I say worst-case scenario, turn your in-laws' antics into funny stories for your friends. Sit politely at the dinner table, listen to all their rude or crazy comments, and take notes on your phone about their "greatest hits." Of course, you can't let your spouse know you're doing this.

Bill: DePandi, that's terrible!

Giuliana: Hey, you do what you can to get by. It also helps to remind yourself that your in-laws raised their son or daughter to be the amazing person you love. They can't be all bad, right?

The Friend Factor

Giuliana: In the beginning of my relationship with Bill, I paid attention to the friends Bill spent time with, not because I'm a possessive freak, but because it said a lot about Bill's personality and values, and I was still learning. And you know what I discovered? That Bill's loyal, generous, and really likes to drink fine red wine. Who he hung out with also told me about what was going on in his life, and what was important to him at the time. For instance, if Bill spent a lot of time with his super sharp work friend Jon, I knew he was negotiating a deal for his company; but if he had a lot of happy hours with his wild friend Jimmy, I knew Bill was stressed and needed to let loose and have a few laughs. Bill leans on his friends a lot, so recognizing the roles they played in his life

When Her Friends Meet His: Lessons Learned

• Two hot single friends don't always make a match, especially if your wife's friend is looking for a husband, and your husband's friend is looking to get laid.

• Seating two friends next to each other, just because they both like vodka, might not be the best idea at a wedding or dinner party. Happy drunks will either lead the gang in a Conga line or hold each other's hair back while barfing in the powder room. Both scenarios stink.

• Pairing lifestyles works! Our good friends, the Harrises, live in the suburbs and have three kids. Our other dear friends the Millers, live in a suburb ten minutes from the Harrises and have three kids. We invited them all out to dinner on a "friend blind date," and now they're buddies for life.

helped me to appreciate him and them. When we got married, it was clear that we had to figure out how friends fit into our relationship. In a lot of ways, they're an extension of our closest family.

Bill: It was very important to me, early on, that my friends were included in certain plans, because I wanted to preserve the friendships I've had my whole life. I didn't want this dynamic to change. To put it in perspective, I'm still friends with people I've known since I was fourteen! I've always known that whomever I married needed to accept my friends. That was a deal breaker in my book. I've seen so many guys I know get married, and then I never see them again because their wives didn't like hanging out with their buddies.

Giuliana: We love seeing all of our friends, whenever we can. I can count my good girlfriends on one hand, but Bill needs an octopus with eight limbs and many suckers to help count his. I like a lot of Bill's friends, though there are a few I'm not crazy about. That said, I include them in our life the same way I include his friends that I do like. If I'm not nice, the only person that hurts is Bill. And why upset him? He also knows who they are, and it almost makes it better because after a bad night, he'll say to me, "Thank you for being so nice to them." And I'll always say, "Of course, honey. I wouldn't act any other way. I'm not going to hurt you because those guys are annoying. I'm not going to let that affect our relationship or your relationship with them."

> *"Once you're married, there's no need to have any sort of relationship with your exes. You can be cordial if you bump into them in public, but beyond that, you're playing with fire if you choose to have casual dinners or talk until midnight as friends."* —Bill

Bill: Giuliana is very patient with my guy friends. More than anything, though, we like to go out with other couples, whether they're married or dating. And if we see single friends, we ask them to round-up a guy or girl for the night. It's easier to go out in even numbers.

Giuliana: We recently went to a Blackhawks game with a new couple we'd met. It felt like we were on a date! The guy plays for the Bears and his wife is really cute, a Realtor. They're cool, so nice, and a lot of fun—and the day after the game, we were wondering what they said about us, if they were going to call, and when we'd see them again. We even mentioned going on a cruise together—how hilarious is that? It's nice to meet people when you're an adult who share your values and interests. It's especially nice because right now we don't have kids, so that gives us more freedom to be social and travel on a whim. Or we can spend time with friends who have kids, and be flexible about when and where we hang out. We're an equal opportunity couple.

At the end of the day, we want to spend time with good people. That's why we don't have a lot of friends in L.A. A lot of L.A types are superficial. Our friends are mostly in Chicago and on the East

How to Win "Best Spouse" Among Your Partner's Friends

• Laugh at everyone's jokes, make a few of your own, and be as accommodating as possible.
• Compliment each person at least twice a night. *"Dude, that watch is sharp! or Wow! I love your sweater!"* It shows you're friendly, confident, and not easily threatened.
• Don't attach yourself to your spouse all night.
• If friends are single, be their wingman/woman to help them meet a hottie at the bar.

Coast. They talk about things that matter and care about how we're doing.

Bill: As much as we love each other and like spending time together, it's healthy for us to go out with other couples. We're still together, but when we take a vacation to the Palms with Jon and Alli or go on runs with Jerry and Missy, it adds some zip to our marriage.

Giuliana: This past year, Bill suggested we go to dinner and a movie for his birthday. "No way," I said. "We need to invite other people. It's a special night!" So I arranged a fun dinner with eight of our closest friends at Il Poggiolo in Hinsdale, a suburb of Chicago. It was amazing. You laugh in a different way with your friends than you do when you're with your spouse. Sometimes I'll see Bill talking to one of his guy friends, and he's laughing so damn hard at everything this dude says, and I'll think to myself, "I am so much funnier than that guy. Bill never laughs like that at my jokes." But it's just a different dynamic, and I realize it's good that we have that. I like seeing Bill do deep belly laughs like only a guy can make another guy do—and the same with my girlfriends. I'll never forget the time I told them how I tripped over my dress on the red carpet, my boob popped out, and I had to quickly get it back in before the photogs made me the next Tara Reid. Oh my God, we rolled until our mascara ran.

Bill: Learning to navigate your relationships with friends and families as a married couple is worth every laughing fit and headache you ultimately experience. Sometimes we have to force ourselves out the door, but when we wake up next to each other in the morning and conduct a postmortem about the previous night, we wouldn't trade *that* memory for the world either.

TIPS FOR TWO: Playing Nice with In-Laws and Friends

• Initiate visits and calls with your spouse's family and friends early in your marriage. This will help everyone feel less threatened, and set a precedent about caring for each other with respect.

• Treat your spouse's friends and family the way you want him/her to treat yours.

• Ingratiate yourself with small but kind efforts, like picking up groceries for your mother-in-law or picking up the tab for your wife's single friend when you're out to dinner.

• If you have problems with your spouse's family or friends, establish boundaries and expectations that help you cope in a civil way. Ask your spouse to run interference if necessary.

• Encourage your spouse to spend time with his/her friends, either alone or as a couple. The unique joy they bring into your partner's life will also enrich your marriage!

14 It's the Gift That Counts

We think it takes tremendous talent to "give good gift." Put simply, the goal is to buy a material item, within a realistic budget, that celebrates a recognized holiday or special occasion. But a present can represent a whole lot more than this, since we often interpret gifts as symbols of how well we think our spouse knows, cares for, and appreciates us. Research shows that a great gift can make couples feel like they're with a kindred spirit, while bad gifts can cause them to question their compatibility. Who knew a bouquet of flowers or new George Foreman grill could take on such loaded meaning? Actually, we did. This is an ongoing, um, situation in our relationship.

Bill really loves putting a lot of thought and planning into his gifts for Giuliana—from expertly timing a surprise vacation with friends to casually noticing a purse she dog-eared in *Vogue* and buying it for her later. Giuliana, on the other hand, is a tad lazy when it comes to choosing and doling out gifts. She likes to blame this on her family, who are rarely sentimen-

tal about special occasions; impressing Bill with a treat to celebrate those days can be a real effort. Giuliana thanks her lucky stars that she married a man who knows how to make her feel special when they celebrate their anniversary or Valentine's Day, but it's complicated and intimidating to return the favor. Consequently, she gives up easier than she should or even tries too hard, and the whole effort falls apart.

Giving your spouse a gift he/she appreciates forces a couple to discover the right amount of effort, thoughtfulness, and understanding that a partner needs. And since gift-giving habits are often rooted in family tradition, it helps to look at each other's pasts. We've found that a good gift is something your spouse wants and not something you wish that person would like—or that you want for yourself. And sometimes the best gifts, like your time, don't cost a thing. Here's how we've handled our own gift-giving debacles, and lived to shop another day.

Giuliana: Any other woman might swoon over a husband like Bill, who enjoys giving gifts as much as he likes receiving them. But to me, this character trait can be a total nightmare to live with. Anniversaries, birthdays, Christmas, you name it—Bill plans to make every holiday as special as he can, and outdoes himself every time. "Our anniversary is coming up," he'll say, at least three months in advance. "What do you want? Where can I take you? How can we make this one count?" Or even more frustrating, he'll say, "Pack a bag! We're going on a surprise trip!" and then kidnap me, drive to Laguna, and check us into a hotel for the night.

I know, I know. I sound like a spoiled brat; a creative hubby is, in itself, a special gift, right? While there are worse things than marrying a gift-giving savant, the bigger problem for me is that I suck at coming up with good present ideas, and I can't even keep up with Bill in this way. I'm more likely to buy Bill a new shirt or watch, maybe before or even after a holiday rolls around (so I can get it on sale), and then ask him if it can count as his gift. This way, Bill gets a treat that he wants and it's one I've given him. This seems like a win/win to me, but Bill rarely agrees.

Last year for our anniversary, I forgot that Bill and I talked about the types of gifts we'd give each other for this occasion, partially to make the whole gift-giving process easier on me. We'd decided to surprise each other with a gift we'd mentioned wanting but would never buy ourselves. Why I agreed to this plan, I have no idea. I can't even remember to buy the right present when I'm told exactly what to get, never mind when I'm not and have to lean on my own creativity and memory. So on the morning of September 1, Bill handed me a beautiful blue Tiffany box with a stunning cross inside. I've always wanted a diamond cross, but I forgot that I'd told this to Bill all the way back when we were dating. He also gave me a beautiful bouquet of flowers with plenty of white hydrangeas, my favorite.

After Bill fastened the cross around my neck, I gave him a big kiss and thanked him profusely. "And *your* gift is coming tomorrow," I told him, with the kind of doe eyes that make Bill melt. "I'm sorry, honey, but it didn't arrive on time." Too bad I was fibbing. I'd had a distracting week at work, and forgot about the vow we'd made to buy the other person a long-desired token. "You didn't get me anything," he said. "It's fine"—though we both knew it wasn't. "No, no," I said. "I did. I did. You just need to be patient. That damn FedEx."

Over the next few days, I panicked and looked for inspiration wherever I could find it. Since I practically live at my office, I spent a lot of time rummaging through old event swag and piles of giveaways that publicists sent the E! Channel for product placement. Alarm clocks, cologne samples, salon coupons—all good stuff, but nothing that was personal enough for an anniversary gift. Eventually I spied a brand-new iPod Nano on my bookshelf, covered in dust but in working order and still sealed in the package. *Ooh,* I thought. *Bill did mention needing an iPod a few weeks ago* . . . There was no time to overthink this present; I had to make good on my promise before too much time passed and Bill began planning for next year's awesome anniversary gift. Just in case an iPod didn't say "I love you" the way jewelry does, I bought a pretty gift bag and tissue from CVS to class it up.

Bill: I waited patiently for this "amazing gift" that Giuliana had promised me for about a week. And then one day, I came home and saw the gift bag on our coffee table. She didn't even bother to wrap the present, and she'd tucked a makeshift card from the drugstore inside.

Giuliana: What?!

Bill: When I opened the bag—

Giuliana: Wait, what? I'm sorry, a "makeshift card"? First of all, people don't wrap gifts anymore; they just put them in pretty bags with tissue. Second, it was an awesome card with a romantic poem on it.

Bill: She's right. The poem was beautifully written, probably by some hairy dude who lives in a cabin in the woods and works as a professional card writer. But inside the bag was an iPod Nano.

Giuliana: They're like $100, retail.

Bill: True, but yours didn't cost that much.

Giuliana: Bill pulled the Nano out of the bag, and flipped it over to check it out. Just as a smile began to spread across his face, Bill took a closer look and then shot me this *You've got* *to be kidding me* glare. "What?" I asked. "Did I leave the price tag on? What's the problem?" Bill shook his head. "You're such an asshole." He laughed.

Bill: The back of the Nano was engraved with the words, "Happy Holidays from E!"

Giuliana: I was mortified but tried to cover for myself and quickly realized that even my crazy brain couldn't come up with a good excuse to get me out of this one. "Busted," I said. "But seriously, Bill, what's the difference between buying you a Nano and giving you one I already had?"

Bill: I told her that to start, the Nano was a pro-bono gift that her boss, not she, had thought of. Unless Giuliana is really good at playing dumb, though, I don't think she realized how bad it was to give me this iPod. I'm sure she thought her gift-giving skills were a little sloppy at the time, but I don't think she understood how easily insulted and hurt I could have felt.

Giuliana: I'm so not a gift person. I don't even recognize anniversaries as holidays that warrant a material purchase. Bill and I don't need anything, so he always says it's the thought that counts. But if my thoughts yield a lame gift, which they often do, then we're back to Bill feeling flustered and unappreciated. I can't seem to get it right.

Bill: Poor, poor Giuliana. Let's not forget that my wife made out with a diamond cross, here. In the end, though, I wasn't too upset and we were able to laugh about the iPod fiasco. I don't like to spend my money. So I was happy that she cut corners, even if it was at my expense. It's not as if this was the first time Giuliana stumbled at gift-giving, anyway.

It's Always Monica's Fault

Giuliana: My sister Monica and I were born three days apart, although Monica is five years older than me, so my birthday comes a few days before hers—and when we were kids, she let everybody know it. The only thing Monica liked more than gifts as a kid was attention, and for weeks leading up to her birthday, she always made sure she got both.

Growing up, Monica acted like God's gift to my parents, and they treated her like the golden child right back. They loved her so much and swore she was destined to achieve great things. "I'm going to be the first female president," she'd tell us during dinner, as I was like, "Awesome. Please pass the cannolis." And my parents believed and encouraged Monica, and even told their friends that their firstborn daughter was going to be the first female president of the United States—never mind that Monica was born in Italy, which disqualifies her. But whatever. Monica didn't turn out to be president of the United States, but she did turn out to be the U.S. sales rep for Versace while she was still in her twenties, which to my father, the Italian master tailor, is about on par with being our country's commander in chief. If your store wanted to carry Versace in the States, you had to go through her, and she'd advise you on what to buy seasons before it was in style. She acted as the gatekeeper for trends at high-end stores like Neiman's, Barneys, and Bergdorf, as she diligently protected our homeland from bad ruffles and pleats. While my sister got the fashion gene, I got the technie gene, and because my parents still can't program their TiVo but will always understand the value of proper stitching and hems, this secured Monica in her role as Best DePandi Daughter Ever.

Now every time Monica's birthday came around when we were kids, my parents made a big deal about it. "What are we doing for Monica's birthday?" they'd ask, forgetting to remember that mine came first. They'd always have some kind of family dinner for me, and then an event for Monica—a trip to the zoo with her friends, or a party with balloon animals. Sometimes it felt like they were too tired to celebrate twice in one week. Why we didn't share one birthday party, I still can't figure out. Maybe because Monica wanted the spotlight to herself. She *is* the center of the universe, after all.

For some reason, I expected things to be different on my sixteenth birthday, I guess because it's such a big milestone for young girls. I'd also just watched *Sixteen Candles* a few weeks before, and told myself that no matter what, my parents would never treat me like Molly Ringwald. On the big day, I waited for my parents to surprise me with chocolate cake, lots of presents, and maybe a surprise party. (I knew a girl at school who got a car for her sixteenth birthday, but I thought that expecting to find a cherry red convertible parked in our driveway was way too much to ask.) Instead, my parents talked about my sister's upcoming birthday plans on my birthday, which I'd hoped was their way of throwing me off for the big surprise that was coming. It wasn't. I let this go until dinner, when it felt pretty clear that my day would come and go without any candles if I didn't melodramatically point it out. "You know, today is my birthday," I said to my parents, all mopey. "How could you forget?"

As my parents began to fidget in their seats, Monica jumped in to rescue Mom and Dad from impending mortification. "This is your fault!" she said to me. "You should have told us it was your birthday. Everyone's busy, so not reminding us is . . . is . . . selfish!" In the end, my mom cooked me my favorite dish, linguini with creamy vodka sauce, and she brought out Sara Lee pound cake with a single candle on top.

Though my Un-Sweet 16 is my most dramatic birthday story yet, it's not the only time my parents bypassed special occasions—downplaying graduations and the Easter Bunny were also typical. Eventually, I became indifferent to calendar days written in red ink, and now, I have a total disregard for most holidays, because they weren't a priority to my family. When Bill gives me thoughtful gifts for these, it always comes as a huge shock, even though he's very consistent. It's been a lot harder for me to value occasions for Bill's sake, because I never grew up appreciating them. I'd been taught that they're frivolous days, but it's not always about me, and how I react to them. I see that now, and I've tried to make nice with my past, but it's a process.

Bill: Giuliana told me this story early in our relationship, so it always helped me understand why she's such a dunce at gift-giving. And I couldn't have had a more opposite experience as a kid. Holidays were always a lot of fun for me and my siblings, and my parents always told us when it was their anniversary; for birthdays, we had parties with our neighborhood friends. So celebrations were a given. They weren't taken super seriously, but they never went overlooked.

Giuliana: I think that my and Bill's pasts have formed our gift-giving sensibilities more than we like, or sometimes remember, to keep in mind. Bill has been very forgiving with me in the last few years, but he gets frustrated that I'm not more mindful about these things. I think Bill is still waiting for me to give him his version of the Tiffany diamond cross, which he thinks would be symbolic of how much I care about him.

Bill: Here's my deal on gift-giving: it's not about the gift or the dollar amount. It's about effort and thought. The reason I gave Giuliana a pass with the iPod is because she *did* put thought behind it: she knew I wanted an iPod, and there was one in her office, and so she gave it to me. When you know another person has put even a little effort into a present or a plan, and has taken the time to think about you, it makes you feel special. That's what life is about: knowing you're loved and knowing someone carved time out of their busy day to make your day better. I try to demonstrate this to Giuliana as often as I can.

Gift Horses with Laugh Lines

Bill: Giuliana gave me a bittersweet birthday gift last year, and at first, I was torn about whether I should feel impressed or insulted. But for the first time, she put a lot of effort into it, which meant a lot to me. It was really funny, actually.

Giuliana: My goal was to help Bill feel better about turning a year older, in a very practical way.

Bill: I was feeling pretty bad about turning thirty-eight—after all, forty is right around the corner. I'd begun to realize that my body doesn't recover after a workout the way it used to, and on days off from the gym, I felt aches and pains that I couldn't account for. I'd also noticed some crow's feet and laugh lines, and I'd begun to feel like everyone around me looked like a teen. So I was in a reflective mood, like, "Damn, I'm really an adult. Adulthood is here." Giuliana's gift-giving extravaganza was themed to make me feel better. It happened over a few days, in L.A. and Chicago.

Giuliana: We started off with a gift that would make Bill feel physically better in his own skin. My husband had been com-

Gift Ideas for Fussy Husbands

• The latest upgrade of his favorite gadget
• Your participation in his best hobby (go to a game, join him on a fishing trip, etc.)
• A day off from the kids, if you have them

plaining about this body, so I thought, *What's a good gift to get aging muscles? A treadmill?* But I thought a package to a Hollywood trainer would be cooler. So I talked to Gunnar Peterson, this brute guy who works with Tom Brady and Gisele, Reggie Bush, Sylvester Stallone, and tons of other muscley celebs and athletes, and asked him to come up with a workout plan to help Bill feel rejuvenated and young again. Gunnar may have taken my request a little too seriously, though, because the day after Bill's training session, he could hardly move—Bill was paralyzed. Gunnar worked him too goddamn hard!

Bill: Giuliana told him to give me the NFL training session, and I thought that sounded awesome. But that workout crushed me, *and* it made me feel even older than I already felt. And Giuliana's next gift, well, that was something else.

Giuliana: Next, I brought Bill to see Giuseppe, a pricey but talented hairstylist in Beverly Hills. Bill still goes to old barbers for ten dollar haircuts, so I thought it would be a lot of fun to try something younger and cuter—maybe a hip cut like Chase Crawford or Justin Bieber. But that's not what I ended up telling Giuseppe; when he and I spoke ahead of time, I got just a little bit carried away, and by the time Bill actually sat down in the chair we'd come up with a completely crazy hairstyle for him. My Italian cohort and I were having such a blast playing around with Bill's hairstyle it hardly occurred to me to ask him how young he really wanted to go.

Bill: Yeah, I looked like Alfalfa in *The Little Rascals*. My wife is a real comedian.

Giuliana: After laughing at him, I took some pity on my poor husband and let Giuseppe do the real deal: He gave Bill a beautifully updated version of his previous haircut. But I'd blown my chance to revolutionize Bill's life. I was zero-for-two.

Bill: The grand finale of my thirty-eighth birthday gift happened once Giuliana and I flew back to Chicago. On that Saturday afternoon, she blindfolded me, walked me to the car, and drove east. I'm not sure why, but I thought we were going to Wrigley Field to sit in the skybox with my buddies, and I was stoked to end my birthday on a high note, with a gift I could really appreciate.

Giuliana: In the car, Bill had his mind set on the game and wanted to make sure it went as he'd mentally planned it. "All right, listen," he said. "If we're going to Wrigley Field, please, please make sure I don't have to sing the seventh-inning-stretch song. Please don't make me do that."

Bill: I did it once, and it was really embarrassing!

Giuliana: And I was like, "Oh, you don't have to worry about singing . . ."

Bill: But when the car stopped and we took the blindfold off me, we weren't anywhere near Wrigley Field. We were in the lobby of a plastic surgeon's office! Giuliana had made an appointment for me to get some Botox.

Giuliana: Bill had been complaining about lines around his mouth and eyes, and on his forehead, and although I suggested staying out of the sun, he didn't listen. So I thought, "Let me get him a little Botox. It'll take five years off his face."

Bill: This was the furthest thing from a skybox I could think of. In the end, I did not get the Botox. People say you give gifts that you want to receive, so maybe Giuliana secretly wanted the package with three Botox sessions she so kindly thought I'd like.

Giuliana: Who doesn't want a little Botox? I thought Bill would be thrilled, but he wasn't, not even a little bit. I'd already paid for the package, so one of my assistants went under the needle instead. In short, for Bill's birthday, I had him injured, butchered, and insulted.

Bill: My thirty-eighth birthday montage was the most thoughtful gift Giuliana's ever given me. And I mean that in a good way—I think.

When Giving Is Worth More Than the Gift

Giuliana: When we go to Bill's family's house for Christmas, gift-giving is a big deal. Everyone gathers around the tree in a circle, and the kids open their gifts first. Then they go into this whole technique of distributing them. It's so organized and systematic. Now I know where Bill gets it . . .

Bill: For Christmas, we do a grab bag. We pick the name of one of our family members ahead of time, and then we buy that person a gift that fits into a $40-per-person budget. It's a challenge to find something that the recipient will like within that price limit, so it becomes a game. Sometimes we spend all year on a hunt for the best gift within that budget. It's good fun.

Giuliana: The whole point of this gift swap is to encourage everyone to be thoughtful, while also saving them money. It's a really smart way of doing things, but it doesn't come naturally to me. I think you have to have done this in your childhood to really master and appreciate it as an adult.

So every Christmas, without fail, I watch the guests at Bill's house open their gifts, and I'm always amazed. They think of the best stuff to get each other, and it's all so personal. Someone's always like, "Thank you, Mom! This is the scarf we looked at that day on Michigan Avenue!" And Mom's like, "I've had it wrapped for seven months." And I'm like, "What the hell just happened?!"

Bill always tells me to stick to the $40 limit, but I never listen to him. Because I'm not too original and creative with my gift-giving, I tend to fall back on gifts with a hefty price tag. Growing up, my Italian family was very stuff-centric at Christmas, so a good gift always meant an expensive one to us. Sometimes, we just got money, which was thoughtful in a different way.

But with Bill's family, I'll buy each person—not just the name I draw, but everyone—the hottest gift that year, like a fancy Nespresso machine, so nobody feels left out. And when they open their boxes, they seem appreciative enough, but I've yet to see one of my chic gifts in their homes. One year I got everyone a high-tech digital picture frame that was popular at the time. *Great gift,* I thought, *because you'd never buy it for yourself. Isn't that what Bill always says?* But there's a reason nobody buys themselves a suped-up frame: they don't use it! The worst was when one of Bill's nieces pulled her frame out of the box to start loading it with family photos, and we realized the frame had a $29.99 annual service fee! So I basically bought a gift that required a pricey membership, and that didn't go over well either with these $40 folks. But you know what they do like? When someone makes them a bracelet. Who cares if I think the beads cost eight bucks and the bracelet looks like something I made in high school when I tried to sell jewelry? The recipient is always thrilled because turquoise is her favorite color.

At the DePandi home, gifts weren't the product of sentiment. Christmas was an occasion to give lavish presents, but mostly because we needed or wanted them, and Christ's birthday seemed as good a reason as any to do it. Once, I crawled under the Christmas tree as a child and tore off a small piece of wrapping paper to peek at the gift beneath. When my parents caught me in the act, they didn't care. "You can open it," they said, which sucked the fun right out of being sneaky. "But don't you want me to be surprised?" I asked. "Nah," Mom said. "It's just a coat."

Bill: Giuliana does try with my family at Christmas. For me, however, she gets whatever is featured on the *E! News* gift guide. I find out what I'm getting when it airs about a week before.

Giuliana: He's right. Every day on *E! News* leading up to the winter holidays, we feature "Gifts for Him" or "Gifts for Her," and when it's time for the "Him" broadcast, I always make sure we're at dinner or out for the night so he doesn't watch it. But Bill has the show on TiVo for me, so if we watch it back, he always says things like, "Oh! A Brookstone wine cooler!" And I'll say, "So, um, do you like that?"—trying to figure out what to edit out of his Christmas list, because ninety-five percent of what I get him is on this guide. I do get Bill one nice gift that's not on the list, though.

Despite my source of inspiration, I fail to see the problem. "Do you want me to be happy that all my gifts were on *E! News*?" Bill said to me one year. "Uh, yeah!" I told him. "That's a new GPS! And the batteries are already inside!" Sure, the box had been opened and it came without instructions, but that doesn't discount the item itself. He also gets bummed that everything on our show comes from Brookstone, Best Buy, or Red Envelope. But let's be honest here: who *wouldn't* want a jumbo remote control?

Bill: Or a wine decanter from RedEnvelope.com . . .

Giuliana: That decanter's really pretty, by the way. We still have it. But I can't win for losing. This past year, I surprised Bill with a beautiful gift that wasn't on our list, but that too was a disaster. On Christmas morning, I gave him two garment bags with big bows on each one. Inside were two very nice trench coats.

Bill: "Which one would you like?" she asked me. "Whichever coat you don't want goes back to the store." Giuliana did her best Vanna White impression, while unzipping the more expensive item for me to see. "This one cost four times the amount of the other," she said, raising her eyebrows.

Giuliana: Bill chose the sleek, more expensive European coat, of course. But he thought it took all the romance out of the gift when I asked him to choose his favorite; he'd have preferred I give him two coats or picked one out on my own, which would have shown how well I knew his taste.

Bill: Who does that? Who says, "Here are your gifts, and now one is going back?"

Giuliana: What's so wrong? I thought I was doing Bill a favor by giving him options. I didn't want to stick Bill with just one trench coat he may not have liked as much. I wanted him to choose what made him happiest, and I wanted him to wear the happy item and think of me.

I pulled a similar stunt on Bill's birthday a few years ago with a suit order, which may explain why Bill was so feisty about the coat incident. Bill has a very similar build to Joel McHale, host of *The Soup*, so sometimes when Bill and I go out, and he needs a great coat, I'll cunningly steal one from Joel's wardrobe. "Here, Bill, you can have this," I'll tell him. And he'll get so excited when I tell him it's an E! wardrobe leftover, though it's

> ### Wives Are Always Thankful For . . .
>
> • Orchids—they're low maintenance and lovely
> • Subscriptions to all her favorite magazines
> • An all-expense-paid night out with her girlfriends

really from Joel's current closet (Bill wouldn't wear something that's borrowed). So Bill will wear the jacket, but he'll want to wear it again, a few weeks later, after I've returned it. "Hey, where's that gray jacket from last week?" he'll ask, and I'll say, "Oh, it's at the dry cleaner." And then Bill will never see it again. So for Bill's birthday, I thought I'd get Bill a suit like Joel's that he could hold on to and call his own.

Bill: I love Joel's skinny suits; the fit is perfect on me. So on my birthday, Giuliana asked me to meet her at work and brought me into her dressing room, where her stylist Jose, who's also Joel's stylist, was waiting for us. "Happy Birthday!" Giuliana said. "Jose would like you to try on a few suit samples, so he can custom fit some suits for you." Custom suits for my birthday? Excellent.

Giuliana: Once we knew Bill's measurements, I told him the suits would arrive in a few weeks.

Bill: That was two years ago. I still haven't seen the suits.

Giuliana: And he still talks about them. Every time Bill's birthday rolls around, I ask him if he'd like some nice sheets or maybe a dinner with friends, and he says, "Are you going to buy me sheets and bundle them with the suit?" Or, "That suit is taking a long time to order. Are you having it made in a town without a post office?" I tell Bill that I don't know what happened to the suits, but I think we never ordered them when we got busy with summer shooting. I always tell Bill I prefer him in his au natural birthday suit, anyway, but he's hard to amuse when he's mad.

Bill: When you're buying or giving gifts, it's not about what you want. It's about what the other person wants. And I wanted those damn suits. You know what else I'd like? A wedding album.

Giuliana: Bill thinks we have no real pictures of us, and that since I'm the wife, it's my job to be the designated memory keeper in our household. "We have no catalog of our memories together," he complains. "We don't own a photo album, and we never download pictures from our digital camera." But this doesn't faze me. "Big deal, Bill," I tell him. "We have a reality show. Can't we can get it on DVD and watch that? Oh, and remember when we were in *US Weekly* last week? That was a good shot." But Bill doesn't think magazines and reality shows count. "A paparazzi pic of us kissing on the beach in Cabo doesn't count," he says. Eh, tomato, tomah-to.

No surprise, then, that Bill also hounds me to order our wedding album. We've been married for a few years, but it's such a chore to choose the photos, organize them with the photographer, decide on a finish and font, blah blah. "My mom would like to see those pictures before she dies," he says. But Bill's mom is fine. She's seventy-five and has a lot of energy. More likely, the photographer we hired may be retired by the time I get around to contacting her . . .

Hey, wait a minute. I think I just figured out next year's anniversary gift.

TIPS FOR TWO: Give Good Gifts

• Don't judge a spouse by his/her gift.

• Always make an effort to let your spouse feel "known" by your gift. If your gifts repeatedly disappoint him/her, ask your partner where you fall short and how you can improve next time.

• Family traditions influence gift-giving habits. Ask a spouse's relative to brainstorm ideas!

• Use TV shows or magazines for inspiration, but always try to add a personal touch.

• The "right" gift can reinforce that we've married our equal, so choose all gifts with care.

• All that said, don't take gift-giving too seriously. Bad gifts make for good stories!

15 The Good Fight

We pride ourselves on marital teamwork, but when we fight, it can become an ugly battle. The alienation that follows can feel lousy, as can the stomach knots and silent treatment—and if an argument's not carefully resolved, its lingering effects can be just as upsetting as the verbal smackdown itself. Vocab to the rescue? A recent University of California, Berkeley, study shows that spouses who use couple-focused language like "we," "our," and "us" fare better during conflicts than those who don't. If tweaking our pronouns helps us feel connected, even when we're pissed off, we're all for it—and we recommend it to you, as well.

The most trivial spats feel awful to us, like when we scuffle because Bill doesn't replace the toilet paper or Giuliana uses his razor without asking. Because our long-distance marriage insists that we make the most of our bursts of time together, we've learned not to sweat the small stuff, but that doesn't mean we don't fight or get damn close to it. On a good day, we choose to talk through an issue and come up with a solution that helps us avoid future conflicts; on a bad day, we might come to this friendly place, but only after Giuliana erupts into tears or Bill stomps around the house. We also like to step away from bigger fights for an hour or so, and return to them with a clear head. Brawls, concessions, compromises, and apologies are part of every marriage, but what we think preserves ours is that we take our vows seriously. When we got married, we told our priest Father Mike that we'd love each other "till death do us part"—not "till one of us drinks all the milk without replacing it." We work hard at aligning our values and goals, and making our marriage thrive despite a rough patch. If we don't, forever can feel like a long time to spend with someone who upsets us all the time.

Oftentimes, the quickest fix to our heated arguments is remembering how good it feels when we don't fight. Rarely do we encounter a misunderstanding that burns us to the core— like when we met with Father Mike during (our second) pre-cana. Here's how we got past that train wreck, plus how we like to resolve our issues so we can get back to enjoying each other again.

Giuliana: Before Bill and I got married in Italy, we did a couple sessions of pre-cana. For those who don't know, this is a course that Catholic couples take before they're wed in a Catholic church; the goal is to help them find common ground on how they feel about certain marriage topics like compatibility, family values, conflict resolution, and so on. But a year after Bill and I tied the knot abroad, I learned that we weren't legally married in the U.S., even though I had a bona fide document from Italy to prove it. I found out when I tried to renew my expired passport, and I was told the wedding certificate wasn't legit, even though it had some Italian dude's signature on it and a fancy stamp that admittedly looked like I peeled it off a bottle of olive oil. "That's not legal here," the agency woman said. "That document could have been Photoshopped onto stationery from any paper store in town. Didn't you go to City Hall for your U.S. marriage license before getting married in Italy?"

Apparently not. I called my sister Monica, who had her wedding eight years before me on the coast of Naples, and asked if she married her hubby in the United States first. "Of course I did," she said, which basically confirmed she was the worst maid of honor ever (she was already on my shit list for wearing a scene-stealing, bright yellow Oscar de la Renta gown, with a train, to my ceremony). "I can't believe you didn't tell me about City Hall," I said. "Look on the bright side," she told me. "You're single again." Ha, ha, funny.

So Bill and I finally got our stupid certificate from City Hall two weeks after the passport incident, and to celebrate our "real" marriage, we had a second wedding in Chicago. But before we got hitched again, I wanted to repeat pre-cana. "But we've done it already," Bill said. I told him I wasn't sure if our prior counseling counted, since our wedding clearly didn't. "I don't want to jinx our legal marriage without doing this," I said.

Bill: I agreed to do "post-cana," but I think Giuliana just wanted an excuse for free therapy.

Giuliana: Let's just say I didn't see the harm in regrouping with Father Mike to talk about the ins and outs of our first year of marriage. Why not improve our relationship while it was still young and malleable? Bill and I check in with each other a lot, but we've never done it with a priest present. We're prone to exaggeration, so we figured Father Mike would keep us honest.

Bill: You mean, keep *one* of us honest.

Giuliana: I thought it was understood that we'd discuss our marital pet peeves with Father Mike. But Bill didn't read the memo, so he wasn't prepared for Father Mike's first question. "What would you like to improve about your relationship?" he asked. And though Father Mike threw Bill a softie, he fumbled. "Um, I don't know," he said. "I think our marriage is good." So Father Mike turned to me. "How about you, Giuliana?" he asked. I pulled out a list with bullet points.

Bill: That list. I couldn't believe she had enough to say about us to even constitute a list! I threw Giuliana a confused look, but she was unapologetic. "You knew what we were doing today," she said, "So what if I came prepared? I thought you would do the same." Can you guess which one of us did well in school, and who flew by the seat of his pants?

Giuliana: I wanted to make the most of Father Mike's time, so I put a lot of effort into my list. I wrote down that I hate when Bill doesn't make the bed and when he leaves his towels on the floor. I also said I'd like for him to compliment me every few days. I didn't have monumental complaints; I just wanted to address annoyances that, if fixed, could make our relationship better. As I ran down my punch list, Bill agreed to everything. "Noted," he said after each comment. "I can do that. Sure." Then I made an innocent request about bedtime noise that started a freaking war.

I explained to Father Mike that at night, I like to go to bed with the TV off. Meanwhile, Bill likes to fall asleep with the television on. I then said that it's especially difficult for me to fall asleep when Bill likes to watch programs that make startling noises and give me bad dreams. "So what kinds of shows is Bill watching?" asked Father Mike.

Bill: Careful Giuliana . . .

Giuliana: Bill likes to watch educational shows on the National Geographic Channel, Discovery Channel, and the History Channel. But when the shows are about, say, how airplanes are made, they make loud "vroom-vroom" noises that startle me while I'm drifting off to sleep.

Bill: But that's not what she told Father Mike. She didn't use the airplane example.

Giuliana: No, I couldn't think of the airplane example at the time, so I told Father Mike that sometimes Bill likes to watch prison movies.

Bill: "That's not true," I said, and I asked Giuliana what on earth she was talking about.

Giuliana: "Honey, you can tell Father Mike," I said. "You watch prison documentaries about those big dudes in jail who gang up on each other . . ." I was thinking about one we'd recently seen about San Quentin on MSNBC. "I'm sorry, what kinds of movies?" Father Mike asked. He gave Bill a startled-but-intrigued look, as if to say, *you just made my job infinitely more interesting.*

Bill: "What the hell," I said. From the way Giuliana explained the situation, and how Father Mike reiterated it and looked at me, it seemed like they were saying I choked my chicken until four in the morning while watching a bunch of jacked-up guys shower together in jail. But I didn't outright explain what I assumed. I just imagined we were all on the same humiliating page, and that Giuliana would soon back down from whatever ridiculous tale she was spinning so that we could move on to a new topic on her list. "Please take back what you said about the movies," I said to Giuliana. "You're making me look like a pervert in front of our priest." I could only imagine what Father Mike thought of us—the crazy porno-loving husband and his unassuming wife.

Giuliana: I had no idea why Bill was so upset. I couldn't figure out what was so skeevy about watching shows on MSNBC. So I thought that if I repeated myself, maybe this time a little more slowly and descriptively, both Father Mike and Bill would hear me out. "OK. We watch movies . . . about guys in jail . . . and they make weird noises . . . that keep me up at night." Father Mike took a deep breath and cleared his throat. "What kinds of noises?" he asked. "The noises go 'clank-clank, clank-clank,' " I said. "Doors open and close, men yell and grunt . . ." I looked at Bill, and I thought his head might explode.

Bill: "You're lying, Giuliana. I do not watch those programs!" I turned to Father Mike: "I don't know what she's saying. I've only watched . . ."

Giuliana: "You swear to God you don't watch prison documentaries?" I asked Bill.

Bill: "I've maybe watched two documentaries with her on, like, the National Geographic Channel," I said, and then: "Giuliana, I'd like to see you in the other room." I walked out.

Giuliana: We went into the kitchen, where I remained confused and embarrassed as hell. "What is your problem?" I asked. "What is *your* problem?" Bill said. "I can't believe you're telling a Catholic priest that I watch prison movies! You're lying in front of the priest." And I'm like, "You're lying!" And he's like, "You're lying!" And we went back and forth like this for a few minutes, until I felt bad for keeping Father Mike waiting and grew too frustrated to continue. We hadn't resolved much in the kitchen, except that each of us thought the other was delusional.

Bill: When we came back into the room, Father Mike composed himself. "What's the real issue here?" he asked Bill.

"What's really going on?" I looked at Giuliana, and she looked at me, and Father Mike looked at me. "What would you like to reveal about yourself to me today?" he asked.

Giuliana: "I don't want to reveal a thing," said Bill. "Not a fucking thing." Now I was mortified, and I didn't understand how this situation had escalated to such an extreme and irrational level. "Bill! Do not say the 'F' word in front of Father Mike!" I screamed, and then turned to the priest. "Father Mike, I am so sorry," I apologized, as I offered him M&Ms for his trouble. "You have nothing to apologize for," he told me. "Let's get back to Bill. Why are you so insecure about prison films?"

Bill: On top of feeling cornered by a lie, it was upsetting me that Giuliana wouldn't stop sucking up to Father Mike: *Bill, please don't curse in front of a priest. M&Ms, Father Mike? I don't know what's wrong with him, Father. He's never acted like this before.* Father Mike tried to soothe my nerves, but I thought he was patronizing at best. "You're very angry," he said. "Very angry."

What's Your Excuse? (These Work for Us)

"It's an Italian thing, that's how we roll."

"The Rancic genes made me do it. They are so powerful, I can't help myself."

"I have rods in my back from my scoliosis surgery. Can you carry it instead?"

"Honey, I just got off a six-hour flight. Can this wait until tomorrow?"

"These hormones are making me nuts and my ovaries are the size of grapefruits, so piss off!"

Giuliana: "Darn right I'm angry!" Bill yelled. "My wife told you I stay up all night jerking-off to prison porn! And I don't!"

Bill: That cleared things up.

Giuliana: It sure did. Father Mike went quiet, while Bill and I realized that neither of us was lying. We'd had a simple misunderstanding—a miscommunication issue. Because I'd used the words *movie* and *documentary* interchangeably, I guess it sounded like I was talking about porn, and with all those seedy details about grunting prison guards, well, you can see how Bill jumped to conclusions. But I don't think like this, and a documentary can also be a movie, so . . . whatever. I get that it totally came out the wrong way, but it took me a long time to catch on.

Bill: A few things set me off. I was embarrassed for obvious masturbatory reasons, on top of the fact that Giuliana had made a long list of complaints about us that seemed insignificant to me. I also thought she was lying to Father Mike to make herself look like the angel in our relationship. On top of all that, I didn't like the way Father Mike sided with Giuliana. I've known Father Mike my whole life—he's *my* family priest, not hers. A mediator should be impartial.

Giuliana: I think Bill was just mad because Father Mike and I are BFFs.

Bill: Well, it doesn't help that he obviously thinks Giuliana can do no wrong. Father Mike studied in Rome for ten years, so he speaks Italian. That's an automatic three points for Giuliana.

Giuliana: Whenever we see Father Mike, he whizzes past Bill to give me a big Italian kiss and embrace. *"Buongiorno, Come* *va? Tutto bene?"* We have these long conversations in Italian, while Bill stands there like a spare part listening to us.

Bill: They humiliate me by speaking Italian. He knows I don't speak the language.

Giuliana: I think I also made things worse by repeatedly asking Bill why he was making such a big deal about the prison movies—sorry, *documentaries*—as smoke was pouring out of his ears. If your husband's that upset, there's a problem. When we went to the kitchen, I should have asked Bill what was bothering him, instead of insisting that he was lying and over-reacting like a lunatic.

Bill: I felt embarrassed, frustrated, and deceived by my priest and my wife at the same time. I felt ganged up on. I also felt dis-respected, because Giuliana knew something was embarrassing me since I was clearly upset, and even if she didn't know what was bothering me, she should have stopped talking about it or at least slowed down. Giuliana can get so caught up in proving her point, and corralling everyone onto her side, that she forgets to notice how I'm reacting to the argument or conversation. She always brings a machine gun to a snowball fight.

Giuliana: Bill stewed for weeks, *weeks,* over this fight. It took him so long to shake how irritated and resentful he felt toward me for that whole priest/porn fiasco, that we eventually had to agree to disagree on this. The fight had become less about what was said and more about the fact that Bill was upset. In the end, it didn't matter if I thought I said "documentaries" or "movies." "Bill, I feel bad about you feeling bad," I finally told him. "Forget the fight. We need to figure out how to make us better." Just saying this calmed him down. I didn't need to do or say anything more.

Somehow, this has turned into one of our taboo stories that we don't like to revisit very often. Religion is important to both of us, so maybe mixing porn and priests in one context really threw Bill off. What's important is that we decided to agree to disagree. And that's OK, too.

If You Must Duke It Out, Wear Kid Gloves

Giuliana: When you and your spouse fight, you don't always need to decide on a winner, loser, or a happy compromise in between. Sometimes the best you can do is agree to disagree, and if you both resolve to do this, then that is satisfying enough. When Bill and I argue, we usually find a solution that works for both of us, and we rarely bicker or nag, but this isn't always realistic.

Bill: We do our best to stay in a positive place, rather than drift into a negative one. I rarely lose my temper with Giuliana too easily, and we definitely don't fight nasty with name-calling or storming out of the house in the middle of a fight. That's the worst. We do our best to talk about our problems and avoid the blame game, even when I'm partly responsible for doing wrong. We choose to confront topics instead of avoiding them by checking in a few times a week. We definitely mess up once in a while, but I wouldn't characterize our relationship by its arguments.

Giuliana: I think it's normal to have the occasional fight, and some might even say it's healthy. Standing up for your opinions in your marriage is worth the random scuffle, if you ask me. Bill and I had a life before we met each other, so our different backgrounds, upbringings, friends, and even finances affect the way we think and behave. We also blame a lot of things on my Italian background and Bill's Midwestern upbringing—it can be a culture clash. But at least we can call it like it is, and often laugh it off.

Bill: Once in a while, a fight can also result from guy/girl differences. Men and women look at things, and problem-solve, differently. That's easy to forget when you marry your best friend.

Giuliana: I think the best fighting-fair advice I ever got had to do with being rational: don't argue at night, and don't argue when you're hungry. That means it's OK to sleep on an issue (as long as you're not furious) if you promise to discuss it in the morning, and if you walk away from an argument to collect yourself for an hour, eat a banana while

> ### Fighting Words
>
> *"You'll hear from my lawyer in the morning!"* is one of the worst things we think a spouse can hear you say, even when you're joking around.

you're at it (it keeps your blood sugar stable). Taking a break from a fight is different from storming out of a room. It promises to pick up where you left off instead of abandoning a conversation, and spouse, out of anger.

Bill: A year and a half into our marriage, Giuliana and I fought about which in-laws to spend the Christmas holiday with. Long story short, we hardly spoke for eight hours! At one point, I left to see a movie and came back with a calmer head, which always prevails. But I told her I was going out for a little while and I didn't just leave without a warning.

Giuliana: Seeing a romantic movie during a fight might not be such a bad idea, actually. It could remind you of how much you love your spouse and how petty your argument really is. We got over that eight-hour fight because we realized that we're in this marriage together and neither of us is going anywhere.

Bill: There is no quitting at marriage. During our fight about the holidays, we said to each other: "I'm not leaving you; you're not leaving me; divorce is not an option." Once you cross that threshold, it feels easier to make amends. So when you take a break from a fight, the way I went to the movies, you're doing it so you can return to the marriage; not leave it. There's no, "Forget her, I'm out of here," going on. And if we have a fight that I don't feel we've resolved, I'll bring it up by checking in with Giuliana. That way we're removed from the situation, level-headed, and can focus on each other.

Giuliana: The one thing Bill and I absolutely swear that we will never do is hold a grudge. It's not even an option. We always try to put our egos aside, and push through the problem no matter how long it takes. It's better to get through a fight sooner rather than later though, and talk about what upset us, and how we can avoid this kind of confrontation in the future. Marriage isn't a duel to the finish.

Bill: During these talks, I always use that old "I feel" trick from talk-show psychology, because nobody can tell you that your feelings are wrong. I don't make accusations or finger point; I state the facts rather than take a personal jab, and then I tell her how much it made me hurt. I don't apologize as much as I should, though I don't know why. Maybe it's because I don't like to admit I'm wrong. I can, but most of the time I just don't have as much to be sorry for as Giuliana does.

Giuliana: Bill! You suck.

I Spy a Pissed-Off Spouse

Giuliana: Though Bill likes to talk about providing lots of solutions to lots of problems, he isn't always immediately clear about what's up. So I have to look for signs that he's upset. For instance, I know I've really screwed up or said something hurtful when Bill's eyes get wide like a kid who thinks, "Gasp! I can't believe you would say that!" And then he clenches his jaw, tilts his head to one side, and looks at me like, "You don't know me, and you aren't who I thought you were." That scares me and makes me feel disconnected from him—like I've massively disappointed him. There've also been times when I just laugh at this face if he's upset over something I think is ridiculous, like when I tried to lift small hand weights a couple of weeks after our IVF procedure against the doctor's orders. Of course, my nonsensical giggling caused Bill to get even more annoyed. I have bad nervous laughter, so I always need to explain myself.

When Bill and I are fighting, the truth about how he feels about the argument, or me at the time, is usually in the way he acts, not in what he says. He might say nothing's bothering him, but if he's on email while I'm trying to talk to him, and he's repeatedly saying "It's fine, it's fine," something is definitely not fine. There's often a whole subtext to our arguments, and most of the underlying meanings in his attitude fluctuations are found in his body language.

Bill: As for Giuliana, when she gets mad, she gets dead silent. I remember the time she was upset with me because she'd spent weeks hinting that she wanted to get engaged on Labor Day, and I hadn't popped the question yet (it was already October). We were en route to Hawaii when she asked me about it, and I told her, "Maybe we should get engaged some time next year? I was thinking the spring?" When we landed, Giuliana gave me the silent treatment for at least three hours—from the airplane, to baggage claim, to the car rental, and then for the forty-five-minute drive to lunch. I knew I could get her to crack by making her laugh, but I didn't know when. So I went into full-blown conversations with myself, as if everything were normal. "Oh! It's a lovely day," I said. "Look at Hawaii. Look at the sun! Look at the ocean!" We *were* in Maui, for God's sake.

Giuliana: "Ah, this is great," Bill said. "Do you like the weather? Me too. What should we do first? Really? OK." I just looked out the window of our rental Jeep the whole time. I was so mad at Bill. When we passed a restaurant called Cheeseburger in Paradise, Bill said, "Are you hungry? Great! Me too." I still hadn't said a word, and when we sat down—I remember that the hostess gave us a great table with a view of the beautiful beach—we just ate our burgers and fries and stared at the ocean. It was so awkward and awful.

Bill: To lighten the mood, I started making fun of Giuliana's skin.

Giuliana: I'd had an aggressive skin peel a week before the trip, and my skin was still red and peeling off like a snake's. As a result, I was wearing a huge, straw hat and giant bug-eye sunglasses to hide my hideous face. This wasn't making the situation any easier, by the way.

Bill: I had to do something to break Giuliana's silence, so I mentioned her face. "You want to go buy another hat?" I said. "You should buy a bigger hat, because that floppy one isn't covering your skin. Why don't we get you some SPF 80 for your scales? I think your face is peeling off."

Giuliana: That did it. I just started laughing. "That's not funny," I said. "I want to go home. I'm miserable." And with that, I started to talk. Because of my tantrum, we missed the first day of our trip to Maui, which wasn't worth it. I learned a good lesson that day, though: If you know you're not going to break up, find some way to work out an argument without the silent treatment. It's tormenting. I still go silent, but now it's less about me being passive-aggressive and more about me sending Bill a hint that we need to talk. OK, so maybe that's a little passive-aggressive. But I'm not perfect, and the short-hand works for us. Bill knows something is wrong if I go silent, so he'll ask me about it. "If you don't want to talk, tell me in one sentence," he'll say, which is nearly impossible for me, so this leads to a long discussion. "Is it because I'm leaving tomorrow, instead of after the weekend?" he'll say. And then I'll tell him it is, and we'll start to talk about it.

Bill: Giuliana's really good at leaving her ego at the door, though. I'll give her that.

Giuliana: I'd rather put my pride aside than have anything go wrong in my marriage. It's not worth it. It is also easy for me to say, "I'm sorry." It wasn't always this way, and it's not simple for me to apologize to other people in my life besides Bill. But when it comes to my marriage, I find it very comfortable to say it, because I think, *If that's what it takes, then that's what it takes.*

I also think it's harder to stay angry at your spouse than it is to make nice; it sucks up all the energy that we could be devoting to having fun. Whenever I'm angry, I always think about how awesome it feels when I'm *not* angry, and how good it feels when our relationship is harmonious. "I've got to get back to that," I tell myself. "This isn't fun." Being angry hurts the other person in the relationship, but it also hurts you. It's emotionally draining. I'm not suggesting that people should bottle up their problems, because then they're living a lie. But when Bill's aware of what behaviors upset me and vice versa, or we can read each other's body language as a fight's heating up, we can diffuse them before they fester. This is probably the reason that the longer Bill and I are married, the less we fight. I think a lot of people find the opposite to be true.

Bill: Six months into being married, friends and family asked us how we like marriage, and we told them it was amazing. "Talk to me in a year," they scoffed. Here we are three years later, and each one is one hundred percent better than the one before. We're making our marriage a ten; we want an A+.

Giuliana: Can I get an "Amen?" Where's Father Mike when you need him?

TIPS FOR TWO: Fight—for Your Marriage

• There's no one way to resolve every fight. Whether one person gives in, you both compromise, or you agree to disagree, what matters is that you both agree that this is the best way to handle it.
• Don't fight dirty. Name-calling or storming out of a room (which is different from telling your spouse that you need to break from an argument, but will resume in a bit) are toxic behaviors.
• The sooner you push through problems, in an open and direct way, the faster you can resolve them. Approach arguments as a challenge to solve, rather than a reason to hold grudges.
• Instead of pointing fingers, tell your spouse how his/her behavior made you feel. Nobody can deny the validity of your feelings, plus pointing out behaviors tells your partner what to work on.
• For us, humor is the great argument diffuser. Try it, and see if it works for you, too!

16 Mi Casa, Su Compromise

Since the beginning of our long-distance relationship, we've had to constantly remind ourselves that being together means caring for another person's needs and desires in addition to our own. While this sounds like a given, it took some getting used to for us, since living in different cities made it tempting to put our own wishes first. As a result, we were forced to learn the art of compromise sooner than most couples we know, and we found that it requires a certain level of self-awareness and communication skills that normally take years to develop.

Early on, Bill had to make numerous time and scheduling concessions to visit Giuliana in L.A. since she has a fear of flying, and when it was time to talk marriage, Giuliana had to consider whether she'd be willing to leave L.A. behind to live with Bill in the Windy City. These decisions required a lot of back and forth to arrive at a verdict that made both of us happy. Most people we know spend their childhoods envisioning a grown-up life they'd like to have, and then they chase it.

But when you don't even begin a relationship with someone who has a shared sense of place, all choices about your relationship from that point on can be a challenge; after all, the town you live in reflects your appreciation for distinct cultures, values, careers, and lifestyles. Though we've opted to thrive in two separate cities so far, it's been encouraging to see how we draw the line between compromise and sacrifice, especially when it comes to hunting for our forever home.

Good thing science says our mutual love for real estate is encouraging, even if it's taken us awhile to decide where to shop for it: Research conducted by the National Longitudinal Study of Marriage found that owning a house is a strong predictor of *not* getting a divorce, partially because it demonstrates commitment.

For us, searching for a home together has helped us keep the discussion going about what we want our lives to look like—from large backyards for barbecues to a sunken tub for alone time. After all, a home is more than granite countertops and ample closet space. It's where you collapse with your spouse after a long day, where you grow a family, and where you entertain friends and loved ones. But home is also where the concession is, since spouses rarely come to Realtor.com with the same expectations. Here's how we navigated our journey on the road to finally settling down.

Giuliana: About six months into our relationship, Bill and I were wild about each other, which meant we traveled a lot to spend quality time together at least four times a month. Unfortunately for Bill, the pressure to hop a flight weighed a lot more heavily on him than it did on me, since he came to L.A. more than I hauled ass to Chicago. The reason isn't because I'm one of those L.A. snobs who thinks the sun rises and sets on Tinsel Town; in fact, I think Chicago has L.A. beat when it comes to its people, parks, traffic, architecture, and real estate prices. (Their men clearly aren't bad either.) No, what made me want to hang back in L.A. is my serious, and often embarrassing, fear of flying that stems from an emergency landing I experienced in a plane as a kid, which traumatized me for life.

As a result of my near-phobia, I spent a lot of time and energy coercing Bill to visit the West Coast when we first dated by inviting him to cool dinner parties or fancy red carpet premieres in L.A. "Honey, you don't have the ocean in Chicago," I'd say. "Want to come out here and hang at the beach for the weekend?"

Or, "I just got invited to a movie premiere. Clint Eastwood, one of your favorite actors, will be there! Are you game?" And if Bill wasn't in the mood to fly west, I'd bust into my best baby talk. "I miss you so much and want to wake up with you Sunday-wunday, so we can roll around naked in bed all day." I'd say

> **Our Happy Home Essentials**
>
> • Sizable kitchen for entertaining friends and family
> • Fireplace for late-night snuggles, just the two of us
> • Sunny backyard to chill out, read a good book, and work on our tans

anything to keep from clocking three and a half heart-pounding hours in the seemingly unfriendly skies.

But after a while, I ran out of excuses and tricks. I suspected Bill's patience would soon hit a wall, too, if I kept begging out of trips to Chicago, especially since our long-distance relationship relied on travel give-and-take. Something had to give. So I decided to find out whether Bill thought we had a future together, and if he agreed that we did, I told myself I'd suck up my plane fears and fly out to see him more. All signs pointed to initiating a "Where's this relationship going?" talk, and let me tell you, that was a hell of a lot scarier than boarding a 757 aircraft.

Bill: We were five months into our relationship, when Giuliana hinted at whether or not I could see us spending our lives together as a married couple. I didn't tell her how much I loved her, what a great time I had when I was with her, or how special I thought our chemistry was. When Giuliana asked me about our relationship's future, I was in no place to lead her on with my feelings because I first needed to hammer down a huge logistic. "I can only marry a girl who will move to Chicago," I said.

Giuliana: That was a shocker.

Bill: Until then, I had been flexible about our relationship details, like where we went for dinner or how often I came to L.A., but settling down in Chicago was a nonnegotiable. And until now, I'd gotten the hunch that Giuliana wasn't crazy about my town because she coaxed me out to L.A. most weekends. I like L.A., but I wouldn't want to live there full-time. I have a close group of friends in Chicago, a strong base; it would be crazy for me to relocate. I also have three sisters, eight nieces and nephews, and a widowed mom I'm very close to. I didn't want to waste any more of my or Giuliana's time if she didn't want to eventually live in Chicago. This probably sounds like me wanting my way, but if Giuliana loved L.A., I didn't want *her* to sacrifice a big lifestyle change for *me* either. I didn't want to rob her of the chance to meet a guy who'd give her the life I suspected she wanted on the West Coast.

Giuliana: Call me a romantic, but I'm a fan of the saying "true love conquers all"—and while I'm not in love with L.A. the way I'm in love with Bill, I didn't expect him to pull what initially sounded like an ultimatum, before he even dropped to one knee. But I heard him out about his friends and family, and did some quick thinking myself. My sister and her kids are in L.A., but my parents, brother, and his family are in the

D.C. area, and my friends are spread out around the country. I do have two best friends who live in L.A, but no matter where we live, we'll always make it a priority to see each other. L.A. is such a transient city that I'm used to dealing with friends who float in and out of my life, anyway. So I didn't feel bound to staying in L.A., because I didn't have the emotional investment in my city that Bill clearly had in his.

More important, I realized that if we got married, our relationship wouldn't just be about what makes me happy. When I thought about the times that Bill was at his best when we were together, I realized it was rarely while doing something "so L.A." He didn't vibe with a lot of the city's traits, especially its lack of community. People are important to Bill. In Chicago, we can't get through dinner without five friends pulling up a chair and having a laugh. That would be hard to leave, even for a nomad like me.

Bill: In Chicago, people don't care who you are, where you work, or what your career is. All they care about is what type of person you are, and if you can have a good conversation and make them laugh. L.A. is the complete opposite. It's so spread out, you never run into anyone. And when you do, it's awkward. We'll be at a breakfast joint, and if Giuliana sees someone she recognizes, neither one says hello, because she may know the person through Hollywood, and who wants to talk about work while eating French toast?

Giuliana: This is all true, but I didn't think about these details until Bill asked me to. My biggest connection to L.A. is that I love it for work. I don't like it for my personal life, but before I met Bill, all I ever knew was my career. I also thought that if Bill wanted to marry me, we'd figure out our living arrangements after the fact. Until now, anyway, our feelings for each other came before commuting issues. I decided that if I wanted a life with Bill, all signs pointed to acting like one of those girls on *The Bachelor,* and breaking out some pride for my man's hometown.

"I hear you," I said. "I'm not as tied to L.A. as you are to Chicago, and I really love Chicago, so I'm open to moving. I'm an East Coast girl, anyway, so the Midwest is a great compromise for me. I'll meet you in the middle—literally, the middle of the country."

Bill looked relieved to hear this, but in coming weeks, I'd secretly page through bridal magazines while he snuck the L.A. versus Chicago topic into conversation to test my sincerity. If we were at dinner in L.A., I'd say, "Isn't this restaurant great?" and he'd sigh. "I think you like it here too much. Are you sure you can leave?" Or if we were at the beach, and I commented on the gorgeous weather, he'd remind me of how temperamental the skies could be in Chicago. *Shut up, and put a ring on it,* I'd think. And then I'd tell him I was positive about leaving for Chicago.

I kept my eye on the prize.

Bill: I did gauge the moving situation with Giuliana a lot, but in my experience, it's always easier to negotiate a deal before it's done, than after. Once it's over, there's no going back. So I wanted to be very upfront with Giuliana about my intentions, very clear and forthcoming, and I wanted to lay all my cards on the table while we still could. I also don't like giving or receiv-

---

Long-Distance Compromise Tips

• *Set phone dates.* Even though you're in two different cities, you can still watch your favorite TV show or eat a plate of spaghetti together.

• *Master spontaneous hellos.* Send lots of "hey sexy" texts, since you can't say it in person.

• *Make travel compromises.* Don't keep score, but do figure out an agenda that feels fair.

ing too many off-putting surprises, so I didn't want to get married and then tell Giuliana a year into it that I was glued to Chicago. I wanted to make sure we were both on the same track. I realize that some tracks change as you go through life, but I wanted our intentions to at least line up at the start.

Part of my insistence, I think, is that I've learned from some of my buddies' mistakes. I've seen people get into marriages that are total entrapments. After the honeymoon, someone is like, "We do it my way, or I get half your stuff"—you know, in the divorce. That's a bad deal.

Giuliana: When Bill talked about his friends this way, I often said, "Listen Bill, I get it!" I never got mad at him, though. I'd just let him talk about the entrapment issue and reassure him that that wouldn't be us. I knew we'd make our lifestyle work because I love Bill, and I'm always going to put love first. And I knew we could always make my professional life work, even if it meant commuting, since E! has an office in New York. I never wanted Bill to think he bought a bad bag of apples with me. I wanted him to know that if he proposed, he wouldn't feel scammed later.

I should add that when I agreed to Chicago, I didn't just roll over and concede. I talked to Bill, quite a bit, about how it was a busy and exciting time in our lives, and that settling down in a Chicago home couldn't happen for a while because of our careers. If I gave in on how we'd spend the future, I needed him to agree to stretching out our present plans. Bill was cool with this, and understood where I was coming from. Unlike a lot of personalities, we know we're riding a wave of popularity that won't last forever. Our fame is a blessing, and we'll go with it as long as we can or until we run out of gas.

Bill: Some women would have said "It's my way, or no way" about the living situation, but you can't always play the game on your home court. We eventually agreed that we'd get married within two years, and we'd settle down in Chicago to raise kids and plant roots. Until then, we'd have homes in both places, and she'd fly out to see me in Chicago twice a month.

HGTV Has Nothing on Us

Giuliana: Since our first date, Bill and I have had four homes in three years—and we're not even in the military. We've always been on the hunt for houses that mirror the kinds of people we are, and when we began dating each other, those qualifiers began to change. For instance, when we met, Bill had a condo in Chicago on Dearborn, a cool bachelor pad, and I had a chic bachelorette pad in Los Angeles, in a fabulous building in Westwood, right outside Beverly Hills. We both had great views, with doormen who got our mail every day. We lived like single jet-setters, zipping in and out of town for work and each other, and we relished every minute of it. But when we got married, we wanted homes that felt more permanent, stable, and grown-up.

Bill: So I sold my bachelor pad in the Gold Coast, which felt symbolic because I'd had some good times there on my own, and rehabbed a hundred-year-old brownstone for us, with views of Lake Michigan. This would be the home we'd settledown in, where we'd raise kids and plant roots.

Giuliana: We wanted to own a home that matched the kind of married couple we expected to be and suited the lifestyle we hoped to live. That brownstone was as much about a fantasy as it was about a practical roof over our heads. It was an accommodating and gorgeous space. I remember the first time I walked through that door, I pictured myself bouncing a baby

on one knee, as Bill made goo-goo eyes at the original wood-
work he lovingly restored. At this point, I still had my apartment in L.A., so we decided to keep that as our West Coast
space.

Or at least that was the plan. About six months after we
moved into the Lake Michigan brownstone, Bill's Realtor,
Laura, called him out of the blue: "I have a great couple that's
looking for a house in your area, and their offer on a home
similar to yours just fell
through. Are you open to
selling?" After he hung up
with Laura, Bill called me
to essentially ask if we'd be
willing to give our dream
home to someone else.
Imagine? "You'll never believe this," he said, "but
we have an offer on the
house." I could hear in his
voice that he was ready to
sign on the dotted line, so I
assured Bill that real estate

> **Biggest sacrifice Giuliana's
> made for Bill:** *"I watch*
> Modern Marvels *on the
> History Channel before we
> go to bed. Do you know how
> steel is made? I do."* **As for
> Bill:** *"I watch* E! News *every
> night so I can see how her
> hair and makeup turned out,
> and if her outfit looks 'cute'
> on TV."*

was his strength, and that I'd leave the decision up to him.
"All right then, it's as good as sold," he said. I was blue, but I
trusted that Bill had a bigger plan for us. He always does.

Bill: I'd given the potential sale a lot of thought before I
picked up the phone to call Giuliana—it was hardly a rash decision. I wasn't anxious to unload it for a few bucks. I was especially sentimental about the space, because I'd spent one
hectic year designing the rooms, closets, and outdoor space to
suit our future family's needs. When renovating a home, you
need to picture yourself living in it, and project that image
years into the future. So I had trouble giving this place up; I

felt as attached to the architecture as I did to the image I'd created of our married life together.

But when I looked at the reality of our immediate situation, the life I'd fantasized about hadn't truly begun yet. Giuliana had just renewed her contract at E!, so I knew we wouldn't live in Chicago full-time for a few years, and we hadn't even started trying to have a child. The home was three stories high, with four bedrooms, and here was a nice family who wanted to enjoy it now, and I really liked them. I thought it was a good fit, so we sold the house. It made sense at that time in our lives.

Giuliana: He had seller's remorse for a while.

Bill: I did. The decision made sense in my head, but I felt an attachment to the home for some time afterward.

Giuliana: I absolutely loved that house, especially the Juliet balcony off the master bedroom, but I didn't want to add to Bill's sadness by reminding him of how much those things meant to me. So to make him feel better, I secretly got the blueprint of the house from our architect and framed it, with the words *Our First Home* inscribed on a little plaque beneath it. That way, Bill could always remember the first home he built us, and this frame would come to every house we'd live in after.

Bill: When Giuliana gave me the blueprint, it was such a bittersweet moment. I didn't want her to think we'd never find a place to call home that she liked as much as that first place. I told Giuliana that I built us a home she loved the first time, and I'd build us an even bigger and better home again.

Giuliana: When we left that house, we moved into a temporary condo in downtown Chicago, and at the same time sold my

L.A. bachelorette pad and moved to Santa Monica, because Bill loves the ocean. We felt he'd embrace L.A. a little more if we were closer to the water. He likes walking on the beach and the smell of salty air first thing in the morning. In Westwood, we were close to shops that were fun for me, but that did nothing for Bill. I love the ocean, too, so I was happy to bend a little, even though my commute was now thirty minutes instead of ten, and Neiman's was no longer down the street.

Bill: She makes such big sacrifices for me. We live on the beach!

Giuliana: And then just recently, we bought our newest home— the replacement for our hundred-year-old brownstone—in a suburb of Chicago. It's really exciting for us, but this space couldn't be more different from the historic one we'd previously occupied. Bill was drawn to a huge home whose previous owners began construction four years ago, but had left it twenty-five percent incomplete.

Bill: They abandoned the project, so I'm coming in to pick up where they left off.

Giuliana: It's a big, gorgeous home, with five bedrooms for guests, parents, and future children. If that doesn't say "Welcome, family!" I don't know what does. I'm just excited by the area. Bill and I grew up in the 'burbs, but I crave that lifestyle more than he does. But Bill will get to build his dream home again, so that makes him super happy.

House hunting for our settle-down home really highlighted our differences, especially in how we define what a home means to us, so compromise played a key role in finding the kind of space that we could make our own. This new place, for instance, seems like a lot of space to me—I'd be fine in a cozy Spanish-style ranch. So I asked for a wine cellar to compensate for the fact that I'm afraid of staying alone in that big house when he travels for work. Pinot noir is always a nice companion.

In a lot of ways, this home suits both our needs. Bill and I both wanted a big yard, since he has dreams about grilling meat, and I long to entertain family with whatever he pulls out of our huge Sub-Zero fridge and cooks on his Weber. Bill was a typical guy about some priorities. Men always talk media rooms and bars, and Bill was no exception. If he could have a bar in his bedroom, where he'd pour himself a nightcap before climbing into bed, he'd be in heaven. The women I know just want a comfy home with an updated kitchen, maybe a garden, and ample space to visit with friends.

Bill: I like renovating homes, and I think it's cool that Giuliana trusts me to do this for us. That means she not only believes in my taste and general contracting skills, but she also trusts my vision of our future. That said, I still don't make any big decisions about the house's design without considering how they'll affect her. I've chosen floors tough enough to withstand how often she drops things and closets that accommodate her crazy shoe collection.

Giuliana: We did have to compromise, though, about what to do with the basement. We agreed on having a little playroom and gym downstairs, but a third of it is also Bill's movie theater . . .

Bill: What? That's unfair. We're taking an existing home, and I have to finish it. The movie theater is three-quarters of the way done, so it's cheaper for me to finish it than to turn it into something else. We've always had certain things that we wanted in our house, and that's a fun one.

Giuliana: Oh, please. It's nothing to be ashamed of. We got a real bargain on that place. So in the theater, Bill wanted home theater seats that recline all the way back in case you're tired halfway through *Borat,* and feel the need to snooze because you're too lazy to go to your bedroom. But I wanted couches—big, plush sofas with cashmere throws so all our guests could snuggle together. Our arrangement? Three rows of cozy loveseats flanked by Bill's classic movie theater chairs on each end. How perfect is that?

Home, Sweet ... Halfway Point?

Bill: Whether Giuliana and I are compromising about a subject as big as where to live our married lives, or one as minor as how we'll spend a Sunday afternoon, the answer isn't always to meet in the middle. I was once told that some of the best compromises in marriage happen when you go back and forth between what each person wants. In a very literal way, this shows real give-and-take in a marriage. So that means if Giuliana and I face an impasse about what kind of car to buy, for instance, I might get to make the decision because cars are important to me, but when it comes to buying a fancy new computer, we lean on her because she's such a techie. The thinking behind this type of compromise is that if you always meet in the middle with your spouse, which is what most people think of as compromising, then neither person is ever one hundred percent happy. That's unsatisfying. This way, we don't walk away feeling like we've swallowed our needs, and our integrity remains intact. And the truth is, unless Giuliana wants something I can't stand, I'm pretty chill about the decisions she makes on our behalf. I choose my battles a lot, and I decide what's worth a compromise or negotiation. We rarely have pissing matches, because a good decision that makes your spouse happy is a good decision for your marriage.

Giuliana: When it comes to our new home, we realized that Bill is good at picking out countertops and materials like the trim on the wall. And when I put my mind to it, my strengths are in design—choosing light fixtures, window treatments, and so on. So we're dividing our responsibilities based on our talents and strengths. He cares about marble countertops, and I know L-shaped couches are cheesy. Bill would have a huge sectional with lots of ugly ottomans if I let him.

There are times, though, that you must meet in the middle to make peace. This is your home. This is where your family lives. That's a big deal. Compromise is imperative to the process of turning empty space into a happy space because you don't want it to be tainted with thoughts like "That's the wall color *he* chose." I feel uncomfortable when I walk into someone's first home, and a wife's like, "Here's the wine cellar that almost caused us a divorce." Or, "Welcome to the game room. It looks like it belongs to a twelve-year-old, but I let him have it so I didn't have to hear him complain."

Bill: I want to have a house where I can live in the whole house and feel part of its creation.

Giuliana: There is also a difference between compromise and sacrifice, and sometimes couples confuse one with the other. The way I understand it, sacrifice means completely letting go of something you want that you otherwise thought was useful; compromise means giving up one thing in exchange for a concession from the other side. You don't want to repeatedly sacrifice what's important to you and lose yourself in the process. This will lead to resentment and anger, as you watch the relationship tilt more to one side than the other. You need to find a balance between sacrifice and compromise in marriage, because the last one means both spouses are contributing to a solution, whether that means flip-flopping, meeting in the middle, or whatever arrangement you agree will keep peace in the marriage.

Bill: When you compromise, you strike up a fair deal. You make a negotiation. You come to that agreement by talking through your original goals and determining a variation on them.

Giuliana: Marriages are partnerships, and neither partner should try to dominate the other. You can still control your own life and support each other at the same time—and man, it requires patience, compassion, and honesty to get there. You also have to listen to each other's sides, get their rationales, and come to a decision together. You need to put yourself in the other person's shoes, too, and think about how you'd feel in a similar situation that mattered as much to you.

Bill: When we come to a crossroad in our relationship, I consider what we

> **Giuliana's compromise that means a lot:** *"I'm terrified of airplanes, but I still fly to Chicago to be with Bill every other weekend. Nothing a glass of red wine (or two) can't make better."*
> **Bill's sacrifice is equally (or maybe more?) painful:** *"I hate karaoke. Listening to people singing badly is not my idea of a good time. Giuliana also hogs the mic, and lets me sing one song for every five she belts out. Yet I still let her drag me to a karaoke joint in L.A. where you get your own room and a huge library of music. I sit on the couch and watch her sing for hours. It is torture, but I stomach it since few things make her happier than pretending she's Celine Dion or Beyoncé."*

want the final outcome to be. Like with the home theater: was the goal to literally have a theater full of recliners or a seating area that's comfortable for us and guests? That said, you can see why we made the concession we did. If I were just out to "win" the discussion, I'd lose, because if Giuliana is upset, she feels unhappy and that weakens our relationship. Happy wife, happy life—that's what I always say.

Giuliana: Me too. Happy husband, happy . . . wait, what rhymes with husband? Oh well. What matters is that with Bill and our beautiful new home, Chicago keeps getting better and better.

TIPS FOR TWO: Agreeing to Concede

• When you face an impasse, discuss the pros and cons of both sides to negotiate a solution. Listen to each other's rationales and come to a decision together.

• Compromise isn't just about meeting in the middle. Try alternating back and forth between what you want and what your spouse wants each time you reach a stalemate.

• Leaning on each other's strengths can also help you reach a satisfying concession.

• Know the difference between compromise and sacrifice. Too much sacrifice can tip the scales in favor of one spouse's preferences, and lead to possible resentment.

• Visualize the final outcome of each side. Making a decision is as much emotional, as it is rational.

17 Sexy Time

Sex. *Romance. Passion.* Just typing those words make us feel all hot and bothered. It's not every day, though, that we hear about couples who naturally nail this trifecta—so if you ever meet one, please tell them to stop bragging. Like any married couple with a busy life outside the bedroom, love comes easily to us, but the consistent sex and romance part takes effort.

Oh, but what delicious effort it is.

Sex, romance, and passion are integral pieces of a couple's love life, though some of these words can feature more prominently in a marriage than others. For us, we can't get enough passion and romance; as for sex, we go for quality over quantity. Giuliana is a sucker for roses, and thinks there's nothing more romantic than when Bill hand-feeds her sushi; Bill feels bursts of passion when he sees Giuliana asking bold and witty questions on the red carpet, as her glamour and confidence shine. Turn-ons are unique to every relationship, but what's key is to know what specific things work for your vibe—and if you're *not* in the mood, how to say that without shrinking egos (among other things), so your lover can't wait to come back for more.

According to the University of Chicago's National Opinion Research Center, the average adult has sex sixty-one times in a year, so a little over once a week. Whether you and your spouse are above or below that number isn't our business (and please don't email us with details). We do, however, think a healthy love life, especially among married couples, must be a priority based on respect, communication, and adoration. Regular romps also make us feel connected, adored, and wanted (the feel-good hormone surge that happens during sex is a perk).

Knowing how to seduce your partner can become increasingly difficult in a marriage over time, maybe because companionship grows deeper every day. But while we think friendship is essential to a happy union, it can't exist in lieu of feeling desired. Creativity, spontaneity, trial and error, and an open dialogue are just some factors that can help up the sexual ante. Racy lingerie and strong perfume can also do it, but as you'll soon learn, that didn't work for us when Giuliana pulled out all the lacy stops on Bill's thirty-seventh birthday. Cue the soundtrack: *Bow chica bow mow* . . .

Giuliana: It's no secret that before I met Bill, the man dated his share of models, pageant queens, and even a blonde and bubbly runner-up in the Miss USA contest. And since I don't have trophies, tiaras, or a ton of call sheets from glossy magazines lying around the house to remind Bill that he married a sexpot, I wanted to reassure him that I'd always put in the effort to turn him on. It's important to keep the romance and sizzle alive in a marriage, and I didn't want Bill to fear that I'd become the type of wife who'd crawl into bed at night wearing shabby flannel PJs with a homemade avocado mask smeared on her face (or at least, not every night). So for Bill's thirty-seventh birthday, a year after we were married, I surprised him with a trip to Las Vegas. I thought it would be a fun and frivolous thing to do while we were still footloose and baby-free.

The day before we left for our trip, I stopped at Victoria's Secret at the mall in Century City, just outside Beverly Hills, to find a look that would make my boobs and tush look ample and irresistible. I gravitated toward flirty baby-doll dresses and push-up bras, but nothing screamed "Las Vegas temptress" the way I'd hoped my birthday outfit would. I'm not usually a lingerie girl, but I could tell that VS was more weeknight sexy than special occasion sultry.

I made Frederick's of Hollywood, a few floors up, my next stop. It's actually right next to The Container Store, and for a second, I was tempted to kiss the whole lingerie idea good-bye and shop for felt hangers instead. In case you live under a rock, Frederick's is a risqué negligee and novelty shop that I suspect is kept in business by exotic dancers, porn stars, strippers, pimps, and desperate wives like me. I felt confident that this place could sell me a look so smokin' that Bill wouldn't be able to keep his hands off me.

When I walked through the door, I couldn't believe all the provocative hoochie mama get-ups I saw. Frederick's sells bras up to size 42 DD, crotchless panties, and entire outfits consisting of lace-and-ribbon bustiers with matching G-strings, detachable garters, and thigh-high stockings. Basically, if a horny male teen could imagine it, Frederick's sells it—and if I think too hard about this, I might get grossed-out about how few adult men outgrow their fourteen-year-old fantasies. I mean, everything in the store had some sort of complex or shimmery detail: rhinestones, mesh, gold lamé, lace, ribbons, eyelets, leather, plastic, you name it—all the better to tease you with, my dear. The shoes were the most outrageous, and as you can imagine, almost all of them had a Lucite platform heel. Even now, the heels on their website feature animal prints, silver studs, chains, and my favorite: a strappy stiletto knee-high patent leather boot with faux snakeskin details. *Meow.*

Once I surveyed the merchandise, I did my best Catholic-guilt wince as I explained, aka fibbed to, the salesperson that I was hosting a silly bachelorette party and needed to buy trashy outfits for all my friends. Then I left with two looks, in case I needed a backup. I could tell that Frederick's mirrors were the flattering kind, and who knew what the neon glow of Vegas would do to my skin tone?

I'd booked Bill on a flight to Sin City that landed later than mine, so I'd have plenty of time to primp in our fancy Palazzo Hotel suite. I'm glad I did this, too, because it took me a half hour to figure out how the hell to tie, fasten, lift, snap, and squeeze myself into an outrageous red-and-black-lace corset, lace garter, thigh-high stockings, and plastic hooker heels.

When I heard Bill turn the doorknob to our room, I threw on a complimentary terrycloth bathrobe from the hotel so he couldn't see the surprise I'd planned underneath. Bill had flown in from a speaking engagement in New York and said he was pooped, so I recommended he take a breather. "Why don't you get settled, take a nap, and we'll go to dinner later?" I suggested, as my tiny G-string crept even farther up my tush. Bill agreed, and crawled under the covers. "Sweet dreams," I said.

Then I dimmed the light, dropped my robe, and leaned against the doorway in my best Paris Hilton sex tape pose.

Bill: When Giuliana dropped her robe, my jaw hit the floor.

Giuliana: "Happy Birthday, honey," I purred. I waited for Bill to do a cartoon double take, complete with a Porky Pig–like stutter, but instead he snickered. "What are you doing?" he asked, but I didn't answer. I held his gaze and slinked toward him. "What's up down there, Billy?" I asked. Apparently, "Billy" didn't know what to make of the harlot version of me, though I suspected his smirk was the nervous-but-pleased kind. "You're so funny," he continued, but when I climbed onto the bed on all fours, he let out the kind of deep, belly laugh you have when you watch *The Hangover* for the first time. "Come on, honey," he said. "What's going on?"

I kept my cool, but I was more confused than anything. "I'll show you funny, baby," I said. "Just sit back and relax." My lines made things worse. "You're playing a joke on me, right?" Bill asked. "Why are you dressed up in that costume?!" I knew Bill could be a slow study, but this was ridiculous. "This costume is called lingerie, baby, and believe me, this is no joke," I told him. "I want to make your birthday *speciaaaal*." The last word came out in breathy whisper.

"Stop goofing around, DePandi," Bill said. "I'm hungry. Change out of that costume and let's go get dinner." And with that, Bill jumped out of bed, went to the bathroom, and left me to change into something more comfortable.

If this was a joke, it felt like it was on me. Would my husband really rather eat a bloody T-bone, than have a piece of *this*? "I'm a little offended," I told Bill, as he grabbed his wallet off the table, and I threw on a dress (what a relief, only one zipper!). "I wanted to do something special for you. And now I'm hurt because this is me being hot for you, and you don't want any of it."

Bill's face dropped, and he felt terrible. "You were serious about that? But this isn't how I know you," he said. "You don't have to be a Frederick's slut to make me happy. I think you're so much hotter when you dress like yourself." I explained to Bill that I dressed this way, because I never wanted our spark to disappear. "Don't worry, baby," he said. "If our fire starts to die out, we'll use your corset to start it up again. I'm pretty sure all that polyester is flammable."

Feeling Hot, Hot, Hot

Bill: The problem with Giuliana's outfit wasn't the lingerie it-self (believe me, I like corsets as much as the next red-blooded American man), but that she made herself look like someone she isn't. In that ridiculous costume, she looked like a bache-lor party stripper or college girl on Halloween night. I could also tell Giuliana was really uncomfortable in the outfit. I never want her to think she has to be someone she isn't for me to feel attracted to her. I'm into the girl who wears my T-shirt to bed and nothing else. What I've always loved about Giu-liana is her authenticity, and seeing her dressed as someone she's not ran counter to that.

Because I didn't want Giuliana to think this kind of dress-up game is arousing, I let her know right away. Had I gone with the flow on my birthday, even though it's only one night of the year, I would have sent a message that this sex object get-up worked for me. What makes me happy is *her*—and what makes me hot for her is when we have fun. That's what we do; we have fun together. Having a good time is so much sexier to me than thigh-high stockings and raunchy perfume that makes my stomach turn. When we have a good time, nobody puts on a façade; we have a genuine connection. If Giuliana were some exotic dirty girl when we were dating, that's one thing. But that's not who I married, and the unfamiliarity of it all sort of bugged me out.

Giuliana: It's true. I never offered him lap dances in a nasty nurse costume when we were dating. I was more likely to sleep topless with cute boy shorts, which Bill always loved.

Bill: We always do romantic things for each other, and I think that's always been super sexy to me. Talking, laughing, laying in bed, holding hands, giving Giuliana a piggyback ride—that kind of fun puts us in the mood. Spontaneity is the most important thing for me, as are random acts of kindness. I don't need something so overtly sexual to turn me on. That does the opposite.

> ### Tantric Tracks
>
> "Wicked Game" by Chris Isaak
> "Lost in You" by Robin Thicke
> "Sexual Healing" by Marvin Gaye

Giuliana: Even if I went about turning Bill on the wrong way, my intentions were good. I think all wives need to remind their husbands that they'll never stop wanting them. Bill should never doubt that I think he's still worth the time and energy I devoted to him when we first met. When we go out, I still make sure I wear short dresses with tasteful heels because he never stopped checking out my legs. I realize I may not be able to sustain this kind of flirting when we're old and crotchety, but I hope I never give Bill a reason to doubt that my heart beats hard for him.

Bill: Sex and romance influence each other, and I think both are best when they don't look like a bad cliché. Sharing inside jokes, slipping a note into my pocket before work, or chilling a bottle of champagne as a surprise are all intimate moves we like to make. There's no reason to skimp on the sexy. I like to call Giuliana in the middle of her day just to say "I love you, baby."

Giuliana: You know what else works? Leaving the toilet seat down or offering me a back rub for no reason. Those are considerate moves, and being thoughtful is romantic. Plus, the more time we spend together, the more our definition of romance changes. When we first met, I thought it was cute when

Bill opened my car door for me. Now I swoon when he replaces my toothbrush for no reason. Another thing I think we do that's hot is drink too many giant, slushy margaritas. Clearly this is the most fun in Mexico, but even at our local taco joint in L.A., it's always nice to get a little buzz when we don't expect it. Tequila always makes us dance, get sweaty, and the next morning we wake up groggy and try to piece the night together. Those times feel so passionate, and we lose ourselves with abandon. It makes us feel young and like we're still dating, though I have been known to slip when we're out and accidentally refer to Bill as my boyfriend. He used to think it was a little insulting, but now he realizes that I do this because I still have that fire inside that I had when we were dating. What we don't do is designate sexy time during the week.

Bill: That's too scheduled, even for me.

Giuliana: I'm rarely in the mood to have sex during the week, anyway, so Bill would never in a million years pressure me or make me feel bad about this, which some guys might do. He understands, and there are plenty of times that Bill's really tired, too, because he travels so much. I never take it as a rejection when he shrugs off my occasional advance, but that's only because he explains himself. "I'm so wiped, I'm about to pass out," he'll tell me. "I can't even imagine fooling around. But don't worry, because I'm gonna come knocking in the morning!" And sure enough, he does. Bill often reassures me by sticking to his word, but it's especially necessary in the bedroom since insecurities and emotions always run higher here. I'd also rather have sex once or twice, really well, than a few times a week when we're too stressed to fill an imaginary quota.

Bill: There's a difference between feeling tired and making up for it later, and just letting the passion fade and spark die out. Who wants to live without sex? Not us. Once you start to think that maybe you can deal with sex once a month, because after all, you do like to spoon . . . that's no good. I imagine this might lead you to wonder if you've married the wrong person, when the real problem is that you didn't keep up with your sex life together.

Giuliana: As time goes on, it's normal for passion and sex to decrease in a marriage, and that time line is different for every couple. We haven't lost our mojo by any means, but I have begun to notice that our feelings of deep friendship, appreciation, and commitment are increasing. Long-lasting couples that we know say that a big part of why their marriage works is because they're such great friends. You just have to make sure you don't lose the sex part of the equation, too.

Sometimes all I need is for Bill to touch me, and I'm ready to go. That's it—just simple skin-to-skin contact can make me friskier than a teen on prom night. When Bill kisses my neck and around my ear, I feel a surge of energy in my belly. It helps that I'm passionate about Bill all the time, and I think you need that, plus sex, to want to get naked with someone as you grow old together.

The funny thing with sex is that it can feel like an effort at first, but once I'm in the middle of it, I think, *My Lord, why don't we do this twice a day?* If Bill's tired but made me feel special by complimenting me or picking up a prescription for me at the drugstore, I'll feel close to him and wonder if he's in the mood to have sex. So I'll start rubbing up on him, and he might say, "Oh God . . . come on, honey. Tomorrow morning—I've been traveling, I'm so

> **Our Afterglow Activities**
>
> • Spooning and baby kisses
> • Eating ice cream in bed
> • Pillow talk, ranging from sweet childhood memories to "So, what do you want for dinner?"

tired." But I know just what to say. "Follow me to the bedroom and I promise you that, in five minutes, you won't be tired"— and then we go at it. Sex is a little like the gym that way. I'm not always in the mood to get myself out the door, but when I come back from a good workout with an awesome endorphin rush, I never think, *Now that was a waste of my time.*

Bill: Because stress gets in the way of sex for us, we like to keep anxiety as low as possible. High-intensity workouts, hiking, and even weight lifting are ways that we like to kill stress.

Giuliana: Bill and I always say that there's no magic pill to a good sex life, but there's always alcohol. I realize that not everyone drinks, but it's our fun go-to thing. We don't do drugs, we don't swing . . .

Bill: Hey, we're willing to learn!

Giuliana: In your dreams, Rancic. A little too much booze is what works for us, and we're not ashamed to admit it. It's not like we have to be drunk to have sex, but we call it like it is. Every married couple needs help at times, and for us, it comes in a tequila bottle. Alcohol can also become code that we want to do it. "Who wants a margarita?" often means "Who wants to get laid?"

When we're home, Rancic likes to use "nap" as a code for fooling around, too. "Are you tired?" he'll ask me. "Come take a nap with your husband." The first time Bill said this to me, I didn't know what he was hinting at. "You're going to take a nap? Great," I said. "I'm going to run to Bloomies for an hour. They're having a shoe sale."

Bill: I remember that! *Goddammit,* I thought. *Why doesn't she know this one?*

Giuliana: It wasn't until Bill said, "Trust me. Come *take a nap*," that I was like, "Oh, OK. I get it. I think?" *But should I change into my pajamas? Take off my shoes?* I got on top of the covers. "Get *under* the covers," Bill said. That's when I knew "take a nap" was code for "do me, baby."

Bill: Giuliana doesn't have a code. She just says to me, like a rapper, "I wanna hit it."

Giuliana: I think that initiating sex, once you're married, can be tricky. When you're dating, it's simply what happened after dinner and drinks, when the guy invited you back to his apartment. But now, Bill and I come home together from a night out, and we have choices. We could watch a movie, brush our teeth, go to bed together, get in bed separately . . . I'm talking limitless options.

Bill: We talk a lot about how marriage shouldn't be work, but how you should put effort into it; well, that applies to your sex life, too. Intimacy should never be work. But effort? I'm into that.

Giuliana: Especially now that he's old.

Bill: Men's and women's libidos move at a different pace. As men get older, our sexual appetites decrease.

Giuliana: I thought guys were always supposed to want it more than we do.

Bill: That's true when the guy is in his twenties. But as we start to creep into our thirties, and late thirties especially, we begin to value sleep almost as much as we do sexy time, as Giuliana likes to call it. So women may want to work extra hard to make their spouse feel special in other ways, and that doesn't include bullying him into being something he once was. I have a friend who's gained weight since he got married, and his wife really lets him know it. "Ugh. I have to go home and sleep with this guy?" she says to us, usually after he eats all the dessert. That sucks.

Giuliana: Did you ever think that maybe being married to fifty extra pounds would also suck? But we have our turn-offs, too.

Bill: Yeah, DePandi's filthy—and not in a way that makes me think of the stunt she pulled in Vegas. She's like, dirt-and-grime filthy.

Giuliana: Bill jokes with me about my grooming habits. They're totally normal, but you have to realize that he showers twice a day, maybe three times. I shower once a day, max.

Bill: Tops.

Giuliana: I'm Italian; what do you want from me? Bill can stink all he wants when we make out—in fact, I think there's something wild and animalistic about it. But if he says to me, "Wanna take a nap?" and I seem interested because I start to unzip my pants, "Great," he'll say. "I'll see you when you get out of the shower, paesano."

Bill: When she's wrapped in a towel and smells like Ivory Soap, I can't get enough of her.

Giuliana: That's just what he says so he can get some action. I'm sure I always manage to miss a spot behind my knee or under my arm. When I shave, I always miss a strip of hair down the backs of my legs, so I can't imagine I hit every square inch with a bar of soap.

Do I Make You Horny, Baby?

Bill: At least we're honest about what turns us on and off. And if something isn't working for us, we say that, too. We're in this marriage for life, so that would be a long time to "just deal" with me accidentally pulling Giuliana's hair or her getting an arm stuck when we change positions.

Giuliana: I've found that this conversation has become much less scary for me now that I'm married. This would have been a super frightening talk to have with Bill when we were dating. Back then, every word I said felt like it might pull him closer or push him farther from me; but now the goal isn't to give Bill a reason to stay, but to make us both feel glad that we did.

When we're talking about things we like and don't like in bed, our voices never sound judgmental. After all, bedroom skills are a cobbled-together, in-the-moment rendition of what's worked with other people, advice from magazines and books, conversations with friends, influence from well-directed movies, maybe snapshots from porn, and who knows what else. We don't realistically expect it to be a five-star performance every time.

Now I'm honest about what feels good. You know how they say in leadership workshops that you should never present a problem without offering a solution? Same goes for in the bedroom. If I complain about how Bill nibbles on my earlobe because it tickles, I suggest how he can kiss my collarbone and shoulder to make me more excited.

Bill: Once in a while, I'll open a magazine for inspiration. It's helpful to be reminded of ways to talk about sex, verbalize fantasies, try new positions, and, yes, even try to improve our orgasms. Once I flipped through Giuliana's *Cosmopolitan* on a long flight, and I tore out a story about seventy-three ways to

---

Foreplay Food That Puts Us in the Mood

• Strawberries and whipped cream—a tried-and-true classic
• Turtle pie, complete with nuts, chocolate chunks, caramel,
and fudge in one delicious slice of heaven
• Chocolate dipped strawberries with champagne
• Any warm cookie that has hot, melted chocolate chips
• Lots of red wine (It's not a food, but it sure gets us frisky!)

---

please your man, or something. I gave it to her, but I think she lost it.

Giuliana: I lost it in the terminal. I'll bet it was about reasons not to wear underwear—I remember seeing that. Men always wish women did that more. One time I wore a dress without undies because otherwise you'd see my panty lines, and Bill put his hand on my butt. "Are you wearing underwear?" he asked me. When I saw the excitement in his eyes, I told him I wasn't. My instinct was to explain that underwear would make my ass look bumpy and unflattering, but I told Bill what he wanted to hear instead. "I'm not wearing underwear," I said. "Later, you'll find out why." He liked that.

Bill: I never knew that was the reason.

Giuliana: Meanwhile, if I were rubbing Bill's back and he didn't have underwear on, I might be grossed out.

Bill: Sometimes I wear underwear, sometimes I don't.

Giuliana: I could run my hand down there and discover that thing just blowing in the wind . . .

Bill: Any given day, you might be in for a surprise.

Giuliana: Who are we kidding? If Bill's not wearing underwear, it's an efficiency thing. If he doesn't pack it, he has more room for his grooming kit and carefully folded shirts.

I'll tell you what else makes me melt: hearing Bill negotiate a business deal from the other room. He sounds so in command, so in control, and a little bossy, too. I love it because Bill is the sweetest, most compassionate guy in the world, but when he goes into business mode, his voice drops and he makes these really great, hot, business points. That's a total turn-on and part of what made me fall in love with Bill when I watched *The Apprentice*.

When we closed the deal on our new house in Chicago, Bill was really tough with the owner. We'd planned to present ourselves as a united front—"Just stand by me as we negotiate, and we'll make it known that we're a team," Bill said—but it got so intense, I went into the other room. "I'm going to look at our future dining room . . ." I said, as I made a beeline out of there, all scared. Around the corner, I could hear Bill do his thing. "I'll take the house for this," he said. "Or we don't have a deal. If you leave it, we'll walk out the door." The owner caved, the two men shook, and my hormones went nuts. "Damn Bill," I told him after. "You were sexy back there." When Bill and I got back to the condo, we had some good celebratory throw-down.

Bill: There are so many things that turn me on about Giuliana, but what I think I love most is watching her work the red carpet. She looks so at ease, friendly, and elegant when she interviews all those celebrities, and then she comes home to *me*. Giuliana's confidence has always been attractive to me. She's calm and graceful. She's good at what she does, but in a natural way. She's a true pro—

Giuliana: I try to make people feel comfortable—

Bill: I can finish a sentence, thank you. It's hard to give Giuliana a compliment, because no one loves Giuliana more than Giuliana. Let me work, woman.

Giuliana: When Bill jokes around, he'll ask me, "Could you ever love me more than you love you?"

Bill: The theme song of our show *Giuliana & Bill* goes: "I love, loving you." But next season we're petitioning to change it. We think Giuliana should sing the words: "I love, loving me."

Giuliana: We can break each other's balls all we want, but we love loving each other, and that's the truth of it.

TIPS FOR TWO: Sexing Up Your Spouse

- Don't force the sexy by being someone you're not. Spouses call bluffs, and that can kill the mood.
- Figure out what revs your hormones. Margaritas? Getaways? Edible undies? Go with it.
- Consider creating a secret code to help initiate sex in a playful way.
- If you're not in the mood for some good loving, give your spouse a rain check to reassure him/her and to build anticipation.
- Share your turn-ons and turn-offs, so your spouse knows how to love you the right way.

The Last Word

Thanks to these two hundred plus pages, you now know way too much about our amusing sex life, messy bathroom habits, and serious passion for ahi tuna steaks. But more importantly, we hope our tips and tales have inspired (or at least, reminded) you to make your marriage the absolute best it can be. By no means do we think we're a perfect couple, but we do pride ourselves on figuring out how to use our ups and downs to become better spouses. We hope you're able to relate.

We've found that the early years of our wonderful marriage have been a series of experiments and negotiations toward finding a happily ever after formula that works for us. Our relationship relies on a strong foundation, built early in our marriage, of shared priorities like mutual respect, loyalty, effort, trust, humility, and good intentions. And while every union is unique, studies show that these tenets are among the most important ones that keep a relationship

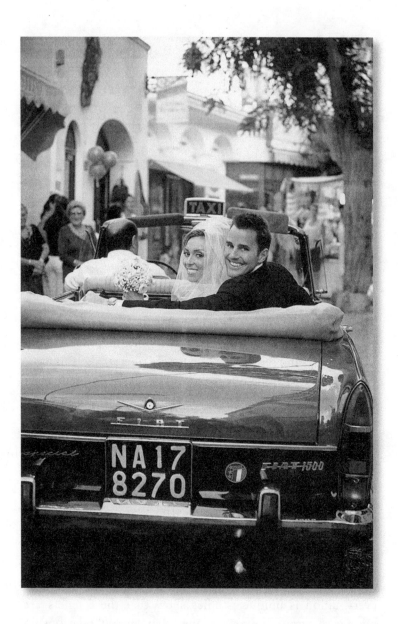

standing. We trust that they will strengthen your bond the way they do ours.

So go give your spouse a big kiss and show 'em what you've learned. You may have reached the end of this book, but we hope that your marriage is about to experience a new beginning.

Acknowledgments

Between the two of us, there are way too many friends, business associates, and Italian cousins to thank by name, without someone getting offended, so a huge thank you to all of you who have enriched our lives.

To our editor, Luke Dempsey, who didn't hesitate to let us tell our story from the moment we walked into his office and introduced ourselves. Even though you wrote a book on bird watching, you are hands down the coolest editor in the biz.

To the lovely and utterly talented Kristina Grish for capturing our story and breathing life into these pages. We thank you from the bottom of our hearts for your devotion and wonderful insight.

To our lit agent, Richard Abate, for believing in our love affair and persuading us to put it on paper for others to enjoy and learn from.

To Pam Kohl, the most fabulous talent manager in Hollywood. Not only do we work together, but we play and laugh together, too. You are a best friend and a confidante. We love you and thank you for always looking out for us.

Thank you, Ted Harbert, for always believing in us and encouraging us to put our marriage on a reality show. You were right, as usual.

Salaam Coleman-Smith for giving our show a comfy home on The Style Network and for advocating healthy and positive programming in an age of some pretty messy reality television.

All our friends at Style, E! and Comcast Productions for all of your hard work and support, especially Jay James, who has been with us from the start.

Thank you to our siblings for putting up with us our whole lives, and to our nieces and nephews for being so damn adorable that you make us look forward to having our own kids one day.

Eduardo DePandi, for being a wonderful father who moved his family to America and worked day and night so his kids could have beautiful lives. You are the epitome of a real man.

Anna DePandi, a true Superwoman, who never says "No" and loves her family with raw passion all while flashing the most infectiously gorgeous smile in the world.

Gail Rancic, the sweetest, warmest mother a boy could have. Your grace and kindness continues to marvel us and make us love you even more every single day.

And of course, Edward Rancic. Even though your time here on Earth wasn't as long as we all would have wished for, the legacy you've left behind is one of honor, generosity, and pure class. We miss you and feel you smiling down on us when we close our eyes and face the sky. Until we meet again, Dad.

Finally, a big thank you to our fans and viewers who tune in to our show each week. The critics said a positive reality show without loads of scandal would never survive. You proved them wrong. Thank you for embracing the show and continuing to laugh, cry, and grow with us. We love you and are forever grateful.

About the Authors

GIULIANA RANCIC (née DePandi) was born in Naples, Italy, and moved to the United States when she was seven. She is the anchor and managing editor of the top-rated *E! News,* a beloved red-carpet interviewer, and the author of the dating book *Think Like a Guy.*

BILL RANCIC is an American entrepreneur and was the first winner of Donald Trump's *The Apprentice.* He spent the next several years overseeing the construction of Trump Tower in Chicago. Since then he has created a motivational speaking career, and is also the author of the *New York Times* bestseller *You're Hired* and *Beyond the Lemonade Stand.*

Giuliana and Bill are the co-stars of The Style Network's hit reality show *Giuliana & Bill.* The two live in Chicago and Los Angeles.

About the Type

This book was set in Sabon, a typeface designed by the well-known German typographer Jan Tschichold (1902–74). Sabon's design is based upon the original letter forms of Claude Garamond and was created specifically to be used for three sources: foundry type for hand composition, Linotype, and Monotype. Tschichold named his typeface for the famous Frankfurt typefounder Jacques Sabon, who died in 1580.